D1160048

Edward Dorn
A World of Difference

Also by Tom Clark

Stones (1969)
Air (1970)
John's Heart (1972)
At Malibu (1975)
When Things Get Tough on Easy Street (1978)
The World of Damon Runyon (1978)
A Short Guide to the High Plains (1981)
    (Introduction by Edward Dorn)
Jack Kerouac (1984)
Paradise Resisted (1984)
Late Returns: A Memoir of Ted Berrigan (1985)
The Exile of Céline (1987)
Disordered Ideas (1987)
Easter Sunday (1988)
The Poetry Beat (1990)
Fractured Karma (1990)
Charles Olson: The Allegory of a Poet's Life (1991)
Sleepwalker's Fate (1992)
Robert Creeley and the Genius of the American Common Place
    (1993)
Junkets on a Sad Planet: Scenes from the Life of John Keats
    (1994)
Like Real People (1995)
Empire of Skin (1997) (Preface by Edward Dorn)
White Thought (1997)
The Spell: A Romance (2000)

Edward Dorn
A World of Difference

Tom Clark

North Atlantic Books
Berkeley, California

Copyright © 2002 by Tom Clark. All rights reserved. No portion of this book, except for brief review, may be reproduced, stored in a retrieval system, or transmitted in any form or by any means—electronic, mechanical, photocopying, recording or otherwise—without the written permission of the publisher. For information contact North Atlantic Books.

Published by
North Atlantic Books
P.O. Box 12327
Berkeley, California 94712

Cover design by Paula Morrison
Book design by Jennifer Dunn

Printed in the United States of America

Cover: Dorn, Santa Fe, September 1961. (Photo by Gordon Clark, courtesy of Jennifer Dunbar Dorn.) *Back cover:* Dorn and Clark, Boulder, Colorado, 1979. (Photo from author's collection.)

Quotations from Edward Dorn's published poetry, fiction, essays and interviews courtesy of Four Seasons Foundation (*Views,* 1980; *Interviews,* 1980; *The Collected Poems: 1956–1974,* 1983), Black Sparrow Press (*By the Sound,* 1991; *Way West: Stories, Essays & Verse Accounts, 1963–1993,* 1993), Duke University Press (*Gunslinger,* 1989), and Limberlost Press (*Chemo Sábe,* 2001). Unpublished Dorn letters, poems and stories quoted with permission of Edward Dorn. All such materials copyrighted 2002 by the Estate of Edward Dorn.

Selected chapters first appeared in *The American Poetry Review, Jacket, Poetry Flash* and *The Poetry Project Newsletter.*

Edward Dorn: A World of Difference is sponsored by the Society for the Study of Native Arts and Sciences, a nonprofit educational corporation whose goals are to develop an educational and crosscultural perspective linking various scientific, social, and artistic fields; to nurture a holistic view of arts, sciences, humanities, and healing; and to publish and distribute literature on the relationship of mind, body, and nature.

This project is partially funded by a grant from the California Arts Council.

Library of Congress Cataloging-in-Publication Data

Clark, Tom, 1941–
    Edward Dorn : a world of difference / by Tom Clark.
        p. cm.
    ISBN 1-55643-397-2
        1. Dorn, Edward. 2. Poets, American—20th century—Biography. I. Title.

PS3507.O73277 Z63 2002
811'.54—dc21
[B]

2002016643

1   2   3   4   5   6 / 06   05   04   03   02

To the memory of Edward Dorn, poet and compadre
and to Fred Buck, tracker and true friend
and to Angelica Heinegg Clark, companion and guide

Contents

Introduction and Acknowledgements *1*

Prologue: We Were There When It Was New
(1965–1968) *9*

I. Son of the Prairie (1929–1948) *43*

1. Tribe *45*
2. Want *55*
3. Reading *61*
4. Confines of the River Town *69*
5. The Soil of Transport *73*

II. A Troublesome Spring (1947/1962) *75*

1. The Story of Morton Draker (Competitive Plots) *77*
2. Distance (Areal Prose) *87*

3. The Brakeman 97

4. Branch Line: Some Further Notes on Dorn
    and Railroads 109

III. A Set of Circumstances and Warps of Destiny (1948–1951) 117

1. A Vast Nothing 119

2. Wherever Intelligence and Curiosity Led 123

IV. Nomadism (1951–1953) 127

1. The Business of Sensibility and Insensibility 129

2. Vagrant 141

3. Sidetrip: Wyo-Booming (1979) 145

4. "C. B. & Q." 149

5. On the Margin 155

6. Woodshedding 161

7. Suspended 169

V. A Light from the North (1953–1954) 175

1. Young Poet in Love 177

2. Love Chaos 185

3. Vocation 191

4. A Serious Business 195

5. A Light from the North ("Relics from a Polar Cairn") 199

6. A Sense of Kinship 209

7. The Difference 213

8. Ice Cream & a Movie 217

9. A History of Yearning 219

VI. Crossing Over (1954–1956) 221

1. Indian Country (Seattle to Illinois) 223
2. Little Differences (Mattoon) 225
3. A Traumatic Enlightenment (Chicago) 227
4. Difference as a Sign of Freedom (Black Mountain) 233
5. Life as If It's Just Started (Mexico) 239
6. Finding Out for Oneself (Black Mountain) 249
7. Testing and Self-Testing (Black Mountain) 253
8. Outlandish Introductions (Black Mountain) 259
9. Star-Crossed (Iowa City) 263
10. Stranded in the Antenna Forest (Mattoon) 267
11. Like Ulysses, Troubled but Unvanquished (Mattoon to San Francisco) 273
12. The Common Lot (San Francisco) 277

VII. "The Geography of My Lunacy" (1956–1959) 287

1. The Bright and Shining Hand (San Francisco to Seattle) 289
2. Hastening to a Dream 295
3. Homesteading (Burlington) 301
4. "1st Avenue": The Formalized Proletariat (Seattle) 309
5. Rain, and More Logs (Skagit Valley) 313
6. Chicken Feed 317
7. Animals ("Hemlocks") 325
8. Interlude: Is "Hemlocks" a Poem? 329
9. Legends of Resistance 333
10. "The Rick of Green Wood" 339
11. The Blue Cowboy 345
12. A Mean Business 349

13. "The Hide of My Mother" *353*

14. The Blackest Hour *359*

15. No Success like Failure ("Like a Message on Sunday") *363*

16. Stolen Riches *367*

17. Assholes & Elbows *373*

18. The Tunnel *377*

19. Piping Down the Valley Wild ("A Country Song") *381*

20. The Magick of Place ("Notes from the Fields") *383*

21. An Expansion of Much Air and Tears *387*

22. A Far Away Look in Her Eye *397*

EPILOGUE: THE LAST RANGE (1997–1999) *401*

Introduction and Acknowledgements

WHO IS EDWARD DORN? We may search for the subject of our study in the historical world of persons, as a particular individual living out his singular existence. Or we may meet up with him inside the frame of the work he has made, as the "truer than life" fictional self there represented. Or again we may hope to find him in his unseen activity, the disposing of words in that work, whereby he assumes another kind of life, as the creator of our reading-world.

Our quest for Edward Dorn will variously try out all three avenues, keeping in mind not only the boundaries between them but the fact that those boundaries are anything but absolute—a further complication the poet himself, in his paradoxical meanderings, repeatedly forces upon our understanding.

"I is now an organ Ization / a pure containment," Dorn writes in *Gunslinger*, Book II (a passage that "resurrects" the poetic "I," a character who has "died"—or been killed off—in the previous Book). And one recalls his fascinating characterization of his novel, *The Rites of Passage* (later retitled *By the Sound*) as "a biography of myself":

> All of it is ... pretty strictly autobiographical experience except
> that I'd say the figure of Carl Wyman [the novel's protago-
> nist] was an attempt, my first attempt, to get myself out in a
> three-dimensional sense and gain that kind of leverage you
> get from looking at yourself when you're not inside yourself
> so exclusively. So in that sense I was able to imagine things
> about myself I wouldn't strictly have thought of otherwise
> and in that sense it's not autobiographical. It's more like those
> parts are biographical. Like a biography of myself which I
> think is a slightly different sense than auto.

In each of the above citations—both from the mid-period of
Dorn's work—we are alerted to some of the perils attendant upon
any attempt to combine into a simple monolithic entity the biogra-
phical person and the frequently (and often deliberately) unstable,
shifting authorial presence in the writing. Even in Dorn's later work,
where there is increasing assertiveness of a centered moral and intel-
lectual presence, seemingly that of "the" Ed Dorn, it remains dan-
gerous to too readily identify the speaker of the work with the
extra-literary person. "When I read my work now," Dorn would
suggest at a public reading in the last years of his life, "it's like I'm
reading my own work. It's like I didn't write it.... Reading it, it's
the eye talking, E-Y-E, rather than the tongue, or some organ of per-
ception." Such comments should provide cautionary advice to both
reader and would-be biographer, reminding us that not the least sig-
nificant of Dorn's instinctive and cultivated distances is that which
separates the "man—located" we are encouraged (by the author
himself, in an early letter to Charles Olson) to find at the center of
his work from the restless wandering man who migrates through
his life with a nomad's resistance to all identifying locations. Of all
Dorn's careful differences the formal distance which he insists on
keeping when he speaks to us in his writing is the one which inter-
ests us and engages our curiosity most.

THOUGH ITS SUBJECT WAS A PARTICULAR FRIEND, a circumstance that has afforded the investigator special privileges while posing special challenges, this book is not intended as the history of a friendship. Neither is it intended as a full-scale biography strictly speaking, for it withholds and reserves to the private domain a second, unpublished "text" constituted by the many sections of chronology not here covered in fully realized and duly proportionate detail. Rather the work is meant to plot out some rough maps of the poet's spirit, tracing back into its complex mysteries the sources of that sense of separateness, difference and singularity which provides so much energizing tension to Dorn's writing. For "rough," in the above sentence, one may read "imperfect." One can be forever getting lost in those difficult, intriguing distances.

NOT THAT MANY PEOPLE DIDN'T TRY TO HELP show this often confused seeker a way through them. Foremost of these people was Dorn himself, who began educating me in these matters—at appropriately long distance—in a correspondence from his then-outpost in Idaho to Cambridge, England, in 1963. A bond of relation substantiated in a personal meeting two years later survived throughout many subsequent travels and vicissitudes and continued until his death in 1999. In addition to the hundreds of remarkable letters he'd written from his various stops over the years, Dorn latterly provided me his generous permission to quote at discretion from those letters, as well as from his other writings: a gift which has here been treated as entailing a serious responsibility. (A representative sampling of Dorn's epistolary genius, in this case *in extremis,* may be found in the extensive late letter-quotations given in the Epilogue.)

Others helped as well. The present book would not exist without the multiple contributions of Angelica Heinegg Clark, who semi-patiently endured the excessive tangential research, quite astutely kibitzed on the writing, valiantly served as the front-line reader, trouble-shooter and editor, heroically typed the whole text, and somehow admirably kept up human relations meanwhile (all this goes beyond the simple meaning of "help," into the dimensions of an

4 / Edward Dorn: A World of Difference

answer to a humble scribe's prayer).

Nor could the book exist in its present form without the precious assistance of Fred Buck, Edward Dorn's stepson. Fred supplied invaluable manuscripts and other documents, family photographs and personal reminiscences; his painstaking, cheerful and unselfish pursuit of biographical data provided not only significant material assistance but a stirring reminder of the kind of spirit in which such labors should be conducted.

The poet's first wife, Helene Helmers Dorn, provided enlightening reminiscences of the Dorn family migrations and much useful guidance, and also generously made available her correspondence of 1954–1959 with her first husband David Buck—an unparalleled source of biographical information for those years of Dorn's life, as well as a highly useful background aid to the understanding of his early writings. Jennifer Dunbar Dorn, Ed's second wife, supplied manuscripts of his late unpublished writings, photographs, and extensive, informative personal testimony, which proved essential in shaping the treatment of two decisive periods in this story, 1967–1968 and 1997–1999; Jenny also made available his 1952–1955 letters to Gordon Taylor, a high-school classmate, which offer a crucial early glimpse into the developing mind of a poet (the letters came to her courtesy of Steven Taylor, the late recipient's son, who is here gratefully acknowledged).

Lucia Berlin and Robert Creeley, Dorn's longtime friends and fellow writers, patiently fielded queries and consistently responded with strong insights. Ed's half-sister Nonna Abercrombie Lytle and half-brother David Abercrombie helped sort out the details of very early biography. His first important teacher and lifelong friend Ray Obermayr spoke with affection about the poet as a young artist and wanderer. Gordon Brotherston, his friend, colleague and collaborator, offered telling witness to the academic politics at the University of Essex during Dorn's time there. Wes Huss remembered Ed at Black Mountain. Anselm Hollo and Peter Michelson gave perceptive testimony on his personal style and intellectual positioning in his later years at the University of Colorado.

The dedicated scholar Skip Fox proffered pertinent research materials. Joe Richey supplied tapes and transcriptions of late Dorn talks. Cid Corman typed and sent copies of Dorn's first published poems from *Origin*. Dale Smith retrieved electronic archives. Mike Boughn contributed useful critical views. John Martin attempted to untangle the publishing history of *Gunslinger*. Steve Emerson provided first-class transportation (Dorn-style) to a Dorn memorial tribute. Last but not least, Juliet Clark devoted an archivist's skills to helping prepare the photo section. (No doubt others assisted as well, and the writer wishes to express his gratitude to them also, and to apologize for any flaws in his memory.)

THOSE JUST MENTIONED who never actually journeyed through the valley of the Rio Grande in Dorn's company are doing so virtually now.

> All may wake who live
> the combination is given
> and Some comb the connections
> in blind search
> there are deaths at birth
> there is death at 21
>   and burial at 80
> each calculation
> involves another century.
>
>   Our company thus moves collectively
> along the River Rio Grande.
>   —*Gunslinger,* Book II

Maybe it's in part because he had such a lonely and precarious beginning in life that later on Dorn always liked to surround himself with congenial company, according to his idiosyncratic lights. In life as sometimes in literature (happily violating that non-absolute authorial/texual boundary) he retained from his middle years onward a certain strange little traveling band, like the ragged but weirdly engaging road-trip company of *Gunslinger:* the cowboy, the dance-hall madam, the poet-singer, the Stoned Horse, among others. The peculiar honor of friendship he conferred on me was to be numbered as an outrider of that party of outriders, along with other diverse disparate friends. Only now that it's disbanded with Ed's death is it possible to understand that this was one group in which membership kept you from growing old, at least in the sense that you were prevented by Ed's intransigent example from losing your sense of humor. ("Entrapment is this society's / Sole activity," he'd write in a signature passage of *Gunslinger,* "Only laughter / can blow it to rags.")

As to his itinerant young manhood out West—of which one can get some sense from an image in a *Hands Up!* poem, "a windborn seed"—I learned a lot from voyaging with him across the upper Plains in 1979 on what was supposed to be a reporting assignment. The alleged objective was to "cover" the Wyoming energy boom for a magazine, but Ed's coverage always went deeper, wider, longer. After cresting the Wind River range in white light and coming down to Moorcroft, Wyoming, Ed drove slowly past the old New Moorcroft Hotel, a landmark in his early story "C. B. & Q.," talking about his drifting days. He found Tiny's restaurant, back of which the half-desert still begins, just as it does in that story. In Ed's day crews of gandy dancers hung out there between shifts. He was remembering his wandering working-life circa 1952, when "You could work endless hours but it was dangerous."

On that same trip he followed the Belle Fourche up toward the Badlands and organized a two-man circumambulation of Devil's Tower. It's a *long way* around Devil's Tower. Reaching the west face, looking out over two hundred miles of prairie, this witness saw nothing, out at the horizon rim the sky trembled and shone, in between the space looked completely empty. Ed then filled it in with the substantial history of everything that had happened out there going back beyond the Plains Indians to the movements of the earth-plates and the ice. He was always giving you everything—the most generous man it was possible to know. "I've always had that Wyo tour as a wild high water mark," he would write to me eighteen years later, dying.

And we are all there together
time will wave as willows do
and adios will be truly, yes,

 laughing at what is forgotten
and talking of what's new....
    —"If It Should Ever Come,"
    from *The Newly Fallen* (1961)

Prologue:

We Were There When It Was New
(1965–1968)

AFTER TWO YEARS OF CORRESPONDENCE between Idaho and England Ed Dorn and I finally met up in person in 1965 at the then-brand-new University of Essex. I arrived from Cambridge in the spring of that year and took a room in a cottage in the North Sea fishing village of Brightlingsea, a half dozen miles from the still-in-construction university site at Wivenhoe Park. Early that autumn Dorn and his family—his wife Helene, son Paul, eleven, stepchildren Fred, sixteen, and Chansonette, thirteen—crossed over from America on the *Queen Elizabeth*. Coming off a dozen trying but illuminating years of wandering "throughout the trans-mountain west following the winde," the family, a tight-knit little group brought closer together by long experience of pioneering, was making its first trip to Europe. Dorn's initial glimpse of the Old World came at Cherbourg on September 13. It was a large moment for him, setting his sense of himself as a poet up against his sense of cultural identity in ways he did not yet fully understand. The next day, rounding the Isle of Wight on the great ocean liner, he thought of Keats's letters— as thirty-three years later, dying, he would retrace Keats's last travels to the Spanish Steps and the Protestant Cemetery in Rome. Five minutes later the tide of feeling had turned in him again, and, as he would report in a letter to his erstwhile mentor Charles Olson, "for some reason the whole thing welled up in me and I started asking abstract questions like do I really want to go to England, do I want to be here on this ship."

By then both questions were purely academic. At the end of a bewildering trail of "altogether nagging occupations" that stretched back to his Illinois prairie adolescence, he now stood at the brink of the first job that would befit the years of intensive autodidactic labor he had put into turning himself from a poor farm boy into a writer and a thinker. That job would provide the credential to enable a peripatetic career in academia. (Ever restless, Dorn would in the decade to come wander from school to school—Kansas, Essex again, Northeastern Illinois, Kent State, Riverside, Essex yet again, San Diego—performing the kind of intellectual migrant work he once spoke of as "'casual labor'—where there's a job you show up," before settling in 1978 at Colorado, eventually to become a tenured professor of English.) With his first "respectable" job would come other transformations he could hardly have suspected in his equivocal moment aboard the liner off the English coast. Those changes are only hinted at in Dorn's capsule autobiographical accounts of these years: "In 1965, a Fulbright Lectureship at the University of Essex turned into an odyssey of upheaval and exile...."

"WE WERE THERE WHEN THINGS WERE NEW," Dorn would remind me in a letter on the occasion of returning to the University of Essex in 1990 for a conference commemorating the school's twenty-fifth anniversary. Back in 1965 he had been appointed to lecture "on the nature of westward expansion" by the head of the then-new university's Department of Literature, Donald Davie. The department was Davie's brainchild; a highly respected poet, critic and teacher, he had left his secure position as a Cambridge don to take up the comparatively risky work of founding a new kind of English Literature program—including in its scope American and European literary studies—at a fledgling provincial school where (as Dorn reported back to Olson shortly after arriving) "the buildings [were] not yet finished, even the ones being used."

Both Dorn and I were Davie recruits at Essex, both of us had come to England as Davie-sponsored Fulbright Fellows. During my two years in Davie's Cambridge college, Gonville and Caius (where he was supervising my Ph.D. research on Ezra Pound), I had observed Davie's growing interest in Dorn's writing. Given the obvious disparity in their training and tastes—Davie had been a disciple of the fiercely canonical F. R. Leavis, Dorn of the equally dogmatic anti-canonist Olson—that interest seemed at first quite unlikely. But there were strong underlying reasons for it. Coincidental similarities of background created surprising common ground between two men of seemingly divergent style and sensibility, the polished don and the hard-edged migrant worker. Both were self-demanding, ambitiously driven sons of Protestant families of the industrial working classes. In his youth Davie had attended a Yorkshire Baptist chapel, a class-parallel with the Methodist congregation of Dorn's childhood: the message in both venues could be summed up by the words of a Scottish-Reform Methodist preacher Dorn considered his earliest intellectual influence, "It's not okay, and it's not going to be okay." Davie's primary role model as a child, like Dorn's, had been a grandfather who was a lifelong railway man (Davie's was a signalman, Dorn's a mechanic and pipe fitter). Early instruction in the pains of upward mobility had left each man with his own particular distance from and distrust of the middle classes: Davie for his part had chosen to express his sense of difference from above, through an enlightened intellectual elitism that had allowed him to prosper in his career among the academic intelligentsia, whereas Dorn had stubbornly maintained an oppositional stance, his identification with the dispossessed of the socioeconomic "basement stratum" not surprisingly retarding his career progress. But Davie would not easily forget his own class history, nor Dorn easily accept the fates apparently attendant upon his.

Davie was genuinely intrigued by Dorn's writing, with its rangy, gestural, highly individualized syntax—once at Cambridge he devoted a session of our tutorial on Wordsworth to a discussion of the comparative grammars of *The Prelude* and Dorn's long poem about New Mexico, "The Land Below"—and its equally idiosyncratic views. But it was the moral depth and complexity of the work that plainly moved Davie most deeply. In an essay on the Dorn novel *The Rites of Passage* for a magazine I edited with fellow Essex graduate student Andrew Crozier, *The Wivenhoe Park Review,* Davie spoke of the qualities in Dorn's attitude which particularly appealed to him: a curious humility and openness, a courageous willingness to moralize directly from experience. "What validates Dorn's lyric voice is, time and again, its humility, the instruction it looks for and gets from people and places and happenings. It reflects upon them, it moralizes on them; but the reflection and the moral are drawn not from some previously accumulated stock of wisdom, but (so the writing persuades us) immediately out of the shock of confronting each of them as it comes, unpredictably."

DORN HAD LONG SUFFERED from an acute impatience with administrative bureaucracy. Two months into his stay at the University of Essex—he unaffectionately dubbed it "the Multiversity," after a Robert Duncan poem about the Free Speech movement at Berkeley—he reported to Olson that Davie struck him as "pleasant and I think he has a good mind, but it might split across the edge of Administration and scholarship. He will tell himself increasingly it can be done but it can't. Already it is a vast school with all the problems and preconditions that enforces. I see it as simply the concept—it isn't how many students you have, you can have [just] one and still be a multiversity, if you think that way. Typewriters and secretaries, rubberbands and paper clips. They are already squeezed between the ultimate memo-pad. But one must say the game is not over, and they do have an idea to make a university civic, like a city, the dorms high rise right in the center of piazzas and enclosed courts."

Physically, "the multiversity" was as yet no more than a loose collection of windswept, ill-matched glass and concrete boxes scattered seemingly at random across an ongoing construction site, with big trucks and caterpillars still moving earth around the formerly well-landscaped grounds of an estate Constable had once painted. Dorn's own office was a spartan glass box in a sprawling concrete and steel compound. I shared a cube-clustered office space just around the right-angled corridor bend; my office partner for a while was a French literature specialist Dorn would draw on in portraying Dr. Jean Flamboyant, the smug mutant-academic expert on "post-ephemeral" subjects who would boast to the hero of *Gunslinger* "I was the flame of my Lyceum / I can fix anything."

The shock of recognition that greeted Dorn with his first taste of "refined" academic politics at Essex—nothing resembling this had come with his four-classes-a-week wage slavery at Idaho State College—was recorded in his letters from England back home to Olson. To the considerable amusement of both poets, it seemed the latter's allegedly "barbaric" influence was an early issue of controversy in the Essex Department of Literature. "There is one American here who bugs me a bit," Dorn reported to Olson in January 1966, "George Dekker, who met Davie when Davie was at Santa Barbara, and both of these men then came somewhat into the very hesitating orbit of [Hugh] Kenner." The "Kennerites," Dorn learned in our weekly departmental seminars, were quite shy of Olson: "This Dekker said you were a Barbarian." Dorn traced the source of the prejudice to basic political leanings—and the intrinsic dishonesty of the academic mind. "The faculty—they're sneaking academic bastards too, i.e. hip academic people—shows itself to me like this: if you seem anticapitalish and no communist they try then to see if you're as sophisticated a fascist as them, like literate and humane, dig you've got to be intelligent, and if you fail that sensual test you come out Zap! barbarian...." He told Olson he had to tread a fine line of neutrality. "I just couldn't get stuck as the champion explainer of your to them (the faculty) abstruse points."

He felt little more sympathy with the department's Oxbridge-bred "liberal" wing, as he told his former teacher. "You can't imagine, or I suppose you can and did already but these types think you *Use* words, like wait a minute!... Or, they got *objections,* which is even cornier. I thought at first because they were more 'intelligent' than the academic[s] I'd been used to in Idaho they were more interesting, but I dig now they're only more boring. I mean that *objection* is a bottomless well; they call it their 'training.' I get so damn pulled apart trying to keep it straight because they are nice men and in no simple sense—they think because the Labor candidate yesterday in Hull won the biggest majority since 1945 everything is simply going to groove."

A POEM DORN GAVE ME for *Once,* the first of a series of mimeograph magazines I'd be bringing out at Essex, showed him doing with his writing what he'd done in all his previous nomadic removals: trying to locate himself in the new place through a close reading of its cultural landscape, history and geography. Titled "A provisional fragment," the poem represented the cultural and historical meanings he'd detected in the air and under his feet during his first months in Colchester. His subject was the confrontation of autonomous local authority with the imposed authority of Empire. He linked the imperialist armies of Rome invading ancient Britain with those of America invading Southeast Asia in the mid-1960s: "Elephants at the Balkerne Gate ... Elephants south of Saigon, under the lazy dog bomb." The heroine of the poem was the local revolutionary Queen Boadicea, celebrated by Dorn for her symbolic—and violent—resistance against Empire. When he gave me the poem he told me he feared it might be too bookish. He'd been studying up on the history of Roman Colchester in C. F. C. Hawk's *Camulodunum,* he said. But there was as always a personal poetic motive informing his studies. His own relation to place was the determining interest. The old Balkerne Gate had stood just up the street from his first English home, a Tudor-style cottage next to a rook-haunted churchyard on Lexden Road, the last stage in the ancient Roman thoroughfare from London to Colchester.

"Colchester is an old Roman town," Dorn reported to Olson during this phase of preliminary investigation. His letter glossed his first "English" poem. "The wall is nice and largely intact. Claudius as you might know took this place first in the reconquest. I guess there was no re- to it, Caesar had no intention like that when he came. But I thought of Claudius the other night when I was looking out the window onto Lexden Road, which went to Stane Street and thence to London, a main Roman street. He had elephants with him when he led the attack. A.D. 43. And then that nasty Queen Boadicea sacked Camulodunum and tore the heads off all the figures of that deified Emperor." Six months later, on the first warm day of their first English springtime, he hiked with Helene up the road to a pub located at the site of the Balkerne Gate. As they basked at an outdoor table in the welcome sunshine, Dorn felt his mind adrift in an ancient past that was suddenly close and tangible, "saw it and heard it, like right under my feet ... Claudius and his chariots & whores were *real* to me, I could smell the dust."

Such moments of virtual presence were gleaned out of an overriding sense of cultural distance. Poking around the town, and trying to find himself at home in it, while yet so far from home, Dorn remained on the lookout for any signs of a familiar world. The son of a grain-rich prairie that had sustained an empire's growth, he decided (as he would later relate) that Colchester's parallel historical geo-economic role as an imperial breadbasket made it a place he could understand—and thus survive. "Colchester is an old Roman grain port. It's where the Romans got their grain, in which respect the province of Essex is very much like Iowa, or Illinois or southern Wisconsin.... So Colchester was a Roman garrison then a British garrison. It was a grain port, and it's still a grain port. In Colchester, I could walk down the street and cross over the Roman wall, still largely intact, and actually know quite a bit about what was going on for the last couple of thousand years. The emotional and the psychological bedding that that gave one to work was just incalculable. To get connected with something Tacitus was talking about made things a lot more exciting. There was a woman named Boadicea here who rode into the marketplace and with her sword took off the head of the Emperor Claudius which had been put up by the Romans as a local deity. So, revolution was in the air. It was ... the mid-Sixties."

IT WOULD TAKE DORN A WHILE yet to find—or forge—a place for himself in local revolution. In the meantime the rather staid day-to-day life of the provincial town would have to do. In the parlance of his neighbors "the local" meant not a geographical concept but the pub across the road. And indeed the poet spent many idle hours that first year at one such establishment, which moreover was located literally right across the road. One night after we'd flung many darts and consumed a pint or two he tried to explain the pub mystique in a letter to Olson. "Does this sound terribly dull? It sort of does doesn't it. But I assure you the Nation, England, is backward and funny but alert in some weird way and it is mostly a strange pleasure to be here."

Still he admitted the secret to the amazing drinking habits of the British remained as yet beyond his ken. He told Olson about the amusing queries he and Helene had received from some neighbors they'd invited to a party following a reading at the university by an American visitor, Tom Parkinson. "These English types are *purists*—we invited a few of the townspeople (as well as university faculty) ... they *all* according to their own lights tried to find out if they had to go to the reading in order to come to the party (read: drink Booze). My gracious wife s[ai]d no, of course not! Oh wow! Charles this is a weird place—this is the Home of Alcoholism—and yet they, as a nation, keep the drinking places closed—they open around 11 AM then close 2:30 PM (the pubs that is) then open ab[ou]t 6 PM and close 11 PM (Sunday 10 or 10:30)—the consequence is they drink like motherfuckers in their Homes—and the English have Homes! And strangely the drunker they get the more sober they seem to get & hence the funnier & stuffier as 'English' they are. I often think I've yet to really see thru any one of them."

"Seeing through" me, on the other hand, was easier for him: we shared a world view, he believed, because we hailed from a common glacial swath. ("We're from the same alluvial fan," he would say to me in a late letter, meaning there were certain things that did not have to be explained between us, and that separated us from others.) By Dorn's culture-geographic reckoning of character, he himself was an escaped sod buster from the tall-corn prairie, I—as he would inform Olson in a late January 1966 letter—"a sharp kid in many ways, a Chicago buster as we used to call 'em, anyway he has a kind of edge of intelligence, spontaneous and practical like how many apples are in the basket and if you take, etc., [which] I like in the middle of the English mind which still is in the more immediate and important ways therefore strange, initially, to me. So we whoop it up once in a while."

We did do a fair share of harmless time-passing according to our lights, hanging out at his house, the pub across the road, the no-frills campus pub at the university, or in his university office, where the whooping got a quantum boost from reel-to-reel tapes of highlights of the 1965 Berkeley Poetry Conference—Olson, Ed Sanders, Robert Duncan, Ted Berrigan, et al.—played over and over on a banged-up recorder that had survived many an epic Dorn journey. As Ed didn't have a car, he was able to visit my own digs in the sleepy fishing village but once, and that only by force of circumstance, one night when he had stayed too late at a party out in the wilds beyond the university and had to hike home with me all the way to the coast. By the time we got to Brightlingsea he was so infuriated by the remoteness of the place and the primitiveness of the accommodations—he'd by then had enough of that sort of thing to last a lifetime—that he refused ever to consider returning.

Once when I'd missed the last bus from Colchester to Brightlingsea the Dorns hospitably returned the favor by offering me the floor of their low-beamed front room to sleep on. I awoke to the flutterings of rooks in the sycamores and bucolic sounds of cowbells from the pastures beyond the adjacent Lexden churchyard. Out the window, North Sea mists were still drowning everything close to the ground. From the other side of the house, where Ed kept his writing office, I heard the intermittent clicking of his typewriter, interrupted periodically by the loud opening guitar chords of the Beatles song "Paperback Writer." He had appropriated his kids' copy of the 45, with "Day Tripper" on the other side, and had evidently discerned the sound of coming revolution. He would type for a while, then play the Lennon-McCartney tune again. His hipster's disdain of pop music had been suspended to entertain a change of sensibility. He already had an inkling he wanted to be part of that change, perhaps.

CHANGE WAS IN THE AIR, Dorn had been caught up in it. His writing and thinking of the time reflect a new sense of the possible relations between poetry, pop culture and history, including personal history. The creative, subversive and revolutionary activities of poet Ed Sanders provided him a significant example. Dorn had been strongly affected by his encounter with Sanders at the Berkeley Poetry Conference. He greatly enjoyed the outrageous comedy of the Fugs, and also admired the curious phenomenon of Sanders' instant celebrity. "Whereas movie stars *think of* themselves as movie stars, Ed Sanders *is* a movie star," he wrote in a report on current cultural developments for *The Wivenhoe Park Review* ("The Outcasts of Foker Plat: News from the States"). "A true Fug-star," Sanders appeared in Dorn's view the forerunner of a New Reformation. "Ed Sanders is John Wyclif 1380 announcing the end of transubstantiation, or the beginning, which[ever] way you choose to look at it." Suggesting Sanders' "Total Assault on the Culture" qualified him as a genuine radical dissenter in the great tradition of the Protestant Revolution, Dorn quoted in full the Fugs song "Coca Cola Douche." "I'm obviously turned on by the paradoxical aspects of thinking," he would say a few years later. His connecting Sanders with Wyclif, he now paradoxically contended, represented "no special conflict." "Groping is not violent, but it isn't, equally, non-violent."

Staying with his paradoxical linking of Reformation history and Sixties Revolution as he turned later in the essay to Robert Duncan's poem about student protests at Berkeley, Dorn boldly traced the origins of that rough beast, "the Multiversity," back beyond the current suppression of academic freedoms through the Oxford town vs. gown battles of the fourteenth century to the "real hydras," the twin heads of arbitrary power and centralized authority. In what Dorn described as a kind of archetypal historical "clash" over the sites of learning, the true heroes had consistently been those dissenting "academicians who defended the liberties of their university against papal interference." In the current struggle only the names and "cover" of the agencies of repressive control had changed; the real malign identities remained. "What in our day, is the Pentagon if not the Papacy. It *is* also the Church. Everyone must have noticed on TV what a fine pair the Pope and Johnson made."

This particular fine point of paradox seemed less seriously meant at the time than it now appears in light of the later course of Dorn's thought and writing, in which his counterposed convictions regarding his own "Protestant" dissenter heritage and the historical evils of the Papacy evolved into something resembling a fixation. At once an expression of a deeply ingrained habit of mind and a deliberately cultivated rhetorical strategy, Dorn's insistent embrace of such paradoxical or "difficult" positions in his work of the later Sixties anticipates the against-the-grain quality of his highly individualized intellectual presence of later years—"a relentlessly perverse skepticism," as his University of Colorado colleague and friend Peter Michelson terms it, "practiced with something like philosophical discipline ... and bordering on being its own faith." The pure products of that perverse approach would include the self-proposed "unrelenting dryness and stiffness of the moral rigidity" of *Abhorrences* (a "corrective" gesture in epigrammatic verse meant to counteract "the abysm of greed ... the moral nadir ... the abandonment to banality" of the 1980s); the impassioned, courageous defense of heresy (historical, and, by implication, personal), of *Languedoc Variorum;* and the challenging, often confrontational, sometimes downright outrageous conversational style that would earn the later Dorn the dread of fools wherever he went. A "cranky cantankerous contrarian," as longtime friend Anselm Hollo would fondly describe him, Dorn was "as dialectical as they come (and then some), conversation with him was always or as long as I can remember (back to the Sixties) a matter of testing the interlocutor's received ideas, or ideas Ed suspected of being such. Almost any take endorsed by the U. S. media, and perhaps especially by the 'liberal' wing of same, was instantly suspect, and Ed's m. o. was to assume the diametrically opposed position."

Dorn's obsessive phobia involving the President and the Pope is a prime instance of the contrarian disposition to which Hollo refers. One recalls the vigorous anti-papist paranoia and prejudice of his later hero Milton, lamenting in *Areopagitica* (a text he would propound in his late teaching) how "the Popes of *Rome* engrossing what they pleased of Political rule into their hands, extended their dominion over men's eyes." See, for the full flowering of this attitude, Dorn's remarkable 1999 death-watch poem, "Chemo du Jour: The Impeachment on Decadron"—written during a chemotherapy infusion shortly after his first visit to Rome—in which the Roman Pope and American President (in this case, Clinton) converge in a hallucinated TV image, the poet's nightmare vision of the Terror of Authority. Ever since his initial recognition in 1954 of the potential of the proliferating one-eyed beast of the "antenna forest" to indefinitely self-replicate, producing more and more monsters in its own image, television had appeared to Dorn an insidious—and dangerous—form of thought control.

"WHAT IS FREEDOM BUT CHOICE?" asked Milton. The televised sporting event, the Hollywood western—forms of public myth, popular democratic spectacle—were the vehicles Dorn chose, in several important transitional poetic efforts of 1966, for discovering the meanings of an intense sense of cultural distance brought on by his self-exile from America. The modes of expression he now adopted—comic, ironic, dramatic—ran stubbornly counter to the painfully singular and earnest sincerity that had distinguished his earlier work.

That summer he provided "coverage," after his decidedly idiosyncratic fashion, of the World Cup soccer series, for two issues of my ongoing mimeograph magazine series, *Thrice* and *Slice*. He'd become intrigued, as he told me, by the idea that poems might be not only new but "news"—instant, topical, immediate. (A few years later, when he started a periodical called *Bean News*, he would reverse the assignment, appointing me his sports reporter.) The results were two long, windy "Quarters," plus an extended "Half-time Script," of a poem of some 800 extremely elongated lines titled "Box Score" (this fragment, all he would complete of the work, appears in his 1983 *Collected Poems* under the title "World Box-score Cup of 1966"). The broadly funny polyphonic political-satire "sportscast" narrated the contemporary struggle between the "Haves" of the "Developed World" and the underdeveloped "Havenots" in the mutated voices of broadcasters remembered from the poet's mid-American past, Bill Stern ("Stern Bill") and Harry Caray ("Harry Kamikaze"). "It represents an initial attempt to get speech into a poem but still inside that narrative thing which has hung with me all along," Dorn would later say of the "Box Score" experiment. "Tom Clark wanted some poems, so I just wrote them. I thought I'll try this out. It seemed like an immediate sort of situation. He'd just mimeograph them ... it was very quick. I carried that on until it didn't interest me any more. I was just trying to make a sportscaster talk in a plausible way, not about sports necessarily, but to turn that into another kind of latitude.... By that time I had become very convinced that the direct onslaught in that sober sense of the political poem was not only very boring but completely valueless." The exploration of "another kind of latitude"—that supplied by the dialogic imagination—would make this abandoned project a significant learning experience for Dorn, a prelude to new freedoms to come. The internal competition or conversation of voices in *Gunslinger,* as it would turn out, would be not quite new for Dorn, having been rehearsed in the quick, casual, low-pressure site of experiment that was "Box Score."

B Y THIS TIME the Dorn family had been wandering from place to place for so long that the lack of a stable home had almost achieved the status of a family joke—"we've been married all these years and we still don't have a pot to put on a window," Ed would tell Olson. In that summer of 1966 they moved from the small but bucolic Lexden Road cottage to a larger, rather gloomy Victorian Gothic flat nearer the center of town, on Victoria Road. The place was dark and chilly, with interior effects out of Poe's "The Raven," or perhaps a scene from *The Addams Family:* "high ceilings—great windows" and "cobwebs built in." It was never quite comfortable to inhabit. In poetic terms, however, the domestic atmosphere, conjured by Dorn in a letter to Olson as cinematically spooky ("I would reckon this flat to be CRYPTO-DANO-IRISH-TRANSYLVANIAN REVIVAL") would provide an entirely appropriate stage for the theatrical entry, in the poem "An Idle Visitation," an enigmatic 114-line dramatic narrative written early in the family's only winter there, of a mysterious visionary gunslinging stranger. That apparitional visitor's knock upon the poet's chamber door would spark the brilliant, bewildering seven-year epic comedy of *Gunslinger,* a work credited by Dorn's fellow poet Robert Duncan as a major breakthrough from "the poetry of process or organism" to a new genrebending mixed-media poetry having "to do with scenario and masque" and driven by the verbal devices of "a screen-narrative voice that takes off as a movie scenario [in] the Western, Marx Brothers style." The project would develop the polyphonic narrative technique Dorn had tentatively experimented with in "Box Score" into a creation of another scale altogether, one that would bring him temporary fame and be proclaimed by novelist Thomas McGuane "a fundamental American masterpiece."

"It came with no thought at all," Dorn later said of "An Idle Visitation." "That particular poem just came and I wrote it and I didn't know what I was doing. In fact, it was very peculiar for me to have done ... later reading it I thought that it, in fact, was a clue to a chamber of my mind that I wanted to go into very much ... I did want to make another exploration."

From reading Dorn's poetry and editing it (for *The Paris Review* as well as for my own modest mimeograph productions) I'd learned that his signature form of lyric realism, variously tender and tough but always and above all *true,* was a style that had never allowed much room for making things up. Yet as was immediately evident, in "An Idle Visitation" he was doing exactly that. An indication of the novelty for him of this surprising "Visitation" came in the early

December 1966 note that accompanied it and another occasional poem Dorn gave me at the same time for *Spice,* my latest mimeo venture. "Here are two for *Spice,*" he wrote. "The cowboy one I don't know what to make of yet, which I'm choosing to take as a good sign."

The second poem in the package was "A Notation on the Evening of November 27, 1966." This poem, which he indicated had been the first of the two to come to him, provides a useful anecdotal gloss on the origin of the gunslinger figure. "A Notation" was written on a night of watery moonlight and chilling North Sea mists, after we'd gone with some student friends "to see / an old classic flick at the Odeon" in downtown Colchester. Ed's poem was about senses of home, an issue of no little complexity for him at that time.

> The moon is a rough coin tonight
> full but screened by lofty moisture
> bright enough to make sure
> of the addresses
> on the letters I drop in the red pillar box
> Frost is on the streets. A soft winter breeze
> comes from the North Sea into my nostrils
> I am at home here only in my mind
> that's what heritage is.
> Turning the corner, only our windows
> along the ribbon of road are lit
> I know that my wife has gone to bed
> and that the gas is burning
> and that my heart and my veins
> are burning for home. Yet those abrupt times
> I hear the voice of home
> I am shocked, the hair on my neck
> > crawls.

The haunting "voice of home" that particular evening spoke in a confusing multiplicity of accents. The movie we'd seen was *The Mag-*

nificent Seven. A gunslinging re-make of Kurosawa's *The Seven Samurai* by John Sturges, a master of the cowboy-picture genre, this spectacular, romantically lyrical Western had a different look for Dorn at his present remove from America and all that was most familiar.

> The magnificent seven introducing
> Horst Buchholz, I'd seen it before
> and *had not* got it that a german
> played a mexican, of course!
> An American foreigner is every body
> navajoes play iroquois
> the American myth is only "mental" a foreigner
> is *Anybody.* Theoretically at least
> an Italian could play
> an English man or a London jew
> if nobody knew.
> Tom and Jenny were there
> and Nick Sedgwick.
> Tom remarked, on the evidence of
> the last scene when the Mexican-
> Japanese said Vaya con Dios
> and Yul said a simple adios,
> "that was philosophical."
> Then the five of us went home
> singing Frijoles!
> twirling our umbrellas
> and walking like wooden legged men in a file
> one foot in the gutter
> > the other on the sidewalk.

The "I do this, I do that" occasional quality of this relaxed account shows Dorn deliberately letting down his rhetorical guard—or anyway seeming to do so. In fact the casual nonchalance of the poem is to a large extent a calculated appearance; the poet, as often before,

is wandering to a purpose. The subtle weave of rhymes—streets /
breeze / Sea; Dios / adios / home / Frijoles!; jew / knew / Yul—rep-
resents a vintage Dorn lyrical tactic, concealing an intuitive but real
formal pattern within apparent informality. Far from casual, the
poem's implications of cultural displacement indirectly signal the
poet's real burden, a problematic confusion of identity.

In its foregrounding of cross-cultural identity dilemmas "A Nota-
tion" may offer some hints as well about the equally complicated
question of the identity of the fictional hero of its companion poem—
the gunslinger of "An Idle Visitation." A composite image, part stock
figure, part personal projection, that hero may have at least "acci-
dental" origins in *The Magnificent Seven,* the hidden link that con-
nects these two poems. Over a post-movie dinner of curry at a
Colchester Indian restaurant that late-November evening we had
discussed the code of conduct of the Hollywood Samurai, a matter
which Ed insisted, in typical out-on-a-limb fashion, had been treated
satirically in the film. In further debate on the comparative merits
of those lethal dudes' six-shooter techniques, he adjudged the anx-
ious, edgy, elegant quick-draw delivery of the character portrayed
by Robert Vaughn "impeccable"—as I remember—while those
played by Steve McQueen, James Coburn, Charles Bronson and Yul
Brynner also received style points. Trivia buffs may harmlessly or
perhaps even usefully ponder just which movie cowboy's "slender
leather encased hands" made their way into "An Idle Visitation."
With this author the proverbial categorical boundary line between
"real" and represented worlds was around this time becoming less
and less immutable: the "ritual of my own person" that in a 1968
prose sketch ("Driving Across the Prairie") Dorn cited as his private
form of salvation included a curiously privatized relation to his own
writings, which seemed for these years paradoxically to incorporate
more and more of his "inside real" existence the more cosmically
provocative and "outsidereal" they became. Thus, in a similarly lit-
eral reading, it's possible to discover numerous points of nexus
between the gunslinger's otherwise obscure statements about his
experiences in "An Idle Visitation" and Dorn's own biography—as

when the poetic stranger, explaining the exhausted condition of his horse and himself, the result of covering "the enormous space / between here and formerly ... we have come / without sleep from Nuevo Laredo," comes very close to describing a particularly stressful chapter in the author's extra-textual personal history, a frantic 1955 exodus across the Sonoran deserts from Mexico City to the Rio Grande.

However, though it's possible to begin to get a referential handle of sorts on the gunslinger figure here in Dorn's early presage, that purchase does not last us very far into what would become an often difficult, sometimes imponderable poem. In its subsequent unfolding into comic romance, epic comedy or mock epic—Dorn's project would increasingly defy or evade conventional genre boundaries as well—the poem's far-traveling hero, here first encountered up close, at a "metropolitan nearness," "in a foreign land," would expand into a character of mythic, even cosmic presence, his interesting movements across the fluid elastic distances of the verbal range not only keeping "the sun, the moon / and some of the stars" in their courses but concurrently governing the entire enlarged metaphysical dimension of a text whose deepest engagement, directly opposing that of Dorn's earlier work, is with not geography but ontology ... "a movie scenario in the Western, Marx Brothers style" whose props and jokes would include the philosophies of Parmenides and Heidegger.

In Dorn's persistent comic confrontation with Being, the personal elements of the early start on the large poem would gradually become diluted into its whole meaning; in the end the personal significance of the apparitional stranger in "An Idle Visitation" must remain, like almost everything else about the *Gunslinger* project, impossible to discriminate, open to speculation. The 1966 newborn "cautious Gunslinger / of impeccable personal smoothness," carrying in his slender gloved hands a rolled-up "map of love" (later the poet would revise this to a "map of locations," thus burying from view a clue to his poem's personal emotional meaning) appears in the light of retrospect a bearer of diverse private runes and auguries—the figure of Dorn's future, arriving at his door?

IN A LAST-MINUTE DUST-JACKET STATEMENT for *The North Atlantic Turbine,* composed in the early autumn of 1967, Dorn suggested the dramatic change that was about to take place in his life and writing. The *Turbine* book, he said, was an extension of his old preoccupation with geography, latterly relocated to "another hemisphere." He had tired of that slow and exhausting kind of exploration. Now his impulse was to move from geography to intensity, he said, from restless surveys of the ground to intensive habitations of the moment: "That non-spacial dimension, intensity, is one of the few singular things which interests me now." The first indication of the transformation of practice had come with "An Idle Visitation." "I wanted to stop looking through these binoculars at the horizon," he would later explain, "I wanted to look at who was standing next to me. Like who was in the immediate room."

By September 1967, the Dorns were on the move again, from the dark, dank pseudo-Gothic interiors of Victoria Road to the fishbowl-like exposure of Linden, a semi-detached "glass house" with a façade of windows and French doors looking out at—and open to be looked in at from—the crossroads at Wivenhoe, a small, conservative waterside village on an estuary a few miles from the university.

That autumn Dorn taught a course on the prose of the American West at the university. In the first meetings of the class an untoward current of feeling began to pull his life in a new direction. It was as if his lines from "Oxford," a *North Atlantic Turbine* poem written earlier that year, were coming back to haunt him: the smoke signals of freedom were sending him the message "it's time / to move on, open up more country...." He informed Olson in a letter that unexplained events had left him "in a fucking hopeless well, of every kind of despair you might imagine." Nevertheless, in creative terms, the desperate and eventful moment was proving a productive one.

By the end of September he'd "finally got going on the Gunslinger,"
revising and advancing the blind-flying projections he'd plotted in
"An Idle Visitation." In October he had a manuscript "of 30 typed
foolscap pages," which he sent off to America to be produced by
John Martin of Black Sparrow Press. "I think it's the best thing I
have ever done," he told Olson proudly, "I mean, I *feel* it that way.
It is nice to get away from the heaviness of what I've been into for the
past, oh, five years.... I am trying for my own life to recast everything
every time I see any motion on the pool at all. It seems time."

> Ah yes, the Gunslinger exhaled
> It's been a long time.
>
> The drifting singer
> put one foot on a chair
> and began
>
> I shall begin he said
>
> the Song about a woman
> . . .
>
> her mouth
> a disturbed tanager, and
> in her hand an empty damajuana,
> on her arm an emotion
> on her ankle a band
> a slender ampersand
>
> her accent so superb
> she spoke without saying
> and within her eyes
> were a variety
> of sparkling moments....

In November he brought the completed Book I of *Gunslinger* to his class for a first airing. Among his students was the young woman who'd been the secret model for his lyric blazon in "The Song about a woman," a 21-year-old London girl named Jennifer Dunbar—one of our little group of Colchester moviegoers mentioned in his *Magnificent Seven* poem of the previous year, "A Notation on the Evening of November 27, 1966" ("Tom and Jenny were there ..."). The "sparkling" Jennifer and her twin sister Margaret (the unidentified fifth moviegoer in "A Notation") stood out in the staid social landscape of Essex as bright exotic imports; their mother came from an aristocratic Russian family, their Scots-English father was the Director of the London Film School.

Looking back on that time of turmoil and discovery—Dorn himself would call it a season of "embraceable revolution"—Jenny Dunbar recalls his reading of *Gunslinger* in class as a first oblique declaration of his love, extended with the masking indirection characteristic of a shy and private man.

> He read a rough typescript of Book I, all of it. ... It was close to the end of term. I don't know how to explain this, but we were both already in love at the start of the semester. Ed was playing that Martha and the Vandellas single "Dancing in the Streets" over and over again, and I was playing Jimi Hendrix and hitch-hiking to school every day like I was getting a ride to another universe. In class his gaze was so intense it felt like we were the only two people in the room. When he read Book I—he pretended it was a poem he'd just got in the mail from another poet—he made it sound like a love song to me. I mean "the Song about a woman" at the end of the book— it's like he already knew. And of course I knew he wrote it. This must sound crazy, but there are several things in *Gunslinger* he wrote about before they happened. Howard Hughes moving to Las Vegas, for example. ... The fact is, although we didn't declare ourselves until December, on this other plane,

we were already together. We talked about this afterward—
which one seduced the other?—and all we could say was that
forces beyond our control had pulled us into this orbit.... We
tried to resist all those months because of course it was
"wrong" and would hurt people, but we couldn't defy the
truth of it.

In the uncollected spring 1968 poem "This Is the Way I Hear the
Momentum," written out of the "knarl of feeling" produced by a
tincture-of-cannabis-tinted visit with Jenny to Druidic sites at Stone-
henge and Glastonbury, Dorn would celebrate the intertwined begin-
nings of his personal transformation and of his verse epic as combined
biological message, organic energy-discharge and cosmic bolt from
the blue: "to arise into the light / *ness* of these limbs / these parts of
the universe having growth / So that the foot of this book / is grown
at last for the book to stand on / thrown away from myself as my
life was given to me / with sharp aim...."

B UT WITH NEW LOVE came a period of domestic agony for Dorn,
as his marriage of almost fifteen years was shaken by its first
serious signs of disunion. Always a dedicated and loyal family man,
he had survived and surmounted many hardships and trials over the
years with Helene—who for her part had forsaken the compara-
tively stable economic circumstance of her first marriage to accom-
pany him on his errant wanderings. "We share a common exile,"
he'd written in "Six Views from the Same Window of the Northside
Grocery," a poem for Helene written during a bleak February in
Idaho ("the most desolate place in existence," as he would call it in
a letter from that time). Another poem dedicated to Helene, "Oh
Don't Ask Why" (also from the Idaho collection *Geography*, 1965)
acknowledges some of the cost his struggle to become a writer had
brought upon them as a couple and as a family.

How you loved me
through all travesty

how you kept those lovely eyes
clear,

their burn
fixed away from some
monument of curiosity,—How
ever can you live like that?

Yes, at moments I did waste
our lives, giving way
foolishly to public thoughts,
large populations.

Are we needed? On this mountain
or in this little spud town in the valley
or along this highway, you held
your eyes on getting us there, repeatedly
where? We

never knew. . . .

Helene keeps vivid at forty years distance the memory of such marathon Dorn family treks as the exhausting September 1961 "caravan" transit from Santa Fe to Pocatello—which followed after the Dorns had moved out of their Camino Sin Nombre place, where they'd relocated from their Acequia Madre place in Santa Fe— "where we'd moved from a stay with Lucia and Race [Newton]; where we'd gone, at Race's suggestion that Ed could work at Claude's [restaurant-bar]; where we'd gone due to Bob [Creeley]'s suggestion, from a stay with Ray & Lorna Obermayr [in Idaho]; where we'd gone totally spent with Burlington, at Ray and Lorna's magnanimous, as always, invitation. It was the first time we left a house we felt was almost our own [Anacortes Street, Burlington] and there was only the Salvation-Army-bought trunk to hold what each one wanted to keep."

Dorn's 1962 poem "West of Moab" memorializes the grueling overland junket from Santa Fe to Pocatello, representing the risks and ardors of the expedition in a stripped-down version of the classic John Ford frontier migration saga. Substituting "tired engines" for covered wagons, filling stations for watering holes, Dorn's strained travelogue retains the familiar essentials of the Western voyage of re-settlement, tracing an arc of feeling that encompasses anticipation and regret, openness to discovery and vulnerability to loss.

The actual collection of vehicles, weighed down with the family's worldly belongings, had included, in addition to the Dorns' "packed to the hilt" station wagon, Ray Obermayr's pickup truck and Bob Creeley's VW bus: Obermayr acting as the welcoming advance sentinel ("I went down to help them load up"), Creeley as the departing escort-guard ("I hated to see them go, so could walk along with them in this fashion for some usefully longer part of the way"). "We led the caravan," says Helene. "I remember checking the rearview mirror to make sure everyone was behind us. There are wonderful photos of Ray and Creeley and Ed sitting on the stove the night of packing up before we left. I was pissed. They were drinking and having a party while I was desperately trying to make sure we had packed everything.... Mother hen who loved to party too but had a household and three much-loved kids to think about. And we did make it, no matter all the drivers must have had terrible hangovers."

Complicating matters was a freak early September snowstorm on the eve of the party's departure, making the highways of the "great / american desert" a challenge. Ray Obermayr, another survivor of the trek, supplements Helene's reminiscence from the wagon driver's p. o. v.: "We had a caravan. Creeley had got hold of some big dexedrines, they were white and large, about the size of Alka Seltzers. We said we'd drive all night. So I took one of those big dexedrines. It was so damn strong I started to hallucinate the center line was rising right up off the road. There were posts holding up power lines along the highway; I was afraid I was going to run into those. Finally I had to stop. We all got together at Cortez, the whole caravan pulled in and we all slept in the cars in the parking lot." Creeley, the second driver (in what the poet calls "the nazi car") has perhaps the fondest memory of all the survivors. "I just remember it as a great and affectionate trip! Actually I recall it was very romantic, as that part of our great country always is."

The tone of Dorn's own verse report is characteristically flat and unselfsparing:

> The caravan wound....
>
> A modern group in cars.
> They travelled north at an angle....
>
> Bitterly cold were the nights....
>
> In the bitterness of the great desert
> they tried to get comfortable in car seats.
> Utterly left behind was
> a mixed past, of friends and a comfortable house.
>
> They felt sorry for themselves perhaps
> for no real reason, there had never
> been in their baggage more than a few stars
> and a couple of moons....

The Dorn's isolated pioneer-life in an outbuilding on Ray Obermayr's mountain-country ranch typified the adventures which had brought them together as a family during these nomadic years. "The first two winters in Ray's studio," Helene recalls, "were pretty basic, no inside john, we went down to the college to take showers, but we all loved it there, and I was certainly used to cooking on a wood stove.... The wood cook-stove we installed was a Garland, which delighted Ed, and we always referred to it as our Red Garland. It was a happy time and not so 'basic' that Bob & Bobbie [Creeley] & kids didn't spend an Easter weekend with us one time—I guess the kids must have bunked up together, can't remember, but I do remember making Easter baskets to the annoyance of all the males. [The film maker] Stan Brakhage came too, at some point. He was then doing those 8 mm profiles of writers."

Obermayr's "studio" was a former chicken house. Creeley, who'd himself once made an earnest attempt to secure a living as a chicken farmer, recalls the Dorns' homesteading in the converted shed above Pocatello: "What I'll remember forever is the extraordinary way Ed and Helene were able to turn the hen house (one of those large houses for laying hens, egg producers, etc.) into such a warm and affectionate home, floored with bricks, a great wood stove—and it worked. I recall visiting there a couple of times and loving the vibes."

Creeley remembers the Dorn famly as a particularly close-knit band in that Western-wandering epoch. "They travelled always as a family, Ed was domestic and enclosing as a family man, they went together. A great poem of that time is 'The Land Below'—there's the park family scene (both theirs and their neighbors') which concludes that poem. Ed writes from a domestic base all the way—and it really underwrites his politics, as in 'The Debt My Mother Owed to Sears Roebuck.'"

In a 1967 visit to the Dorns in Colchester, Creeley got the impression the repeated moves had begun to have an attenuating effect: he cites as the central text of their nomadic ethos an early Dorn tale of the hard side of the drifting life. "Being so 'on the road' in the 'C. B. & Q.' mode was part of their life for years and years, as was still [now] in Colchester—in a rented house that rained in the kitchen when one used the stove." Later that winter after Dorn had left his wife and family, Creeley met up with him again in London, now in company with his new love and seemingly infatuated with the possibilities of the cultural moment. (Jenny's "swinging London connections" referred to by Creeley included a sister-in-law who was a pop star.)

Recalling Ed and Helene sitting in that immeasurably dank house in Colchester, Helene's back bugging her, them both with ultimate runny noses, feet in tub of concoction of mustard and hot water—I think Ed just said silently, fuck it—I've got to get out! And Jenny with her modest but real swinging London connections, the brother and Marianne Faithfull, etc.—her tone, her hipness, her brightness—wow! Fuck pioneering, man—on to London! Ed reverted to ONE on the instant, not glibly, but truly—he'd been stepfather/father for three very pleasant kids, had done damn well by them, and then it broke—the feeling between him and Helene, who continued for some real time to love him and feel confused, but she was not really in that world he wanted and finally did enter. It was she who was the pioneer—her initial break with her first husband was heroic.

The tensions of Dorn's life—the wariness, displacement, opposition—were no longer containable within the structure he had created for himself, Creeley suggests. In "the world he wanted"—that world of "large populations," previously engaged only from an edgy distance—presence appeared interchangeable with the presentation one made for oneself:

> I think one's well advised to keep conscious of how deliberate and worked for were Ed's "self presentations," like the white linen jacket Helene [once hand-sewed] for him, the intense self-consciousness and awareness of others he demonstrates insistently. "Gunslinger" is a successful "Ed" in obvious ways, and Gunslinger's company is ideal indeed, a comfortably hip woman and a talking horse, another "Ed" as it happens, in an echo at least of the TV series—and "I" gets finally what he / she/ it deserves. Stoned.

By the time Dorn brought the first book of *Gunslinger* to read to his class, he had ceased work on the poem, and would not take it up again until he'd returned to America with Jenny the following year. The epic "exploration," like much else, would have to be put on hold until he had resolved the crisis of heart and home. Things were growing daily to seem more fraught. "Sometimes I find myself saying 'we must go on' flat and simple," he confessed to Olson on November 9, 1967. "But I can't figure why, always. I am so confused in my own work now, not what to do but the endless delay in doing it, i.e. my own fucking requirements are so multiple just now, and at a time when I want a simple and open shot at it.... Look, I don't know why I'm saying this, Sunday afternoon, fog, and cast in the form of our own problems unquote." A month later, term had ended, and Jenny had gone back to London, but nothing was clear, and the trying situation at Linden had not improved. "It is more desolate around here than I would care to tell you," Dorn wrote to Olson on December 15.

He now made several trips to London. Helene flew with the kids to New York for a visit with her brother. When she returned in January there came further torments. "I am now the stranger to my own life, or traveler in small circles—utterly confused inside inner confidence," Dorn told Olson on January 24 after a long silence. He mustered the nerve to spell things out at last. "The reason I have not written ... is difficult to speak of in any sense—because it doesn't seem easily to lend itself to *believable* sense—OK—Helene and I have been thru a very difficult 2 months and one result is that I live temporarily in a hotel—until the end of this week simply to make life easier because we had come to such impasses of 'talk' that it was all we c[ou]ld do ... the whole thing is particulary injury prone and painful and ambivalent because we are so damn closely tied—etc., Love, etc.—oh wow you know how much I *don't* have to say to you. So here it is—Six months more confinement in this close-out white-sale so-called country and then home...."

He and Jenny made a trip to Paris in company with a small party of Essex "politicals" whose purpose was to observe the revolutionary upheavals then in progress among their French academic compatriots. Returning to London for a reading in the last year of his life, Dorn would cast an emotional glance thirty years back to that revolutionary idyll of the spring of 1968—a moment of "bucolic" innocence and intuitive simplicity, as he latterly remembered it. "I just can't imagine how bucolic life was then, I mean in my memory. If you went to the Sorbonne, which we did, and, you know, saw the *situationistes* spilling over the balconies and explaining the L. A. riots, it all made some kind of sense. It was beautifully intellectual and feasible and containable, embraceable ... and now it's so cheap, you couldn't give it away."

"We did attend lectures at the Sorbonne," Jenny recalls, "going from room to room to catch the range of polemic from structuralists to situationists. Jean Baudrillard, *par exemple,* whose work Ed always admired. His French was very poor but he seemed to understand quite a bit. It was exciting. We saw the students rioting in the streets, cars on fire, cobblestones uprooted."

The idyll in Paris brought unintended results, forcing the covert romance out into the open. A member of the small contingent of Essex academics with whom they had traveled to Paris, says Jenny, sent back a manifesto of sorts to the *Times* from the cross-channel ferry, advertising the expedition as a gesture of support for the "revolution." "He listed all our names—including Anna Mendelsohn who was later arrested with others for having a bomb in her house (can't remember what they intended to blow up) ... the point is that the telegram was published in *The Times* and announced to everyone that we were going to join our fellow revolutionaries in Paris, and of course it served as a public announcement to be read by Helene, Donald Davie, et al. that Ed and I were off together. We did not want to be part of this official revolutionary group and it caused us some embarrassment."

Back at Linden came the final split. Helene took the children off to Barcelona to live. "Break-ups are a nightmare," she would say long afterward of that time of painful upheaval. "Worse for the person who's left behind, but hard also for the person who is going. Ed said to me, 'I guess I want the bright new coin.'" On a day when the early spring weather turned "very cold w/ gale wind from land to sea," Dorn wrote Olson to break the news of the dissolution of his marriage. "Helene and the kids settled in Spain.... All the 'explanation' of this scene, the guesses one might make as a 'result' are still too preposterous to think a[bou]t much less talk—I can only take heart from such people as you ... and you are almost single in this respect—i.e. Creeley was cautiously understanding—which is understandable of course—Helene and I never shared anything if not all friends etc.—But regrets seem unavoidably loaded to me at this point and in that sense I haven't been wholly free of paranoia. Anyway I have no idea what can happen—Colchester to Kansas—can this really be the end? ... Still it is a 'situation' and one of my own flawless manufacture—Jenny, I almost hesitate to say—i.e. break the silence as it were a bubble of brilliant color—is lovely, like a fine day."

Dorn moved back into Linden, stowing all the rented furniture—big settees, stuffed chairs and sofas—out on the front lawn and setting up with Jenny and a few pillows and psychedelic posters in the empty house. All the world's curious crossroads passers-by now stared in, or so it seemed to the sensitive couple (not "wholly free of paranoia"), and invidious "talk" seemed concurrently to be spreading behind their backs at the university. In *Love Songs,* Dorn's lyric journal of the love affair, there is a defensive bristling of resentment against the various phantom presumptions upon the lovers' privacy: "all the people looking / over the wall / are frozen ..." "we both fly off ... Away / from the flat rancorous smell / of their insinuation."

Gordon Brotherston, a Spanish-Americanist, Dorn's colleague in the Literature Department and later his collaborator on several translation projects, remembers the American poet and his young English lover being "stigmatized" more or less on general principles by the highly conservative neighbors at Wivenhoe Cross—who, says Brotherston, had already perceived the "new people" at Linden as "quite different," even before the latest developments (e.g., the furniture on the lawn, "like the set of a French movie")—as well as by the conservative majority in the Literature faculty.

Caught up in the confusions of his own life, in his concurrent flirtation with "revolution" Dorn now found himself playing a largely inadvertent role in the academic history of Essex. Events of that spring at the provincial university were following a particular course toward confrontation on the Parisian model. In April, in a climactic faculty vote that pitted radicals against authorities, Dorn declined to side with Donald Davie—by then ascended to Pro-Vice Chancellor of the university and as such the local figurehead of established power. The debt of gratitude he felt to Davie constraining him, the American poet equally declined to vote *against* the man who had brought him to England. Instead of committing himself either way, he attempted to distance himself from the issues by abstaining, stating that the matters at stake were local to the university, thus strictly none of his business as an American. Davie, however, understandably misinterpreted Dorn's abstention as a sign of disaffection—in effect, at this time of great pressure, a betrayal. "Ed's decision was a matter of principle," Brotherston says. "But Donald's sense of betrayal regarding those 'parlous times,' as he called them, ran very deep. Loyalty was the issue for him. His spiritual withdrawal from Essex was affected by that vote." At the end of the spring term Davie abandoned the program that three years earlier had been his brainchild, defecting abruptly to Stanford. He would continue for some years to harbor a strong reactive animus against Dorn—a "lulu of morality," the latter would comment on reading a late Davie memoir about Essex.

At the height of the spring 1968 Essex student/administration clash, demonstrators "closed down" the university, declaring the birth on the institutional site of the Free University of Essex. "The lecture theater block became the daily focus of public debate," Brotherston recalls. "Ed was very, very present in the Free University. He kept on meeting classes, but lecturing under the Free University auspices. It was an extraordinarily interesting time—for me, because I was very, very involved, and I'm certain for Ed as well."

Freedom was the tone and color of the time for Dorn. Having "reverted to ONE on the instant" (in old friend Creeley's words), he found the complications of the past months—and years—

dissolving in the rarefied air, until, as he wrote in *Love Songs,*

> I am nothing
> anymore at all
> than in myself

Getting ready for his return to America, he sent Olson a short note containing a draft of what would be the first lyric in *Love Songs,* with an accompanying note from a life that love and loss had winnowed to a fine airy thinness: "This is just simply to send you something because there is nada else—I don't know whether life gets empty or is that pure? Pure Life?"

> *After   Ours*
> *After   Thot*

> It is entirely true going from here
> from the old world to the new
> from Europa home
> the brilliant scrolls of the waves
>   wave
> the runic secret of homeward
> no sense in old towns
> got to have
> Newtowns of the soul

I.

Son of the Prairie
(1929–1948)

I.

Tribe

O N A COLD DRY NIGHT of downslope Chinook winds lightly agitating the unseasonably thin snow cover of the Front Range, in the second week of the last month of the now-gone century of which his writing is still a green and interesting memorial, surrounded by loving kin, his second wife Jennifer Dunbar (descendant of the fifteenth-century Scottish poet William Dunbar, who penned "The Lament for the Makers"), his daughter Maya, his son Kidd, and his half-sister Nonna, Edward Dorn passed away at his Denver, Colorado home. It was, coincidentally, the first house which this light-traveling son of the open prairie had ever in his wide-rambling life owned.

Where shall we look to "place" this poet of our distances and spaces, now that he is gone and only his written word and our memory of him remain to guide us? One of Dorn's last poems, "Tribe," yields some hint. Composed in the final months of his life, in a direct unornamented language that suggests there's no time to waste, it is a calm yet urgent statement of personal and genetic location. A "breed" of common origin is identified and celebrated in an inscription that is as much clan kinship testament as individual autobiography.

My tribe was lowdown struggling day labor
Depression South Eastern
Illinois just before the southern hills start
to roll toward the coal country
where the east/west morainal ridges
of Wisconsin trash pile up
at the bottom of the prairie, socially
a far midwest recrudescence of Appalachia
my grandfather French Quebecois
Master pipefitter in the age of steam
Indian fifty percent, very French
who didn't derogate himself
as a breed, showed none of those tedious
tendentious tendencies. Came down
from Chebanse, from the Illinois Central
in Iroquois County, to the Chicago &
Eastern Illinois line's division at Villa Grove
in one of the Twenties boomlets,
the last precipitous edges of the great development

A poet of multi-dimensional signaling, Dorn in his best poems typically offers apprehensions variously geological, geographical, cultural, social, historical, continuously interlaced. The descending median line that is the downward gravitating formal center of this poem is drawn by the final lobe of the last great late Pleistocene glacial surge, festooning the land around and below the southern tip of Lake Michigan (Dorn's east-central Illinois native country) with the makings of a rich soil turned in the century before the poet's birth to tilth—and wealth—by pioneer prairie farmers. But for Dorn a geological or geographical idea about a landform variation cannot be separated from a historical idea about the cultural differences that landform variation makes. Here his patented spring-loaded syntax, source of a characteristic mode of irony, spills the geographical/geological thought of "morainal trash" over into the socio-cultural thought of his own Appalachian "trash" migrant ancestors—a breed of people who'd long worked but never held significant title to any of that rich, fertile, black-loam corn-and-hog prairie country. And then sinking down further into history pure and simple, the descending axis of "Tribe" plumbs the life and career of Dorn's half-Indian French Quebecois grandfather, William Merton Ponton.

In the 1920s, Ponton, a railway steam-pipe fitter, had quite literally *come down* out of Iroquois County, where he'd worked on the Illinois Central, the great empire-building line of the Illinois Valley, seventy track-miles south to a job at the C. & E. I. division center at Villa Grove, a farming and railroading town of some two thousand souls situated on the Embarras River twenty miles south of Champaign. Ponton married a daughter of "pure Kentucky English" pioneer stock, Edward Dorn's maternal grandmother Bessie Hart, and they moved into a "nice clapboard house" in old-town Villa Grove. "My french canadian man," as the poet affectionately addresses him in the early 1960s poem "Obituary" (from *Hands Up!*), Dorn's grandfather Ponton was the most important male figure in his early life. "Obituary" is remarkable for the sheer detail with which the mature poet retains his commemorative inventory of his grandfather's many trouble-laden stops to deal with winter leaks and dirty pipes in nowhere burgs on the several railway lines for which his life was spent scaling and fitting steam-pipes. Beyond an obvious admiration of his grandfather's tough frontier-railroad trouble-shooting expertise, though, there was Dorn's more important private reason for quietly honoring the man (and on a return trip to Villa Grove in later years, for stopping off to pay a respectful visit to gaze a while at the peonies on his grave). The reason for that special honoring involved Ed's mother, Louise, William Ponton's and Bessie Hart Ponton's daughter.

Louise, at age twenty-one, had been wed and then just as promptly abandoned by a railroad boomer nearly twice her age. The fellow was a brakeman on the C. & E. I., a somewhat mysterious drifter out of the Ohio Valley named Dorn—of whom, after this feckless act, little else was ever said around Villa Grove, if indeed anything was ever known. "I asked Mother once about her first husband," Louise's daughter Nonna Abercrombie Lytle recalls, "and she said, 'He was like all railroaders, he had a woman in every stop,' and it was taboo to ask any more." William Leslie Dorn had turned up in town on a gust of freight-train grit around 1928 and by the next year was gone on a vanishing caboose, compelled by the first stiff winds of Depression joblessness, leaving no forwarding address. (In the poet's private symbolism, railroads would come to signify forced separation, division, alienation, dissociation, abandonment—see his poems "The Sundering U. P. Tracks," "La Máquina a Houston," "The Cycle of Robart's Wallet.") This William Dorn figures as the missing man whose unexplained absence is the enigmatic sign in the "meaningless map ... meaningless riddle" of lost childhood space Dorn graphed in the early poem "Goodbye to the Illinois."

> Where out of the black dirt
> screens are put up, shocks
> men come blindly to harvest ...
> heat giving rise to plants of illusion,
> soft winds blowing yellow pollen across the rows
> and in seclusion babies are born,
> in spring ...

For the departed brakeman's young wife the shame of divorce was terrible, and the social stigma was made even worse by her secluded early-springtime bringing into the world of a son: Edward Merton Dorn, born on the second day of April, 1929. Events left both mother and child thrown back on the family custom of William Ponton and his wife Bessie, a naturally generous woman, the sort of small-town housewife who around that time left fresh-baked pies out on the back steps of her clapboard house for the starving tramps who were starting to turn up along the railroad right-of-ways of the prairie as thick as the locusts and grasshoppers in the suddenly dust-choked fields. Louise herself became something of a wanderer. Using her father's railroad passes, she took her small son to visit her mother's Hart relatives in Michigan, as well as several of her own scattered siblings: one brother had gone to find work in Flint, Michigan, another in Gary, Indiana; a sister had migrated to Adrian, Michigan.

And then with the demise of William Ponton in 1936—he died at sixty-one of overwork, "wasted like a job," as his grandson would write—the Dorn family trials of "depression nomadism, / wandering work search, up and down / the bleak grit avenues of Flint, following / other exodus relatives," alluded to in a subsequent stanza of "Tribe," became even more pressing. For Edward this was a displaced, precarious time in his life that in this strong late poem about kith and kin survival-struggle became the basis of his characteristically provocative claim to be *a Kurd:*

> But I'm as proud of my tribe as if I were a Kurd,
> my pure Kentucky English great grandma—
> it would take more paper
> than I'll *ever have* to express how guiltless
> and justified I feel.

DORN THEN LEFT US this powerful and valuable clue as to how we might begin to address him. "Tribe" places him. Noted surveyor of our edges and boundaries and scout of far-off spaces and distances, rightly valued for his attentive survey of the western continental ground, commentator on its cultural development, seer of expanding extensions at its lonesome margins, this poet was in fact originally and finally a child of the interior, of the heart and center of the national body. "Thus the surplus numbers shipped out to the West by the North were by definition asocial outcast wanderers," he wrote in a resonant "subtext" to another late work, *Languedoc Variorum.* Dorn was a class-exiled rural upper Midwesterner who never gave a thought to moving back, yet persistently returned to the interior in his writings to rediscover his root meanings.

His 1968 tale "Driving Across the Prairie" provides a specific text to remind us just how deep and conflicting those homecomings were for him. The trip back to Illinois was a psychically relocating reality check, revealing just how far his life had ranged out of the orbit of those "old gods" who, with their "crippled" and "maimed" values, had prevailed over an early family scene he now looked back on as painful and an adolescence in which, as retrospect suggested, his sense of social disadvantage—and thus of his existential "difference"—had grown finally too acute to bear. The latter circumstance became the subject of his most thoughtful revisitation, the virtual return made in the 1962 uncompleted novel "A Troublesome Spring"; in the abandoned work, Dorn engages and tests those rejected gods and values, revealing their continuing negative role in his imagination of his fate.

In the draft novel's analysis, both prairie and son are disclosed under a sign of abandonment. "Lostling," an evocative epithet from one of Dorn's early regional landscape sketches after the manner of W. H. Hudson and Thomas Hardy ("Notes About Working and Waiting Around"), perhaps applies generally here. Loss pervades Dorn's early writing in both poems and prose concerning Illinois, which is elegiac rather than nostalgic in feeling. It gazes out over the vast featureless prairie cornfield distances as if reproducing the view from the eye of a disaffected son; or its melancholy yearning glides away toward far-off horizons that turn out to hold very little hope— thus imitating the perspective of the son's mother in "The Debt My Mother Owed Sears Roebuck," "a little melancholy from the dust of the fields / in her eye" as she maintains the silent watch for the family's forever missing man. The elegiac tone of such work functions beyond the instances—the images—to signal a larger absence: "Oh mother / I remember your year-long stare / across plowed flat prairie lands" ("Goodbye to the Illinois," from "Three Farm Poems"). The writing is all the more powerful for that—the moving way it refers us out on to that endlessly disillusioning Midwest landscape, where the dry, dusty cornfields of Depression summers and the flat, nearly black plains of still-barren early springs frame the hesitant, singular, unfledged being in the center imaginatively intent on taking off above the sentinel fences and never coming back. It is a landscape of rectilinear grid sections stretching off endlessly past a thousand single-family homesteads toward an exhausted Christian eternity of frugality, thrift and constant killing work. The larger elegiac lyricism of *The Newly Fallen* (1961) and *Hands Up!* (1964) is founded in that vast spiritually endarkened landscape.

Dorn was a child of prairie sparrow skies who in his writing developed an attitude of lyric realism from inner dispositions to which his lonely early reflections under those skies disposed him. In that deep sense he is a ruralist if not a pastoralist. Unpretentiously, he grew up in Villa Grove, a river town on the Embarras. Like paradox, paranomasia was a favored Dorn mode: he enjoyed the pun on *embarrassment* in that local river, though he of course knew it was actually pronounced *am-braw*. (His habitual recourse to the rhetorical technique of going against the grain—i. e., getting under people's skin with language—may remind us of the etymological pun of irritation and provocation hidden in his name, which in German signifies *thorn,* and farther back, in the verbal substantive of its Indo-European root, "the piercer.")

The courses of rivers that watered the Illinois prairies of Dorn's youth also charted kith-and-kin histories simply by floating the continuing local resettlements that went on up and down them. The length of the Embarras supplied him a winding, lingering trickle of later memories. An embarrassing adolescent sexual quest recounted in "A Troublesome Spring" leads the alter-ego hero of that work across the river (to ignominious failure). The river also migrates in a poetic displacement into "An Idle Visitation," the 1966 precursor-poem of *Gunslinger.* In Dorn's boyhood the Embarras still flowed through old-town Villa Grove under a venerable overhead-girder bridge. When in the late Sixties he came back after an extended absence and found that bridge torn down and replaced by something much simpler and more "efficient," he realized that "there was never a connection with the universe here, but that bridge was a beginning. (And of cosmology these people were able to add nothing to what the red man left)...." River water was drawn up from the Embarras and stored against dry years in the town water tower,

Villa Grove's largest and most imposing structure.

After passing out of Villa Grove the Embarras meanders down-stream to the southeast some sixty or seventy miles before reaching the Indiana line and emptying into the Wabash at Vincennes. Along the way the river wanders through Camargo, where in 1941 Eddie Dorn and the other eighth-graders from Villa Grove's one-room ele-mentary school had to go by bus to be handed out their graduation certificates. "All my friends," Ed remembered, "looked exactly like me because they had red faces, their wrists stuck out and they were dressed like that for the first time." The Embarras accepts a small input of tributary waters near the town of Newman, where, as Dorn reports in a *Hands Up!* poem, in his youth he was a tireless dancer.

Ed's longtime friend, the writer Lucia Berlin, recalls his touching account of coming back from an early trip to Southern California and attempting to make a minor splash at one of those summertime Newman, Illinois, Saturday night dances. "He was about sixteen," Lucia recalls. "That's when the pachuco kids out in L. A. were wear-ing zoot-suit pants. Ed, with his great sense of style, had brought back home the most beautiful pair of pants. He loved to talk about those pants, they were brown-and-white striped gabardine, they had these big wide pleats, he went on and on describing the weave and the fabric of those pants. They were so fine. Well, he brought them back to Illinois, wore them to the dance—and nobody had ever *seen* such a thing!"

> Oh perish the thought
> I was thinking in that moment
> Newman Illinois
> the Saturday night dance—
> what a life! Would I like it again?
> No. Once I returned late summer
> from California thin from journeying
> and the girls were not the same.

You'll say that's natural
they had been dancing all the time.
— "In My Youth I Was a Tireless Dancer"

THE WHOLE STRETCH of Illinois prairie ranging from Villa Grove southwest to Mattoon, where Dorn's mother and stepfather would later relocate, and then back east toward the Indiana line, provided the poet a deep rift of private image-reference. Even in later years when he thought he'd left that country behind, it stayed with him, getting more complicated in his memory's projections. There was his poem "Sousa," which came up one time when we were talking about the whole matter of the "brood structure" he'd left behind in Illinois. "That *did* mean something to me," he said. "In 'Sousa,' 'the octagonal / stand, Windsor, Illinois, the only May Day / of my mind'—all that came back to me from playing a record of Sousa marches, much later on, when I was living up in the Skagit Valley. I found to my surprise I was actually a lot more isolated in the Northwest than I'd ever been back in the Midwest. So the actual experience the poem is about is the ritual social custom of my brood structure back in the Midwest, the family reunion bandstand, the box elder, the 'northern madness / which no one values any more.' Just the *fact* of all that is probably a lot more interesting to me now as a possible human arrangement than for any possible nostalgia it might generate. 'Sousa' is a memorial to family reunions before the war, with all the exodus relatives, the Mertons, the Parks and the Harts. They'd hold these reunions in parks in places like Turkey Run, Indiana. Naturally we'd all go. They played Sousa in the band shells, always . . . all that ended with the war. I suppose the poem does keep the memory of all that green, in a way."

2.

Want

I was never middle class nor were my parents. I mean our
safety was never public. Our poverty was public.
 —"Driving Across the Prairie" (1968)

IN THE MID-1930S Dorn's mother remarried to a local hired farm
mechanic of Scottish descent named Glen Abercrombie. Young
Eddie, to whom the tractor-driving Abercrombie at first seemed a
wholly admirable figure, eagerly encouraged the union. Dorn's step-
sister Nonna recalls her father's story of "driving a caterpillar and
this little boy sitting on a hill watching him, so he would take his
lunch and eat with him, and Ed asked if he would like to meet his
Mom—and that's how Glen and Louise met." Soon, however, the
once-admiring boy found himself at loggerheads with the reliable
and competent handyman. As the dynamics of the new family took
shape, Eddie began to reveal a proud, stubborn, mischievous streak.
For the first time he became subject to physical correction; Aber-
crombie, revealing a severe side to his own temper, rewarded the
boy's obstreperous displays with whippings. Yet in the boy's testing

gaze, the strict disciplinarian his stepfather was at home gave way, at the farms where he worked, to a pathetically submissive servant. True to the family pride bred in him by William Ponton, the youthful Dorn at once disdained and was humiliated by what he perceived as his stepfather's lack of spirit.

In early Dorn farm poems like "On the Debt My Mother Owed to Sears Roebuck," the tractors that chug along "pulling harrows / pulling discs," as well as the "mechanical bare heart" that breaks under a farm boy's bare feet in locust-infested fields, relate to Abercrombie. So does the nominally fictionalized account of a farm household of the late Thirties in the bleak and moving autobiographical chapter, "The Early Days," from the novel *The Rites of Passage (By the Sound)*. For "father" here, one may read "stepfather":

> Carl had hated his father for his helplessness without knowing anything about him. Was his father then the rabbit you could knock in the head and walk away? Without a shred of remorse look back on as the man kicked in the dirt, and return to finish him off? He had hated him abstractly. His mother encouraged that in spite of herself. With her digs at him she must have covered the entire range of her own fruitlessness. But there it is. The meanness they lived in ruled them, was their boss, those men who owned them simply came across the fields toward "their" lives as the agents between them and their simple, tentative existence. They hardly knew they were alive. They hardly felt it. Even the sharp edge of real poverty was taken away with a wage. Just enough to support a thin shell of dignity around them.

The stable providing figure for the boy in this rather fraught family landscape was his mother, Louise. Having been through a good deal together, mother and son were particularly close in a way only the combination of blood ties and mutually experienced straitened circumstances would allow. "It seems to me that men are multiple and women are singular," Dorn would later suggest in an interview.

"When I was growing up, that was my mother. After that it's been one Woman.... I think the only unit in human society that's interesting is the family. And that's got, as I know it, a woman ... there's no need to take on anything else." Louise's central place in the household went unchallenged, whatever disciplines may have otherwise applied to the boy. She and her son shared many qualities. Both had a native curiosity about things, both possessed a gift of intuitive judgment, both were tough-minded, individual and outspoken in their views, and self-taught in them. In adult life Dorn's notebooks record moments of amusement—and shock—as he repeatedly discovers small gestures and physical mannerisms, as well as reflexive responses and habits of thought, which he identifies as deriving from an unconscious mimesis of his mother.

At the same time, though as the years went by his own cultural horizons expanded vastly, hers remained strictly local and circumscribed—her information sources on current events were television, scandal sheets, *The News of the World*—causing a certain wariness between them and also bringing about occasional moments of stubborn mutual incomprehension such as that inscribed in the telling episode of television-watching in "Driving Across the Prairie." In that tale, contemporary "issues" of death, starvation and poverty—leaking from an educational TV show about famine in India across electronic space into rural Illinois and "the inside of an American lower middle class house which has been robbed of life in a way death doesn't really cover"—divide mother and son into opposing ideological corners, obstinate in their respective, violently contradictory views. Even in that scene, however, Dorn presents himself as ultimately unwavering in his role of dutiful son: "as the son, I shall always make an attempt."

A little more of the complication of Dorn's close relation and affinity with his mother is suggested in a poem of a decade earlier, "The Hide of My Mother." In that black-comic family-snapshot account of Louise's visit to his Northwest migrant homestead in 1957, she's represented as half-seriously proposing the "hides" of the poet's young children be made into rugs. "My mother / never

knew about the world ... Whorled, like a univalve shell / into her-
self." Her cut-off self-containment, moreover, was seemingly some-
thing Dorn did not really disapprove of in his mother. What he
himself had learned about the world suggested it had less to adver-
tise itself to her than once might have been hoped. "People who
don't like me have hung this poem around me as though it showed
I had some *problem* with my mother," he told me in 1985. "Actually
I got along very well with my mother. She was very critical and she
taught me to be that way, too. I've always been grateful to her for
that."

IN DORN'S 1964 POEM "The Sense Comes Over Me and the Wan-
ing Light of Man by the 1st National Bank," a long, dark and
harrowing retrospective of a childhood of contained want and denied
need, a forced austerity is lived out imaginatively in a reviewed early
scene of loss, pain and wasted abundance:

> ... there, of course, we were
> alone
> and it could be said there were questions unformed
> for the lapse of any plausible answer, the walnut dropped
> literally onto the ground in the woods
> and rotted there through the year, and the people cried
> out in their ineffectual way for white flour and pork,
> canned peaches my aunt brought once was a ceremony
> I almost
> waited under the table...

The "ceremony" of his aunt's canned peaches is the closest thing
to an ecstatic childhood memory the adult poet Dorn carried. His
poem reminds us the deep Depression years brought specific hard
times for the severe, broken-spirited hired hand Abercrombie and
his family. There was little to eat beyond a subsistence diet of corn
meal. Grocery shopping was a primary magical ritual. Each week
there was Saturday night at the market, almost a religious event. If

cash was short Louise would have to "borrow the money to get gro-
ceries on Saturday night, she'd go to town, they'd all go, and park in
front of a store called the Grab-It-Here, everyone called it the Grab-
It. A ten pound sack of flour and some beans and two pounds of
oleo." Years later, Dorn still remembered the momentousness of
bringing home and unpacking the sacks, touching the meager food-
stuffs. The oleo packets became play-fetishes. "He liked to break
the little package of color and mix it."

In bad weeks or seasons the color of the time could drain off into
hunger's single-minded concentration. With the coming of Eddie's
half-brother, David, and half-sister, Nonna, there were five mouths
to feed. Louise supplemented the monotonous staples—corn meal,
flour, pale oleo—with occasional chickens she butchered herself,
vegetables from her own garden and sometimes too with wild greens
gathered alongside the C. & E. I. tracks (the same tracks Eddie's
genetic father had followed out of their lives). The desperate tone
of Abercrombie food gathering activities was something that never
completely vanished from Dorn's memory, as those close to him
could see. Dorn's stepson, Fred Buck, recalls a visit with his mother,
Helene Helmers Buck, to the bachelor suitor Dorn's austere Seattle
digs: "My first memory of Ed must have been summer 1953, Helene
taking me and my sister to visit her friend. Ed had a basket of nuts
and hard candy and I ate most of the candy. Helene told me later it
was the only food Ed had and it was tough for him to watch me
chow through it. Ed was always deeply generous with food, that
Depression hunger pain must have been strong."

Hard times for the Abercrombie household continued into the
1940s. "In Villa Grove in 1946 we farmed for a doctor 'by the
month,'" Nonna recalls. "That was what they called it when you
worked someone else's farm. For a very low wage you got a pig to
butcher and half a cow and your own garden space. Since you didn't
have a freezer you had to can all the meat or smoke it; but one thing
I remember, Ed hated to milk with a passion and he said, 'No mat-
ter what I do it won't involve a damn cow.' And back in those days
flour was bought in cloth sacks and I remember if Mother had two

sacks alike I got a dress but if there was only one sack one of the boys got a shirt. Ed never got a bought shirt until he entered college. Everything Ed done to get his education he done on his own. It wasn't that Mother and Dad didn't want to help but they didn't have it, so he done it ALL on his own."

The narrow margins of such a childhood as Dorn's framed all experience within constant perimeters of constraint. Louise Abercrombie practiced and promulgated a strict domestic care for frugality, cleanliness, lack of waste. This pattern, created and maintained more or less out of necessity by his mother, was one Dorn would borrow and carry over into the domestic space of his own first marriage. The habits and responses of his childhood stayed with him.

In 1966, as a visiting professor in England, he at one point moved with wife Helene and their three children into that large, gloomy Victorian-gothic Colchester flat where "An Idle Visitation" would be written. The flat had been left in an appalling state by the previous tenant—who happened to be an eminent Irish bard, W. R. Rodgers. With Helene (and young Cambridge don Jeremy Prynne) he would spend a full week trying to clean up. The epicenter of the mess was the kitchen, which was coated with grease. "There were maggots in the food [Rodgers'] wife left in the cupboard," Dorn reported in horror to Charles Olson. "After 7–8 days of scrubbing," he reached a realization about his own personal history: he had never been able to stand living in filth. "You know we're not *clean* folk, but still my upbringing, I begin to see, was so poor-white, civilized or scrubbed ... " He left the sentence unfinished, for Olson to draw the implication. The kitchen of the flat on Victoria Road as it had been left was a place Louise Dorn Abercrombie would not have brooked. "I see it," Dorn said, meditating perhaps upon a scraped and scoured farm kitchen of some lost decades before, a spotless table whereon his mother had served up the meager fare of hard times— and whereon, on one occasion, a country doctor on a house-call had surgerized him for a painful infection that had ensued from a botched circumcision.

3.

Reading

BOOKS AND READING WERE an early Dorn habit, fables, tales, narratives, adventure stories, legends of freedom, words a way of filling up the lonely prairie spaces and distances. His mother, he would later say, "read to me, before I could read, the things that she knew, that she had been read, I don't know where in the family that comes from. Among people who were not literate in that conscious sense, there nevertheless was a habit of reading, say, Defoe's *Robinson Crusoe* or Stevenson's *Kidnapped.* ... I got the stories, like 'Jack and the Bean Stalk,' not from these books that are now fashionable, especially in English-looking editions with period drawings and considered *good,* but they were told to me by my grandmother and mother. Many stories were told, because there weren't books in the house much." When he was four or five, the boy was taken for the first time ("probably by my grandmother") to the Villa Grove public library—"a little brick Carnegie across from the Mercury Garage on Main Street"—where he read a book called *Dicken Among the Indians,* "about growing up stranded among the Massachusetts." The book would haunt his imagination for years, unearthed from memory finally to supply an image of freedom that culminates some reflections on Thoreau in a poem written at the age of thirty, "The Land Below" (1959): "In America every art has to reach toward some / clarity. That is our hope from the start. / Dicken among the indians. / A very new even surprising element (a continent is a surprise)...."

For young Dorn, stranded in the cultural vacuum of the heartland, written myths of space and American geography became, early on, an escapist continent of continual discovery and surprise. The tale of Dicken among the Indians was a story in Eddie's imagination which he could substantiate when at Thanksgiving the children of the one-room school made a large communal mural of "an Indian tribal scene ... a big poster with the outline drawn, and we'd color in. It would depict a big scene, and everybody worked on it. We'd also be reading about it and talking about it." The teachers of the one-room Villa Grove school were all women, usually "wives who had been away at teacher's college, and had children of their own, so there wasn't that much difference in form being at home or at school," as Dorn later remembered. These motherly women's encouragement of him, to read and use the library, supplemented that of his mother and grandmother. "It was very much of a brood structure"; the adult poet would look back on the birthplace of his interest in formed language as a warm, nurturing, endeared matrilineal site.

In high school, it was also a woman teacher who, as Dorn later told his half-sister Nonna, "convinced me to get my education." This teacher, Helen Harrington, motivated the nascent writer to excel: "She said Ed was almost failing everything when he started high school," Nonna recalls, "[yet he] graduated with high honors." Dorn later claimed he "knew he was being a poet" as early as high school, then qualified, "although I didn't write poetry that much, not more than anybody does ... [but I had] a general tendency to conceptualize the world; and feelings which are characterized by saying they're 'beyond one'; a desire to look at reality as if it were reproducible as language." Over the remaining years of his formal schooling, he said, he tried various languages to express that inner quality of feeling: "I made certain motions ... architecture, journalism, painting—[but] none of those other forms of expression went beyond poking around."

What appears to be true is that the thoughtful, proud, private youth was from a very early age an omnivorous reader, though no more than an occasional writer. At Villa Grove High School, he edited the student paper, joined the drama club, and penned a few short stories of his own. Perhaps more important in the long run than these first "literary" productions, however, was the early reading habit, a hunger for words that from high-school years onward seems to have comprised one of the significant drives of his life. The laborious self-imposed project of reading his way through a small library was something he would take on again in more than one small town, later on.

The story of Dorn's early reading is a parable of the advantages and drawbacks of autodidacticism. His first experience with the rigors of the mother tongue came when he was "around sixteen, trying to read a book by the Englishman Kingsley, called *Westward Ho!,* purely because of the title." It was "one of my first penetrations of the jungle entirely unaided." Charles Kingsley's 1855 extravagant historical novel of England's maritime triumph over the Spanish in the sixteenth century, a thick blend of British patriotic sentiment and swashbuckling heroic romance, yielded another "West" altogether, a far cry from the expected rawhide, ranges, and frontiering. Dorn later recalled a great struggle with Kingsley's narrative—his difficult first encounter with the "high" rhetorical style of English historical prose of a Carlylean strain. To the self-demanding, intellectually underprivileged young reader, Kingsley's "extremely tortuous prose, not what I'd had in mind from the title," was both daunting and an obscure delight. Curiously, the dense shadow-plotting of the Kingsley novel, with its "profound concentration on the minutiae of [English] history, which is lengthy," and its plethora of pedantic anti-papist "historical" detail—Jesuits deviously plotting the fall of England, inquisitioners cruelly torturing Protestant prisoners, cooking them alive, etc.—anticipates the obsessive anti-Catholicism and preoccupation with religious torture in Dorn's late, salient historical sequence, *Languedoc Variorum*. And in the same late period the Kingsley title re-emerged as a homophonic subtextual ghost behind the title of an ambitious, difficult Dorn comic epic of the High Plains, *Westward Haut*.

That there was in Dorn's youthful self-presentation a certain edge is suggested by some anecdotes he told of his high-school years, usually humorous, concerning the "dark" side of his nature. One pastime he mentioned was playing pool for a dime a point with the Villa Grove undertaker, whose line of work seems to have interested him. Another was seeking out the most reputedly disturbing books in the high-school library, like *Crime and Punishment*. Upon first looking into Dostoevsky, young Dorn fancied himself saddled "for a while [with] a sensibility profoundly unsuited to life in a small prairie town." But this spell of alienation seems to have been safely contained within the Capra-esque small-town setting. While still in high school he picked up his first regular job, as a printer's devil for the town newspaper. Before long he'd learned to set type and run the presses. Hanging around the print shop, rubbing shoulders with editor and reporter, gave him a worldly feeling of expertise and accomplishment that carried over into a sense that newspapering might be his calling. It was that sense, in turn, which spurred him to take up the first volume of poetry he'd ever read. It was the light verse of James Whitcomb Riley, journalist-bard of the Wabash Valley. Partly because Riley "was a newspaper poet, and known—my part of Illinois, east-central, is close to Indiana where he wrote," and partly because Riley's sentimental regionalism struck a cord of feeling in him, the Hoosier poet became the first young Dorn actually "got."

A T THE METHODIST CONGREGATION the family attended, young Dorn put in weekly Sunday-school hours at Bible-reading studies and took part in youth discussion groups on "contemporary" spiritual issues. In such sessions the lean, quiet, cornstalk-blond farm boy could show a surprising proclivity for asking hard questions, a habit he seems to have got from his mother. Even this early, it seems, he liked trying to get behind the easy veils of assumption that close around things, shielding painful truths from more "normal" minds. Throughout one whole high-school year he was a member of the Villa Grove Lodge of the De Molays, young man's subsidiary of the Fraternal Order of Free and Accepted Masons. In the doctrines of freemasonry young Dorn encountered a system of representation more complex than anything in Whitcomb Riley, a mystifying grammar of arcane beliefs whose elaborate symbolic ceremonies reflected "hidden" iconographies of spiritual and intellectual resistance. Residual traces of that para-religious instruction would provide an essential tincture in the virulent anti-authoritarian rhetoric of *Languedoc Variorum*. Jacques de Molay, last Grand Master of the Knights Templars, renegade crusader, defiant victim of Pope, King and corrupt authority, brought with his Knights before an inquisitorial court, charged with heresy, tortured, burned at the stake, became a convenient emblematic alter-ego for the mature Dorn at a period when he sensed himself (or projected himself) in a beleaguered and exposed defensive position, persecuted for his own expression of anti-authoritarian intellectual views. During a 1992 teaching year in France, Dorn toured the Languedoc countryside, "rediscovering" the figural patron of freemasonry's youth order. "I just remembered my De Molay year in Illinois," he summed up the experience in an epistolary travel report to me.

On that expedition, Dorn would also say, "I got into my Protestant roots. That's real unfashionable actually—but I was raised a Methodist, and I've been a Methodist ever since. You see, I think Martin Luther was the greatest revolutionary. The Protestant Revolution precipitated all other revolutions, and all the other revolutions were failed revolutions. The American Revolution came out of it, the French Revolution came out of it. The basic proposition of the Protestant Revolution was that authority is inherently corrupt. And you know, Machiavelli said that one of the most salient things about Christianity is its pious cruelty. If torture hadn't already existed, the authority of the Church would have had to invent it, to have *something* it could do with heretics."

That Dorn's latter-day "recovered" Protestantism was intellectual, spiritual and political, rather than strictly theological, or related to any religious practice, should be evident. So too should be his seriousness about it, and its consistency with the development of his character, as made plain to all who knew him from his days as the "country skeptic" and dissenter of Black Mountain. (To Robert Creeley, encountering him there for the first time in 1955, Dorn seemed "a lovely, resistant man, [who] tested all of experience.") Looking back in a 1998 conversation, he located the original recognition underpinning that skepticism and dissent which was his constant habit of mind, that edge of question and test which individuated him and defined his singularity, in an incident that occurred at a Methodist service in Villa Grove in his late teenage years.

"The first truly educated person I ever met," he said, recalling this small, telling moment of the coming-of-age of his mind, "was a preacher who came to visit my church in what would have been about 1948. Scottish Reverend Aldridge was the first preacher I had heard talk to the congregation like they were adults. Other Methodist preachers of that day were educated on the whole. But they tended to be pretty syrupy and soupy, and they talked down to the congregation. But this Scots Methodist definitely did not. And in fact it was the first time I ever heard somebody actually address a group of people in that straightforward way without trying to make things easy or softening, or 'it's going to be okay.' None of that. It's not okay, and it's not going to be okay was the message. That was always the premise, but what followed was an interesting sermon about pretty common stuff that you had never thought of that way at all. So, in a sense, this guy, the Reverend Aldridge, was my intellectual baseline. I also found that this Scottish person had a pretty deep understanding of Midwest American life, and I suppose that he had in his background immigrant relatives."

The stern "message" brought by the Scottish preacher, a confirmation of everything the fatherless young man's poverty-margin rural upbringing had taught him, would have multiple echoes in poems to come. Dorn, one might say, became the Reverend Aldridge of Postmodernism. The adamant rhetoric which arms the decisive moral gestures of middle-period Dorn poems like "The Sense Comes Over Me" projects a curious aggrieved, sermonizing tone that sharply points its argument, an angry protest against institutionalized capitalism: "All the children / were taught the pledge of Allegiance, and the land was pledged / to private use...." In the moral outrage and high rhetoric of Dorn's insulted outcry against a corrupt human condition, one of his most sensitive critics, fellow poet Robert Duncan, noted the withering edge of a fire-and-brimstone rural preacher. It was, Duncan accurately suggested, the "fundamentalist character" of such Dorn poetry—the irascible, exacerbated, uncompromising, lofty, defiant, abiding "burden of righteousness"—which supplied the verse its paradoxical expansive gravity, that quality very much Dorn's own.

4.

The Confines
of the River Town

there was a girl
who was a resolution
with whom I walked the empty streets
and climbed the watertower for one night
to show off, she standing a spot of white summer
on the ground, and looked out I did
over the lights of a realm I thought grander than

THE IMAGE OF DOWNTOWN VILLA GROVE, in Dorn's memory of the 1940s, was shot through with layered recollection of a still earlier time, like the "pictographic scratches" inscribed on the silver paint of the town water tower that exposed a prior social geography in "The Sense Comes Over Me." There is the scene of his looking down from the catwalk of the tower on a June night—Eddie and his high-school sweetheart Phyllis Sprinkle, daughter of the owner of the town's only Rexall drugstore, in their senior prom duds, he in a powder-blue suit, she in a white dress, at the brink of their respective unanticipated lives. Dorn told this story more than once to friends. As he told it to Robert Creeley, it was a tale of "climbing to the top of the local water tower, and looking out on the world, literally, on the lights of the town, the flatness, the unrelieved real life that still had to be hopeful...." To Creeley, the image was of a young man's deep, longing "care, or humor, or anger, at what the world wants to do with itself." But in this Dorn poem about the occasion, there is a crucial shift of perspective, as the young man's surveying gaze from the catwalk zooms back in from the vista out over Villa Grove's dimly twinkling evening—"the lights of a realm I thought [myself] grander than"—to the scratches on the tower's silver paint, hieroglyphic signs of what had transpired in the 1930s in those streets below:

> men vomiting from hunger
> on the thin sidewalk below, a lonely mason
> with his business ring on, but beyond,
> in the little shoe repair shops the men,
> part of a hopeless vigilante, exhaling the slow mustard gas
> of World War I. My mother, moving slowly in the grim
> > kitchen
> and my stepfather moving slowly down the green rows of
> > corn
> these are my unruined and damned hieroglyphs.
> > > Because they form
> the message of men stooping down
> in my native land, and father an entire conglomerate
> of need and wasted vision....
> > the walnut dropped in the autumn on the ground
> green, and lay black in the dead grass in the spring.

Dorn's retrospective, shifting "double" view from the water tower contains a self-reflexive, time-action panorama, showing him caught in his native place's confining, negating atmosphere of waste and decay—one recalls here, significantly, the "confines of the river town" in which a beloved is left behind at the outset of his 1966

poem "An Idle Visitation," origin of *Gunslinger*—and also show-
ing him escaping, while hardly free of its lingering effects.

> Sharp
>   and keen the fever
> this thrill of spring in the Lord's prayer
> which I carried and still love as a vague solace
> I carry, confused
>   that ceaseless speculation over
> the ways of love
> into the darker borders
> of my wounded middle years...

S OMEWHERE BEYOND "the ways of love," the poet met up again
with the girl he'd left behind in the confines of the river town. In
1983 Dorn wrote to me that he'd encountered her real-life proto-
type, by surprise, after a reading at the University of California in
San Diego. "During the usual bullshit questions, an attractive lady—
she'd be about 50 now—came up to shake hands and look me Right
in the Eye and say 'You don't remember me do you?' There was
nothing I could say, I didn't. She said 'Drugs!' Her father owned the
only (Rexall) Drugstore in town, altho that was meaningless to us
then. I thought, oh my god! Does this have something to do with
my dopey past? She said 'I'm Phyllis.' So. It was my high school girl
friend, I mean we were constant for 4 years. I hadn't seen her for 33
years. I was totally bashed. I realized how much I don't know now
about where I come from."

In the 1968 sketch "Driving Across the Prairie," that transpar-
ently autobiographical account of his return to Villa Grove, Dorn, as
narrator, learns his former sweetheart has married, moved to Cali-
fornia, given birth to a deformed child. In Dorn's tale the crippled
child becomes an unpleasant symbol of the pure products of his
home town. "I want to be able to look back into the faces of the old
gods," he wrote then. "That lineage, that result, the crippled stem

of this country is made with the mind." He had changed his own mind, by that time.

But after their 1983 re-encounter, Ed began to write to Phyllis, who, having lost her husband, was left alone in middle life. It was a gesture of sympathy characteristic of him. In the summer of 1991 he received a phone call from a friend of hers notifying him that she had died. On the day of her death, he was told, she'd received a note he'd sent her "and was very happy to have it at that moment." It was, he thought, "an amazing co-incident arrival at her death." He wrote a poem in his notebook to commemorate that river-town girl he'd left behind. The verses were spontaneous and private, lit by an intense, shy, thwarted passion momentarily aflame in his heart again at sixty-two as it had once burned at nineteen.

> Her eyes were as dark as agates
> in 1948, so dark I stayed
> an extra year, just to be with her.
> It was the only thing to do.
> I'd been so slow and distracted
> when the war ended
> and the country was
> suddenly engorged with
> the youth of five years earlier—
> full grown men thrown
> into the dead air peace,
> some back to the scheduled
> combustion of the Railroad,
> some saddled in the
> tyrannical throb of cultivation....

5.

The Soil of Transport

"**A** WOE OF THAT LOWLY ORDER became my sign and weight in that / land / I became that land and wandered out of it," Dorn wrote in "The Sense Comes Over Me."

Abandonment and flight from the heart of the national or family body were patterns Dorn came to understand better with further observation and analysis of his experience over time. "It's always fleeing in this geometric way," he averred to me in a 1980 conversation about the paradoxical self-losing abundance of the prairie. "It's going to the Southern Rim, or it's going to the coast ... on the other hand, it's still the place that's always the richest. Because it's got surface, depth of surface. That's the whole meaning of the prairie. It took millions of years of Nebraska, Kansas, Illinois glaciers coming down and making the broadest river plain that ever was. Which is called the prairie, and it was six feet of loam."

His incisive, tellingly titled *Hello, La Jolla* poem "If Somebody Asks Where You Come From Remember" reduces this thought about prairie soil as metaphor for a paradox of cultural retention and dispersal—a thought originally derived from Dorn's readings in the work of the geographer Carl Sauer, who had said of the historical ecology of the Illinois prairie, "there was no stage of extractive or exhaustive cultivation"—to the kind of stripped-down propositional statement we find in much of his later epigrammatic verse (which at times emulates the pre-Socratics in its epistemological directness). In the poem, Dorn distinguishes two categories of soil, the soil of transport (to be found "anywhere between the Appalachians and the Rockies") and the soil of disintegration ("which can be found anywhere, especially in mountains"). "Runoff goeth down to the valley / into the soil of transport." The extracted or exhausted soils of the intermontane West, Dorn believed, were ultimately disposable and depleted. They defied settlement. The soil of transport, on the other hand—he believed—always endures, drifts, abides. Thus speaking, of course, he was addressing not only mineral contents, but, by metaphorical extension, human qualities.

However, in a middle-period poem called "The Stripping of the River," Dorn also suggests the "green heart" and "true richness" of America's central, sustaining "continental tree"—i.e., his native Midwestern country, and all that was good of human nature in it—may have been finally "cloven from this plain," enfeebled and wastedaway by successive waves of diaspora, each bearing its promise of a pot of gold at the end of the prairie horizon as well as its potential for national and private loss. This perception of his work's real subject, the nation's interior "crippled stem" (as he'd called it in "Driving Across the Prairie"), ultimately made Dorn a tragic writer. That "spiritual genius so apt ... to migrate to the neutralized / and individualizing conditions of the coast" was a value that perhaps could not be renewed and stored after all.

II.

A Troublesome Spring
(1947/1962)

I.

The Story of Morton Draker (Competitive Plots)

Morton had always had a difficult time doing anything with an inner sureness. I suppose it is true he never did, and never shall. There were long ruminating days during the summer, on the farms in Illinois....

AMONG THE MOST INTERESTING and telling of Dorn's several unpublished early prose works is a lightly-fictionalized autobiographical sketch of some 6000 words concerning his uneasy coming-of-age—and discovery of a world of difference—in the period around the end of and just after World War II. A determinedly if incompletely distanced portrait of the artist as self-exiled prairie son, the sketch deals with a tenuous life-passage otherwise absent from Dorn's writings.

The work was produced during the cold spring of 1962 in the converted shed of an Idaho ranch where the writer was dwelling with his wife and three children. The surviving draft appears to represent a start on an autobiographical novel that would remain unwritten beyond a single completed chapter (Dorn's typescript is followed by another few handwritten pages that may have been intended as a prelude to further action). The draft he left behind among his papers when he departed America in 1965 was later recovered and preserved by his stepson and loyal archivist Fred Buck. It bears the handwritten title "a troublesome spring for a young man," with the final four words incompletely effaced.

Dorn submitted a draft of "A Troublesome Spring" to Scribners for their 1962 *Short Story* competition, a widely respected annual showcase of new fiction talent. Along with the autobiographical sketch he included a piece on his Seattle waterfront wanderings (later published under the title "1st Avenue"). It was not Dorn's first attempt at the Scribners prize. He'd started shooting for it two years earlier, when invited by Robert Creeley's editor at Scribners, Donald Hutter, to submit a manuscript. On his initial try Dorn had sent three pieces from Santa Fe, including "Notes About Working and Waiting Around" and his tender lyric portrait of "the slender Beauty" of New Mexico, from a novel in progress.

The autobiographical sketch fared no better at Scribners than Dorn's earlier entries. Donald Hutter would later report to Creeley—as Dorn's informal representative—that while he'd found signs of promise in the "very direct, alive fragments of ramblings along the Seattle waterfront," he saw little commercial hope for Dorn's accompanying "longer, more 'rounded' narrative dealing with a cross country runner"—i.e., "A Troublesome Spring." Through Creeley, Hutter then asked for a look at Dorn's novel of life and work in the Skagit Valley, *The Rites of Passage*. In its turn *that* "more 'rounded' narrative," too, was turned down. Similar failures greeted the same Dorn material at Grove Press and William Morrow, where *Evergreen Review* editor and anthologist Donald Allen was promoting it. The cold hard facts of Dorn's negative marketing prospects, as they became clear, could not but have represented to him a return of the old social gap, original source of his estrangement. As for his autobiographical project, he was left to lament with Blake "the desolate Market where none come to buy." For whatever reason or reasons, he abandoned "A Troublesome Spring."

THE MAIN ACTION OF THE PIECE takes place in 1947, during the spring and summer of the alter-ego protagonist's final year of high school in a "small obscure town" on the Illinois prairie. "15 years ago is a short time," Dorn's narrator declares, stating the mode and motive of the work in its opening paragraph: "Still, almost any meandering of time back will give a difference to a reality, as it is remembered."

The story line of Dorn's autobiographical sketch involves his hero, Morton Draker, in parallel competitive plots. In each of these plots the youth is aided by his natural gifts and by a certain measure of stubborn determination, but impeded and finally overcome by a disabling social deficiency. The concentration on issues of class and status suggests Dorn intended to project social disqualification as a critical thematic concern in telling his early life. Here he attempts to account for and reckon with a determining disadvantaged condition perhaps best summed up in the epithet "embarrassing," reiterated at key moments.

Dorn involves his hero in twin competitions, parallel avenues of struggle that appear to converge in a common objective: the young man strives to become the best 440-yard runner in his rural secondary-school conference, and to attain the social prize represented by the favors of the most widely coveted unmarried girl in town (not coincidentally, she is also among the wealthiest). Both efforts culminate during the troubled spring of his final high-school year in stinging, humiliating defeat. While Dorn relates these matters in a dry, matter-of-fact manner, doing his best to retain a storyteller's objectivity, the subtextual tensions created by the autobiographical purposes of the piece contribute much of its urgency. The writer is belatedly toting up the psychic toll of his own tenuous, trial-and-error-riddled emergence into adult life.

Though he loses crucial races to certain particularly defined rivals, and the girl to another, unidentified rival (who eventually marries her), it is Morton's class-fate, rather than any individual or individuals, that seems to blame for all his losses. In the case of the protracted, problematic love relationship, a disabling mutual incomprehension between the youthful principals, Morton and Pat, is traced by Dorn to the dramatic disparity in their families' socioeconomic status. While Morton's mother and stepfather are caught in a bitter struggle to keep the family above the rural poverty line, Pat's father, a merchant, operates a respected and successful local business—a "monopoly in town.... An important thing to own in a farm community. And with it went the self-assurance that goes with a monopoly." (In Dorn's text, the girl's father owns the only hardware store in town, whereas the father of her real-life prototype, Phyllis Sprinkle, had in fact owned Villa Grove's only Rexall pharmacy.) Pat herself, with that golden self-assurance in her blood and in her air, reduces the socially maladroit Morton to awkward confusion with her first smile: an unexpected hero's trophy proffered upon him toward the end of his sixteenth summer in the privileged precinct of her "monopolist" father's place of business, marking the beginning of the courtship with an unsettling augury of things to come ("He was so nervous and flattered he forgot what he had come in for, something for his step-father"). Later on as well a class-related confident assurance seems to typify the girl's behavior, at least in Morton's mind. Stunned at first by her evident willingness "to be his steady girlfriend, even though she was very pretty and the daughter of the most important man in town," as time goes by the earnest, self-doubting youth comes to distrust this inexplicable favoring, and grows worried he's actually being toyed with— used by Pat to spite a pack of her well-heeled suitors, who would presumably be impressed by her ability to claim anything she desires as her own: "that she could have had as a companion the son of a dentist was certain, but it [i.e. going steady with Morton] was her way of saying she was too ambitious to put up with the best the town had to offer, and thus made her independence clear." (By specifying the competition as "son of a dentist ... the best the town had to offer," Dorn privately referred to Gordon Taylor, the closest male friend of his early years.)

Pat's outward appearance of social assurance is the thing that distinguishes and empowers her. Morton himself, disadvantaged by a specific deficit in family social position—direct result of a dire lack of money or property—is possessed of no such protective veneer. At critical social moments he is afflicted by a disabling habit of betraying himself. Making himself over for other people, he loses himself, slipping out of touch with his own insistent, nagging reality. A reader winces along with him when the girl's curious gaze falls upon the exposing commodity signs of his poverty: the contents of the Draker family's grocery bag. "She saw a box of Ritz crackers and mentioned she liked them. He was very embarrassed although he didn't say so. They were a luxury for his family, something they shouldn't even have had. He couldn't get the thought out of his head."

We make out in this episode as in many of the revealing incidentals of "A Troublesome Spring" an initial structure of shaming, giving us cause to further read Dorn's shy distances as self-recovering withdrawals from the constraints and embarrassments of the social—that "World of iron thorns" of which he wrote in an early poem ("Like a Message on Sunday"), in which the humiliations of his class situation accumulate and intermingle to create complex thickets of pain. The small obscure town on the banks of the Embarras comes into focus at key moments in Dorn's autobiographical text as a theater of ritual trial in which the hero's bouts with secret guilts and shames represent at once the perils imposed in the course of his persistent aspiration and the proof of his unworthiness for the prize. How could a poor farm boy like Morton ever truly qualify to take possession of this elusive girl, object of the whole town's desiring gaze, most precious commodity in a community built on farm futures, material goal of what we see to be an impossible idealistic quest?

> For many years he would dream of this girl. He loved her very much the first time he saw her in the store. She had large brown eyes and a nice way of laughing. And a wonderful quick way of looking away when you looked at her. But he could never afterward remember her voice. When he later

became really close to her he loved her no more than he had that first time. Because then the whole preoccupation was how to hold her, how to one day be great and successful, although he never knew it was success that seemed to be demanded, but it was a sense of some mean[s] to hold them together always.

Morton's pursuit of the middle-class entry credential, the socially-determined, legitimizing "means" to securing the approval of others, traps him in an anxious repeating cycle, his touchingly futile upward-mobile efforts followed inevitably by awkward, painful falls from grace. In effect he is running to keep up, all through this story; the "means" remain just out of his reach. Dorn's detailing of the ambitious youth's near-misses recalls the earnest futility of Dreiser's heroes. Morton makes a bid to gain the girl's respect by his athletic feats, scoring "several early triumphs on the track"; she is discouragingly "not impressed." He toils at his books in order to earn senior-year academic honors; she takes him to task for having been so lazy earlier. The cheap yellow carnation corsage he buys her for the spring prom wilts before he gets it to her door, and when they hit the dance floor he's embarrassed to note that "all around them there were girls wearing more substantial orchids."

Dorn occasionally represented himself in conversation as having been a high-school track star, but in this unselfsparing autobiographical account it is his failures down the stretch that preoccupy him. Morton Draker's lack of self-assurance haunts him even on the cinder track, causing him to wilt at decisive moments in the presence of more substantial "orchids." In one race during a meet in the neighboring town of Newman, he semi-deliberately "holds back," putting out only a halfhearted effort in a tacit gesture of concession to a particularly "cock sure" competitor. The rival, Anderson, is known for his social-sexual prowess. He "had been around ... had a reputation with the girls not only those who live[d] in N[ewman] but those in the surrounding towns too, which is no small accomplishment because those towns are terrible in their clannishness, their restrictions." In the wake of this galling if partially self-inflicted defeat, humiliated loser Morton revisits the rival's town to exact a pathetic symbolic revenge by pilfering turnips from a farmer's patch, a further compulsive self-shaming. "It made the boy a little ashamed when he thought of going to Anderson's town and committing such a petty and unimportant theft. It punctuated in his own mind his ineffectuality."

The comically inept sexual self-education of Dorn's young alter-ego hero reminds us of the autobiographical chapter "The Early Days" from *The Rites of Passage,* in which the farm boy's first solitary fumblings with the instinctive and imposed meanings of the body are darkly, if matter-of-factly, recounted. Here in "A Troublesome Spring" Dorn's inventory of Morton Draker's early sexual history begins with school days and yields a single bathetic incident: a study-hall proposition that somewhat to Morton's surprise wins the girl's consent, but leads, after a trepidated stroll through the willows by the river, to balky embarrassment in the patriarchal shadows of a barn doorway and terminal loss of nerve ("he hesitated not knowing what exactly to do beyond the major idea he maintained in his head"). Notwithstanding his sexual unknowingness, however, Morton is far from incapable of loving. His love for Pat, we are told, inflicts a "certain sharpness of feeling," and is felt keenly for years beyond the end of the relationship. Though acute, the feeling is largely idealized. Physically, Morton's love for Pat remains to the end "unrequited," or at least unconsummated, the closest call coming two years into the courtship, when front-porch necking results in Morton's inadvertently soaking the girl's dress with an uncalculated ejaculation. Dorn treats the incident as an embarrassing and confusing *faux pas,* an ironic reverse fulfillment that leaves the innocent young couple in anxious dismay: "She cried and wondered if she would become pregnant, Morton assured her it was impossible but thinking about it more and more wasn't sure."

For all Morton's earnest but unsure amatory striving, ultimately the frustrating relationship, with its long history of mutually yearning youthful inexpressiveness, simply evaporates, as he and Pat finish school and the girl goes off to college.

> But that spring was the last of their love. To the end unrequited and painful to the extent that they [Dorn first typed *he,* then by hand amended it to *they*] wanted to really love no matter how uneasily. This spring they were both to graduate. Usually they dated on Friday, Saturday and Sunday nights. And of course saw each other during the week at school. But for most of all of every day Pat was in the thoughts of Morton. He had to learn from a friend that she was going away to school in Western Illinois. The last day he saw her was after school had ended, he was walking up town with a friend past the tennis courts by the community building, he had a book of hers and asked his friend to go over to her house and give it to her. He waited by the courts. When his friend returned and they had continued their walk toward town he asked how she was, hardly wanting to hear the reply, and hardly hearing it. He had nearly given up hope of ever seeing her again. It was intensely true to him that his entire body choked up at the fear of losing her, of never again holding her in his arms and talking intimately with her as they used to do.

In the disappointed aftermath of love's troublesome spring Morton again is driven to indirect expression of his sense of defeat. With some companions, he sets a series of fires in abandoned buildings around town. (These destroyed structures remained landmarks of vacancy and absence for Dorn as late as 1968, when in "Driving Across the Prairie" the returning son is driven through Villa Grove, "past some places which are not there now because in our youth we burnt them down.") Though Dorn's hero "passively" masterminds the gang of "amateur arsonists"—"he didn't exactly direct the event but when they had shown signs of backing out he urged them on"— he escapes retribution even as his accomplices are apprehended. Though "grilled for days [by] the sheriff," they decline to implicate him, out of pity "because his parents were so poor and wouldn't have been able to pay the fine." At the level of the law, "Morton got off scot free." Unpunished but guilty, the boy observes the penitent "conversion" of his co-perpetrators to his own Methodist congregation. Though he boasts a perfect attendance record at the church youth league, he too senses there is a debt to be paid, and is forced to quail alongside them under the baleful "cocked eye" of a stern "new preacher." The latter figure is drawn on Dorn's powerful memory-image of the dour Reverend Aldridge, he of the grim burden, "It's not okay, and it's not going to be okay." But the righteous judgment of the severe congregational reformer, instead of relieving troubled conscience, only exacerbates its pains for the boy. Here the fable within the sketch disperses Dorn's authorial persona into past and present projections, as judged and as judge. One recalls his comment around this time to Olson that he couldn't help gazing upon his own surroundings with "a cocked eye."

Morton Draker's difficult season of coming to age reaches its bitter nadir in a scene of confrontation with his stepfather. Dorn here indicates another major stress point in the psychic rift system that threatens to fracture his hero's identity into so many ill-fitting pieces, churchgoer / juvenile delinquent, would-be lover / ineffectual loser, loyal ("good") son / ungrateful, rebellious ("bad") son. Long masked by his shy, diffident, somewhat dreamy manner, Morton's inner tensions finally "come out" into the open in this passage of the sketch. The blowup ensues when, driven by lovesick distraction to stray overnight from home, Morton is accused of asserting a wayward "independence," and receives a dressing-down from the angry stepfather. The tender trigger of the boy's self-questioning, his sensitive not-yet-manhood, becomes the point of attack.

> This spring has been a turmoil inside Morton, going and coming from school and many evenings not returning but staying in town with a friend rather than go home to the bitter resentment of his folks, who are busy with their own lives but who think Morton demands too much independence. His stepfather one morning stopped Morton in the garden. He was

standing with the hoe in his hand. Why don't you ever think of your mother he said, why do you stay away without letting us know, you're not a man yet, not by a long shot, and if you think you are I'll let you have it with this hoe. It was too much for Morton. But all the shame he felt for neglecting his parents, for staying away days at a time, came out in the bitter feelings of don't I take care of myself, and what do you care anyway, what does anyone care about me.... Morton was afraid he was lost.

At this stage of impasse hints of a struggle over the hero's mother hang in the air, but remain unresolved, and the eighteen-year-old's momentary exposure of carefully concealed feeling only renders him more ashamed, conflicted and isolated than ever. For the troubled young man the losing battle over manhood with his stepfather represents the original unequal competition.

2.

Distance (Areal Prose)

Morton had not always lived in the Small Obscure Town, though he was born there. His step-father always had a hard time finding work, especially during the Depression which Morton only vaguely remembered. In their travels back and forth across the farms of the Mid-West they had lived in many different places but finally, after only a few years returned.

—"A Troublesome Spring" (1962)

we scoured the ground of the earth
to start fires
in these rickety geographies
we knew no better than to call home

—"Oh Don't Ask Why," (c. 1962)
from *Geography* (1965)

Escapees are not home seekers. The number of people who came west seeking a home must have been *very* few. A man will linger twenty years here, and want to go home.

—"The New Frontier" (1963)

The objects which exist together in the landscape exist in inter-relation. We assert that they constitute a reality as a whole that is not expressed by a consideration of the constituent parts separately, that area has form, structure and function, and hence position in a system, and that it is subject to devel-opment, change and completion. Without this view of areal reality and relation, there exist only special disciplines, not geography....

—Carl Sauer, "The Morphology of Landscape"

There would seem to loom only facts: that boulder, this moun-tain, these store fronts, his greed, her compassion, water, no water, prayer, arrogance, futility, loneliness, a swindle, an even break, the dandy charmer, the slothful soilbound fanatic, the dream and of course the inevitable dreamer. History has always seemed to me lying on the table, forgetful of age, or not pres-ent at all. And geography is not what's under your foot, that's simply the ground.

—Preface to *Idaho Out* (1965)

DORN LEARNED THE TERM "AREAL" (as of "the associated or inter-dependent phenomena that make up an area") from one of the central texts of his intensive self-education, Carl O. Sauer's 1925 essay "The Morphology of Landscape." He would credit the Sauer essay with instilling his own aspirations to an attentive, educated "love of the formation of the land." "I knew of Sauer from Charles [Olson]," he would tell an interviewer in 1972, "I got interested in Sauer because he was the first one, especially in that 'Morphology of Landscape,' who spoke to me with that kind of love of the for-mation of the land. Which was beyond what I could see as an aes-thetic, as an alternative. Superior to an aesthetic because it was like handling the constituents, the bones of America." During his Idaho sojourn of 1961–1965, the period which yielded "A Troublesome Spring," the final draft of *The Rites of Passage,* and the poems of

Geography, an areal aesthetic inspired by Sauer's thought provided the "bones" of Dorn's work.

At the outset of the chorological journeying-poem "Idaho Out"— which is perhaps the representative poem of this period—Dorn actually installs the unassuming geographer as a symbolic presiding figure in the "hopeful" birth of a new redemptive poetics of space. The poem is headed by an unattributed Sauer quote (from "The Morphology of Landscape") which announces the poem's immediate theme: "The thing to be known is the natural landscape. It becomes known through the totality of its forms." In his opening lines Dorn pictures the unassuming Sauer as a Prospero, a visionary master who has a magical power over the land forms; we see him "with his hand in the air as well," and hear that this art of the "areal is hopefully Ariel" also. The poet clearly wishes us to link Prospero and Sauer as conjurors of the morphological reality of the phenomenal landscape. Dorn's gesture of recognition and acknowledgment toward the master geographer—"the poles have been strung for our time together"—openly implies his intellectual indebtedness to the man who fathomed the forms of discrete cultural landscapes from "The Barrens of Kentucky" and "The Pioneer Life of the Upper Illinois Valley" to "The Road to Cibola" and the *Early Spanish Main:*

> Since 1925 there are now no
> negative areas he has ignored
> the poles have been strung for our time together
> and his hand is in the air as well
>
> areal is hopefully Ariel

The symbolic figural placement of this percipient hero's hand in the air creates an elevated perspective (aerial) that doubles the controlling pun, which now becomes areal = Ariel = aerial—three ways of fathoming space cleverly compacted into a triple homophone on which the poem pivots. When Carl Sauer then disappears out of the poem, making way for roadside characters, notably roadhouse women, like "The Beauty of North Fork," we move closer to the center of the poem's intuitive cultural morphologizing. "You go through it as though it were / a planet of cotton wadding ... and love / its parts as you do the parts of a woman / whose relations with earth are more established than your own." A poem that begins in the air and ends on the earth, "Idaho Out" takes the characteristic Dorn form of the search-through-space that turns out to be a search through the mind.

The "task of geography," as Sauer prescribed it, involved cre-ative action "embracing the phenomenology of landscape, in order to grasp in all of its meaning and color the varied terrestrial scene." Dorn suggested something of his idea of how this "embracing" applied to poets in a heroic verse encomium to his prior master Olson, *From Gloucester Out* (1961). "To play, as areal particulars can out of the span / of man" was the special gift Olson was endowed with in this poem, another integral piece in this period of Dorn's "areal aesthetic." Olson, Dorn here implies, has grasped the areal forms of his own proper precinct, Gloucester, and *played upon* them as only a poet is able. Sauer, as Dorn knew, had recognized that cre-ative writers—from Herodotus down to W. H. Hudson, one of Dorn's primary models of place-writing from the late 1950s on— are often the best geographers. By placing the forms of the earth (areal) at the center of one's writing, a writer may displace the func-tion of the "I" to the free imaginative play of the mind's eye (ariel): from this premise, contained in his critical play on words, Dorn develops in his more ambitious works of this period the active field of narrative distances and differences through which his writing freely ranges at play, tethered neither to the lonely ego that seems to hang back behind the singular diffident voice nor to the social forces against which that voice insistently poses itself in resistance.

"The objects which exist together in the landscape exist in inter-relation...." Shifts in areal relation supply the main action in "A Troublesome Spring" as in Dorn's other prose and longer poems of this time. Those moments of areal displacement are the small shocks which bring the restrained emotional tendencies of the writing into focus. In the autobiographical sketch the shifts are both outward- and inward-tending movements: the view of small-town prairie landscapes recedes out into a long horizon offering distant vistas both of loss and hope; or swings back in through intersecting containments of mapped space and earth history to old haunts of the soul on forsaken soil.

Coming to address specific instances of the workings of these movements in Dorn's tale of his "birth-place," it may be useful to consider as a parallel description Carl Sauer's account of Illinois prairie life in a time not too long before that of Edward Dorn / Morton Draker, when the cultural patterns that shaped the writer's upbringing were being established.

> [The] last great movement of land settlement was out on to the prairies and differed largely in manner of life and kind of people from the settlement of the woodlands.... The hard pull was to get enough capital to improve and equip the homestead, and this was done by hard labor and iron thrift. This is a sufficient explanation of the work ethic and thrift habits of the Midwest, often stressed in disparagement of farm life ... it was necessary to keep to a discipline of work and to defer the satisfactions of ease and comforts.... Dispersed living, the isolated family home, became most characteristic.... The General Land Survey established the rectangular pattern of land description and subdivision for the public domain. Rural land holdings took the form of a square of sums of squares, in fractions or multiples of the mile-square section of land. The quarter section gradually came into greatest favor as the desired size of a farm and became the standard unit for the family farm in the Homestead Act.... Four homes to the square mile ... gave the simple general pattern for the rural geography of the Midwest. The pattern was most faithfully put into effect on the smooth upland prairies. Here the roads followed section lines and therefore ran either north-south or east-west, and the farmsteads were strung at nearly equal inter-

vals upon one or the other strand of the grid. It is curious that this monotony was so generally accepted, even a clustering of homes at the four corners where the sections met (and giving the same density) being exceptional.

Writing here in the early study "Homestead and Community on the Middle Border," Sauer emphasizes many of the same features foregrounded in Dorn's writing about his youth in rural Illinois: the monotonous, rigidly geometrical regularity of the prairie landscape, the internal social distances its conditions of physical isolation imposed, and the stringent work ethic required to sustain a life upon it. What Sauer portrays as a discrete and coherent cultural pattern, however, comes out "played upon" in Dorn's refractive areal workings, turned back upon itself to reveal its negative internal aspect, its capacity for cruelty, its abiding absences, its catalogues of pain and loss; "World of iron thorns," that phrase from a Dorn poem of this period, perhaps expresses the Methodist-bred prairie exile's summary view of the same areal particulars Sauer notes.

In "A Troublesome Spring" Dorn appears to have concocted the name of his alter-ego hero Morton Draker in part out of his own— Edward Merton Dorn, commemorating the railwayman William Merton Ponton. The source of "Draker" is harder to identify, until we recall that this is a tale of a high-school track runner from the prairies of the Midwest at mid-century; in that time and that region, the largest track meet of the season was the Drake Relays. The traces of geography in Dorn's protagonist's name are hints that the actual most important character of the piece is not an individual but a place, the landscape and culture of the tall-corn prairie. In fact areal values establish not only the setting of this tale but its determining symbolic structures. Morton Draker's iron-thorns world of intersecting confining spaces is drawn on the same template as "Homestead and Community on the Middle Border," a grid-sectioned "graph" of various rigidly-bounded restrictive distances, here pictured as the harsh symbolic matrix against which the sensitive, more or less helplessly skewered hero struggles to become a man; his character is exposed negatively, as a series of defensive reactions to the cultural situation that leave him defined as rebellious misfit and ungrateful (or damaged) son.

The unwavering and merciless geometries of the physical place are repeated in Dorn's character-presentation of its flat, planar, spiritually rigid denizens, their minds as reflective of socially imposed constraints as their enclosing property-limits. "Those towns are terrible in their restrictions, their clannishness," he writes. In this world boundaries and distinctions are opposed by distances and vistas. The prairie's long horizons, potentially open and assuaging, are broken up, with the tightening of Dorn's retrospective focus, into the socioeconomic geometries with which he overwrites them, the right-angled, section-squared, mercilessly unwavering dividing-lines that strain and break the heart. An important plot of the piece occurs in the play of the mind's eye over these signifying distances and containments, which we read as multivalent signs, alternately indicating emptiness and openness, loss and freedom, desperation and discovery. This play takes place in Dorn's areal interiors, the complicated remotenesses charted-out in one early lyric of utopian hope as "the geography of my lunacy" ("Geranium").

The distances and "flatnesses" of "A Troublesome Spring" reflect the structure of an inner landscape also. In the portrait of his young hero Dorn writes the preface to a history of determined lonerhood. "There are times when I not only want to be alone but want to be lonely, which is more complicated," he declares in another unpublished sketch written a few years earlier in Santa Fe ("A Bitter Laugh"): "These are times when I concede that I too am insane." Morton Draker betrays the early signs of just such complicated longings to be lonely. Morton is not unpopular at school, but his bearing is shy, aloof, self-effacing; he hangs back, failing to assert, consistently having "a difficult time doing anything with inner sureness," and settling for the self-isolation that ensues. Out of his true element amid the small-town hubbub of the Newman, Illinois Saturday night dance (a five-piece band blaring *Talk of the Town* vaguely in the style of Lombardo"), this serious, thoughtful, socially-uneasy, rather dreamy youth actually appears calmest when alone with his obscure yearnings, most at home with himself when trudging back from school through darkening cornfields or in idle stretches between chores sprawled in motionless reverie: "At sixteen he still would lay in the hay-mow for hours staring up at the gable, or out the great window at the end of the hay-rack, looking at the sky." Pure type of all Dorn's wistful distances, the primal Illinois prairie sky, with its endless meanings, none entirely consumed, is a vehicle that temporarily transports the hero of "A Troublesome Spring" beyond himself and outside the painfully-experienced trials of a self-defined "ineffectuality" brought on by social striving. This lonesome farm lad's capacity for tender feeling, which like his marginal socioeconomic standing marks him off (at least in his own mind) as an outsider, goes largely unexpressed, and finally seems diminished almost to insignificance—a further self-losing—by the great, uncaring prairie sky.

Dorn mediates the intricate tensions he has laid out between an iron-thorns world of power and property and a resilient, giving earth by an areal "mapping" of these opposed forces as relational structures. Consider the following passage from a section of the sketch that has the ostensible narrative business of conducting the hero, with his high-school track squad, to a neighboring hamlet for the spring season's first meet—and the more important underlying purpose of situating the reader amid the larger meanings of the landscape.

> They rode over in a great hulking underpowered yellow school bus. The interior of the bus was distinguished by smells as was the awakening world outside where the trees were just now breaking green, inviting the red and black box-elder bug to swarm around their bases. The interior of the bus smelled of salves and ointments spread on pulled muscles, and iodine which had been applied to knees broken and scraped by cinders. Over the tops of the osage hedge which in summer will bear light-green hedge apples with the surface texture of a

wart, can be seen the elms that surround a farm house. The country is wholly flat and the singular markings of the hedge rows form a graph of where the roads go, and where the distant fields end. These vistas are always hypnotic if you give yourself to them, riding along.

Here the liberating point of view slips away from the almost comic infirmity of the boys inside the bus, above the tops of the osage, beyond the lonesome farm house, vulnerable among its sentry elms, and out over the rectilinear-patterned hedgerows ("a graph of where the roads go") that indicate the ruler-straight dividing-lines of country roadways; beyond lie distant fields, far vistas and the anticipated bounty ("... will bear light-green hedge apples") of a full, fruit-bearing summer. A writerly verbal opposition, yielding the "primitive information," as the Romantic poet John Keats called it, of contrastives, sets off the burgeoning promise of spring's natural orders ("awakening," "breaking green," "inviting," "swarm") against the defensive vulnerability hinted at by the elms whose business it is to protectively surround the farm house, osage hedges which conceal roads that lead nowhere. The place speaks itself, by such internal oppositions; they remain tacit in the images, and are not argued in any editorial way. From the picture of land as material possession (the farmer behind the hedge is implied), Dorn's areal narrative lifts off or takes flight into "hypnotic vistas" that offer a new, enthralling kind of possession—conditional only upon fulfillment of the writer's injunction to give oneself away, as one rides along. These vistas promise no more nor less than one element in the rural landscape not transformable into a commodity, sky.

In a second passage, relating the end of the same trip, a similar arc of expanding perspective traces the spring's troubled ascent from latent hopes "which hadn't come up yet" to a "later" of generous rewards.

The track was at the far end of town past the large frame houses which no one can afford to build any more, sitting along streets guarded by massive spreading elms all of a familiar shape fanning out and interweaving with each other at the tops from which it must be true could be seen the signs of the landscape of the slowly forwarding order of spring: the long rows of planted corn which hadn't come up yet, the closer parallel lines of sowed soy beans, everything black-brown now, later to be scored by the green of new growth.

Gathering contemplative sweep and quiet authority of tone from a subtle deployment of vistas and vantages, this areal sentence moves from closed to open, from spring's tentative anticipation to summer's certain harvest, from a dark acknowledgement of power to an awakening promise of growing things raised up to the light, from the looming of the large frame houses that no one can afford to build any more and the massive elms that guard them to the sudden release and elevation of treetop perspective. At the level of that lofty aerial perch the hopeful augury of the landscape may be read, spelling out the prairie year's black-brown, slowly-forwarding progress, "later to be scored by the green of new growth." It is a birth that will happen in a place that is soon to be abandoned by the troubled young man of the story.

3.

The Brakeman

"I was born in a railway town / the whistle blew in my every dream"
> —"Methodist Child: Slow Train through Denver" (notebook poem, 1998)

"I WAS RAISED IN A RAILROAD TOWN," Dorn wrote in a middle-period unpublished essay, "and I am railroad progeny." By a poetic irony, the manuscript of his autobiographical sketch, as he left it, begins and ends in a contemplation of railroading images. The typed draft of "A Troublesome Spring" opens with a mention of picking up relatives at a small-town railway station "on the only east-west line going through that part of Illinois, the B & O." ("This difference," he notes, "gave a town that was otherwise of no importance at all, some importance.") After the typed draft breaks off, a three-page handwritten epilogue—perhaps intended as the beginning of a never-finished second chapter?—offers a picture of the railway depot in the "small obscure town" of Morton Draker's birth. A remarkable evocation of Villa Grove in the Age of Steam, this passage may have been intended as a staging-point for Morton's departure into the wider world of subsequent scenes. As the surviving text stands, however, the two passages bracket Dorn's tale in a way that creates a haunting thematic echo, none the less striking for the fact it may have come about by accident.

> The town's main street extends four blocks from the river which flowed in a great bend thru it, to the depot standing by the railroad track. Once the town had been a busy division on the line which runs from Chicago to St. Louis. On winterish nights, or cold fall nights, and on harsh spring nights, and some occasional times during a rare summer fog, the depot will be obscured from a point one block away from Main Street, the heaving mixture in the air of moisture and cold with the steam of great 2000 class Baldwins sitting by the depot or pulling into the roundhouse thickens the air, there is a likewise thick and heavy smell of wet coal ash, of the smells of the mixtures of hot water calcium deposits, and of coal dust rattling along the conveyor belt to the top of the massive shadowing black chute, a great landmark of timber saturated with the sifting falling dust of Indiana mines. When the wind is from the south floating cinders then drift into your eye, and it appears you are crying, still you cannot see the depot. Or a lonely brakeman emerges vaguely as a charcoal drawing from a late restaurant looking at his watch. People return to the town because they were born here and still have friends. The railroad carries diesels today, the smoke you smell is like that of the highway off to the south running rather straight between Springfield and Indianapolis.

In a 1958 letter to Charles Olson from his isolated homestead in the Skagit Valley, Dorn accounted for the "presentational immediacy" Olson had found in his use of images in prose by explaining he was consciously attempting to fashion his narratives around "landscape shots": "I am trying an hexperiment, to write out of the concentric rings of my location." At the moment of the letter to Olson his locating image was one that also happened to be quite familiar. "Railroads! A little silly but I seem to always see them, live close to, etc. Right now, looking thru the window, afternoon, the red of boxcars thru the cedar trees (we live in a cedar grove) two blocks distant I suppose, then, a caboose.... I don't know what for I insist on those landscape shots in the middle of my prose. Probably a misplaced affinity, because I am very close to those flatnesses (I really can feel Peru rubbing on my left ear, when I face West). Probably the impurity of my mediums, no?" Notwithstanding the self-deprecating tone characteristic of Dorn's comments on his own writing to his respected mentor, these remarks could hardly be more germane to an understanding of the procedures he describes.

The complex recursiveness of Dorn's "impure mediums," with their stubbornly individualized ways of arranging things, their switchback ratiocinations, their discontinuities and "flatnesses" (rhetorical distancings, tonal self-constraints), seems to drive this writer's thinking to branch out along many side routes, moving sometimes for a while parallel to yet in the end usually quite apart from any narrative main line. His technique in long poems *(The Land Below, Idaho Out, From Gloucester Out, Gunslinger, Recollections of Gran Apachería),* built out of the structural knowledges he had gained in narrative prose, was a development of this meandering, digressive layering-of-"concentric-rings" procedure, adapted to the varying materials and speeds of the verse line. When we look more closely at the functioning of this procedure here, in the building of the appended railway depot scene, we see a characteristic recursive circling action of thought, advancing not in a straight line but in an open, looping orbit. The writing enacts a wandering progression that happens both on the narrative surface (here and now, the present, 1962), and down much deeper, where Dorn evidently meant to descend when he suggested to Olson the "concentric rings of my location" he wanted to display were actually circuitings of *himself* ("tidal shores of, etc.").

In his epilogue's portrait of a vanished technological epoch Dorn inscribes several kinds of history. The writing digs up meanings lost and gone by the moment it occurs. The reader is reminded this is time-past, before the railroad's conversion from burning coal to burning diesel oil—"the smoke you smell is like that of the high-way." Still a strong sense of the physical immediacy of an experienced present pervades the prose. Dorn's concentric-layering technique ("to write out of the concentric rings of my location") reminds us of the articulate fathoming of space Keats termed "stationing." In building the scene he establishes a set of "concentric rings" as successive circles of enclosure. Cold, moist seasonal fogs of the prairie enshroud the small-town depot, which is enclosed again within a second containing layer of obscurity created by the "heaving mixture" of air with the steam of the great pulsating locomotives. Moving further in, a third and still denser aromatic medium is composed of a particularized mix of odors—the thick heavy smell of wet coal ash, the smells of mingled hot-water deposits produced by engine boilers, and the smell of coal dust clogging the air around the depot. Looming over this choking atmosphere, the rattling conveyor belt and the death-black massive-shadowed chute project their dark amorphous presences. The whole scene is shot through, clouded, saturated and made historical by the further siftings and fallings (into the receding past) of coal dust imprinted in the archaic timber of the chute, an unreadable hieroglyphic pastness that surrounds presence with a brooding absence. A south wind arriving, beckoning possible relief, instead fails to clear up anything at all; the encircling veil only becomes more confounding, filling the eyes with tears. In this vale of forced tears it is as if one wept, merely to see into the past. At last a blurry yet singular form begins to take shape out of the endarkened world: at the center of "the concentric rings of my location" the writer's impure mediums—a curious tonal unevenness allowing the carefully restrained picturing voice to be interrupted and enhanced by small intensities of phrasing ("the heaving mixture," "a great landmark")—show their particular impure strength. We understand something more of the complexities of this railway son's ways of meaning, the several-dimensional worlds that his resolute "flatnesses" are never quite so strict as to fully conceal. Stepping from the coal-

dusted semi-obscurity of its third-from-last sentence vaguely as a
figure from a half-forgotten dream to haunt the autobiographical
sketch, the lonely brakeman emerges, looking at his watch. At the
areal center of the concentric rings of a lost past Dorn locates him-
self—and perhaps finds his wayward father.

The Chicago & Eastern Illinois brakeman William Leslie Dorn
was a question mark on a mystery train forever vanishing down
elliptical memory tracks into a foretime which preceded the lostling
child's birth. We are reminded of the testimony of Edward Dorn's
friend Lucia Berlin, who recalls the poet's insistence that once in the
blurred, half-buried memory-tunnel of early childhood he had
glimpsed his father's face; the remembered or recovered moment
had occurred, he told her, on a train. Was it a dream-construction,
compounded out of childish wish worked upon by adult need?

A MORE SOLID, FLESH-AND-BLOOD William Dorn would unex-
pectedly resurface in his son's life two years before "A Trou-
blesome Spring" was written. In February 1960, when Ed was thirty,
living in Santa Fe and struggling to write a novel while supporting his
wife Helene and their three children on an assistant research librar-
ian's small salary, he received a hand-written registered letter from
Indiana that left him thunderstruck. It was from his presumed-dead
blood father, who announced he was very much alive and working
as a conductor on the Pennsylvania line, running out of Indianapo-
lis to Columbus.

Mr Edward Dorn

Writing you this letter to get a Better aquainted after so many
years we have Never Knew each other and I Dont suppose
you ever thought I was still living. Well I am and doing ok.
and I have often wondered what Became of you. after going
through Depreciation and worlds war no 2—there been an
ofal change in this large world....

Now seventy, recently recovered from surgery, weary of railroading after thirty-four years of it, and plainly concerned with material security, William Dorn evidently desired the reassurance of family to secure him in the lonely retirement years ahead.

> Well we have never met But Hoping we Do some Day and get Better aquainted. Well Edd. you have a half Bro. By my 1st marrage he's an army man ... sta[tioned] at Tapeka Kansas. Well I suppose you wonder what I look like well I am 6–1— weight 190 lbs.—No grey hair and Not Bald. got good set Hair. Brown. Wear good close Drive good car. have a good Bank account and own 220 acre of Land in Ohio Near Portsmouth Ohio that where I was Born and Raise I am having my will made out and my Lawyer said to get your full name and add. and Location so I can put you in my will Now you and William Robert Dorn the one in air service is only ayers [heirs] I am single at present and Don't Intend to Ever get Married so Now I have told you about all I know at present.

"For all the world I am floored," the shaken son wrote his intellectual "father" Charles Olson. "It seems like a repossession. You know the example, the dispossessed child.... I guess I am crying. It seems so strange." A day later, though, Dorn experienced "a funny reaction." After weeping "like an idiot" over his father's letter, he told Olson he'd been overcome by a second wave of powerful emotion, this time a dark access "of dread, about my mother." Had her year-in, year-out "year-long stare / across plowed flat prairie lands" all along contained some hidden signal to him, some subliminal hint concerning their original riddle—a clue about the missing man, or even a warning? "I think maybe she did tell me things in the way that has no language, those forces which inhabit us, looks, the black eyes, dreadful. A sigh, a shifting of the hands, imperceptible, but the power. Now I am bewildered a little and wonder why the son of a bitch comes in so late, when I am thirty, as if that's how long he had."

Understandably wary, uncertain where it might lead but nonetheless consumed by a compelling fascination, Dorn wrote back to his father. Encouraged, William Dorn began his belated account of himself and his reasons for disappearing from Villa Grove, running out on his wife and the unborn Edward. "Long came the Depreciation and I got out of work or was Laid of like lots of others and had to leave those small town are No good when a Depreciation hits this country." In those hard days of the early Depression, the semi-literate revenant labored to explain to his son, a man couldn't get any help from the government, couldn't expect Social Security: "we Did Not have Nothing like that those day and I was Laid of till 1937 Before I got back to work mean time your mother found a Nother man and got a Divorce. this is what cause us Not Know each other well I guess things will happen this is a Big Cruel world—and we got to make Best out of it."

"Thirty years," Dorn marveled to Olson, "and I don't even know what he looks like." Pretty soon the father sent along a snapshot of himself: a big-boned, powerful man with prominent brow, large nose and jutting jaw, posed stiffly in suit and tie before a prospect of water (perhaps the shores of the Ohio). Genealogical research conducted after Edward Dorn's death by his stepson Fred Buck shows that the Ohio-born William Dorn was of German descent (*not* Dutch, *malgré* Ed's stubbornly reiterated protestations on that score). Son of a stone mason, he hailed from Scioto County, near the Ohio River town of Portsmouth, whereto he would return to live out his final years. With the photo in hand there is no mistaking the physical resemblance between father and son.

An epistolary relationship of sorts ensued, tentative but interested on both sides. Over the next year further letters and photographs were exchanged between Indiana and Santa Fe. Vague plans were made for a meeting, which kept being postponed. At one point, news of his son's straitened circumstances prompted William Dorn to provide the young family with a modest but helpful infusion of funds. The financial assistance came accompanied by a certain tacit but insistent bonus of advice from the senior Dorn's realistic, hard-knocks-school store of practical wisdom.

> well Edd what are you going to Do are you always going to
> stay out there in that country if you Dont make lots money I
> shure would Not stay there.... I Been out through that west
> I worked years ago in Spokan Washington on the Great North-
> ern Brakeman I Don't like it out there I Don't see what you
> see in that country How Big is sant fe population cant be very
> mutch and a cold country, like it is here, worse.... have you
> gained anything By traveling out through that western coun-
> try when there all these Big City to work in Back here and
> they are close to gether Not far apart there Indianapolis and
> Dayton O. Columbus O. Cinnati O all these Big Place and
> lots employment.... you said something a Bout Being a writer
> and was writing a Book on your life out west and that you
> write for some magazines well Do you Rec. Very good money
> out of that kind of work....

When during a visit to the Idaho ranch of his former college art
teacher, Ray Obermayr, Dorn received an offer of a patch of moun-
tain land on which to build a house for his family, he relayed the
news to his father. The longwinded reply was full of more caution-
ary advice. William Dorn renewed his urging to his son to move
back to the Midwest: "you Never Do any good long as you stay in
that Bush Country.... I would give that Country Back to the Indians
you could get good job here with an Insurance company or car sales-
man or office job." The elder Dorn sternly advised against a relo-
cation to Pocatello. "Ed you said your friend would give you couple
Acre of Land well wat there Friend would give you would Not
Amount to mutch if he would give you the Hole state of Idho he
would Not be giving you any thing Dont depend on any one get
your self a good Job Be Independent that way I operate I Dont
Depend on No one."

The unsolicited individualist imperatives exacerbated an old
wound, emphasizing to the estranged son and struggling family man

the differences that would forever separate him from his lifelong-loner father. By late 1960 Ed had left off communicating directly with William Dorn. His father, however, met up with Helene's mother in Indianapolis that November, and indicated he planned to visit Santa Fe the following summer. In April 1961, Helene resumed correspondence on Ed's behalf. His father was informed that the family was again in difficult straits, there was trouble paying the bills, they needed a loan to help them through. It was not until midsummer of 1961 that a reply arrived.

> What trouble I have not Heard from you. I wrote you a few Letters 3 i know in Jan. feb.—But you would Not anser But as soon as you Needed Help your sent for Loan But I was Not Here for 2 months after the message come from your wife. Shure was supprized to Rec it for Not knowing you long that I would Rec that kind of mail well if I knowing you and of meet you I would of known how to Handle your case of shortage. Dont you have a Bank account what Do you Do with your money you stated in one of your letters about Intertaining Lots Company you had lots Friends. that who you spind your money on and go short I Don't spind any money on Free loaders. I cut them out yrs ago you can always find lots of them Floating around. I thought I was Pretty Nice to send you 40 Dollars Not Knowing you. Does your Friends send you money. I Bet they Dont as I told you if you was Not making a Decent living out there in that Cow Country I would go where I Could Do Better a man with Education you say you have can always get a good job in this country here they are hiring Every Day here things is going good. . . .

William Dorn closed with the announcement that he was no longer able to work and was about to take his pension and go back home to Portsmouth in the fall. He had himself to look after. There would be no loan.

Robert Creeley, who at the time was as close with Dorn as anyone in Santa Fe outside his family, recalls the effect on him of this last exchange with his father. "It was not an easy time for him at all. He and Helene had a very pleasant place on Camino Sin Nombre, but Ed wasn't ever that comfortably at home in Santa Fe, and he had continual need for money. There was this distant connection with his father, who'd reappeared from the past. Ed's sense of that was hard to read. He was intrigued, certainly, but all along he played it down. He'd be ironic about it: 'Hey, wouldn't you know it, all of a sudden, he wants me to be his son.' He was hanging back. After all, it had been a long time, he'd heard nothing all these years. They were planning to move up to Pocatello; finally I did drive up there with their stuff in this old VW bus. Some time before the move there was a hassle with the father about money. Ed told me he had asked his father for a loan, and been turned down. That just blew him away. 'It was only a small loan,' he said. 'I told him I was good for it.' The point was, he did have a job, he was going to get paid, then he'd return the money. It was some small amount, maybe no more than fifty or a hundred dollars. It was for some unexpected need. Ed was shocked to be turned down, and obviously he felt pretty bitter about it. '*After all, he is my father.*' In his mind, there shouldn't have been anything more he'd have to say."

Despite the growing tensions between father and son, apparently William Dorn did follow through with his planned visit to Santa Fe later that summer. "We all did see W. L. Dorn," Helene recalls. "I'm pretty certain it was in Santa Fe at Camino Sin Nombre. Fred, too, has a distinct memory of his visit. Which was most unpleasant for Ed and I ... probably [for] W. L. as well. We were nothing like he'd imagined & vice versa."

Once the conflict of their respective distances had erupted into an open dispute over finances, the fledgling relationship between father and son was doomed to fail. Contact broke off abruptly after the fiasco of the paternal visit. Dorn's chagrin and pain would continue to haunt him, but now there appeared to be no going back. To lose a parent a second time represented a doubly crippling blow. In later years he avoided speaking of his father, and after the latter's death in 1968, he tore up a photograph William Dorn had sent him. The destroyed snapshot had shown the railroad man posed proudly in front of the 1957 black Pontiac, which by his last years was his most significant worldly possession. (Scioto County probate records reveal he left behind total taxable property valued at $1,340, of which $200 was sunk in the black Pontiac. His sole heir was a son, William R. Dorn of Marysville, Tennessee.)

4.

Branch Line: Some Further Notes on Dorn and Railroads

Almost any meandering of time back will give a difference to reality, as it is remembered.

—"A Troublesome Spring"

"Notes About Working and Waiting Around"

In the early prose sketch "Notes About Working and Waiting Around," begun in the Skagit Valley in the later 1950s, completed in Santa Fe, and published in LeRoi Jones' magazine *Yugen* in 1962, Dorn defined his wandering, ruminative, unhurried mode of meditative place-writing by its time-signature, as a kind of idling reverie, like that of a slow train on a branch line to nowhere: "It is the pace that comes from sitting, and listening to the soul, as it meanders back through its former homes." Equal parts narration and reflection, the purposeful meandering of this image-freighted areal prose gathers meaning in a cumulative, incremental progress, making many stops and carrying a substantial burden. In "Notes About Working and Waiting Around" Dorn's intention is to explore the fragile nature of hope, discovered surviving "in its pure state" among railroad bums and drifters. One of these itinerants in particular is given voice to speak the central matter of the piece: a tramp named Tennessi, who preaches to a group of fellow drifters his vision of heaven as the hobo's end of the line, located somewhere on the U. P. beyond Odgen, Pocatello and Spokane. "The old boxcar rattles on": in that tenuous, doubtful transit the poor wandering unfortunate may yet ride the rods to whatever form of paradise awaits the economically marginal and the socially excluded. "'Tomorrow may not come here, but *there,* it's NOW, and that's a fact.' And he slapped his palms together." The desperate certainty of Dorn's eloquent hobo, a sort of last prayer flung defiantly in the face of unpromising facts, expresses also the tenacious hopefulness of this writer, who finds along the ragged edges of power's cruel right-of-way repeated instances of such courage holding out against the odds, and devotes his lyric-realist sketches to their elegiac memorial.

ROLLING STOCK

In the early 1980s Dorn started a newspaper called *Rolling Stock,* a venture designed to live up in both style and substance to what he later called "the suggestive and western railroading feel of the name." The paper's cover logo, drawn by artist Jim Howard, featured an oncoming steam locomotive, full front. The motive of the project was a freewheeling critical resistance, borne out by the humorous outlawry of the lead article in the paper's fourth issue, "RATTLE-SNAKE AMBUSH: Dobro Leaves the Tracks." The story, penned by Dorn's friend the hobo swing musician and Montana rambler "Dobro" Dick Dillof, told of a gratis coal-car ride from Billings to Bozeman, courtesy of "Burlington Northern Tramp Lines." Dobro Dick's hobo prose was illustrated by a vintage photo of a solitary observer in overalls and stovepipe hat watching a locomotive coming around the bend of a river under a full head of steam. If anything, the paper was meant as a vehicle to conduct its marginal crew toward the impossible dream of a drifter's hope. Like the testimony of the eloquent outsider Tennessi in "Notes About Working and Waiting Around," its thematic assertion of the poetic authority of the hobo carried on Dorn's old sympathy for the itinerant class-victim who once survived at the margins of the system by a clever and persistent vagrancy.

"THE SUNDERING U. P. TRACKS"

There is nothing sentimental or nostalgic in the poet's treatment of western railroading in "The Sundering U. P. Tracks," a bitter diatribe of a poem about imperialism that was composed during his period of transatlantic exile, as a concluding statement to complete the 1967 sequence *The North Atlantic Turbine*. The poem is set in the onetime railroad boomtown of Pocatello, where Dorn had dwelt from 1961 to 1965; in another, uncollected piece written some years earlier he'd described the place as "a miserable accidental town even the / Union Pacific abandoned in the forties" (and suggested that he felt both accidental and abandoned there himself—"few people / are as lost as I am"). In the later poem he explicitly figures the railroad as an implement of domination and division, apportioning western lands into determined corridors of power and turning open space into private tyrannies of ownership and use. An agency of separation and alienation serving the acquisitive motives of distant speculators, leaving on "every little bogus town on the Union Pacific . . . the scar / of an expert linear division," the iron regime of the railroad is here viewed as a form of "rapacious geo-economic surgery" that slices "right through the heart" not only of the hardwood forests of the Northwest but of the interests of soft-tissued sensitive creatures all along its route: "Each side of the shining double knife / from Chicago to Frisco / to Denver, the Cheyenne cut off / the Right of Way they called it / and it still runs that way / right through the heart / the Union Pacific rails run to Portland. / Even through the heart of the blue beech / hard as it is." The U. P. tracks of the poem provide a tracer of the space-greedy vectoring of capital development, a practice of "majestic legal theory" linking classic railroad robber barons like Vanderbilt and Harriman with current U. S. foreign policy. (The latest of the Harrimans, William Averell, son of the empire-building Edward Harriman, had inherited the Union Pacific and thirty years later had been appointed a special roving ambassador by J. F. Kennedy—"Harriman, the old isolator, / that ambassador at large," Dorn calls him, relating monopolistic class-exploitation with the political imperialism of the Vietnam Era.) In the anecdotal plot on which his occasional poem is founded, concerning a visit to Pocatello by a black friend (photographer Leroy McLucas, Dorn's collaborator on *The Shoshoneans,* a book about the Indians of the Range and Basin region), the sundering tracks become emblematic also of "how many thousand years" of racial and territorial divisions, the boundary lines that partition-off black and white sections of a town, or impose a borderline of cold distance between a sympathetic heart and its "desires." For Dorn that "other" side of the tracks would always be a district fraught with complex meaning, often occupied by those he loved.

"The Cycle"

"For some while we parallel the train / whose shining rails are closed at both horizons." The railroad's mechanical effectuation of difference would serve Dorn's symbolic uses again. In 1970–1971 he interrupted the trajectory of the mock-epic *Gunslinger* after the first two books in order to interpolate "the Great Cycle of the Enchanted Wallet," a comic rendition in quatrain stanzas of the mystery-cloaked historical (1966) passage by rail of Howard Hughes from "the Sacred Commerce of South Station," Boston, to Las Vegas. As Dorn learned from his study of Hughes biographies, that secretive transit had passed in part over the same stretch of right-of-way pictured as the corridor of exploitative power in "The Sundering U. P. Tracks." This time, however, Dorn extends the suggestive range of his symbolism into an area very close to moral allegory. The extension is consistent with his working principles in the poem, which differs from his previous efforts in the multivalent density of the referential field it activates—in turn a product of his developing intention, as stated in a 1976 journal note, to "write *(Gunslinger)* for an audience which has used, or at least been exposed to, the inflation of University Vocabulary." As Hughes' train rolls along behind its nineteenth-century steam locomotive, for example, the click of its couplings is heard both as realistic detail and as a rumor of something more, the deception and duplicity of speculative deal-making, "as urgent and quick as a whisper / Into the ear of a corporate being." Here once again the railroad figures as instrument of a ruthless greed for power, but the symbol now reaches beyond the political and economic realms to implicate (and undermine) the cognitive function of the single-track mind. When the rich man's private "car tacs / To the Main Line," Dorn spells out the expanding intention of his fable: "this is not about haulage ... this is the Inventory / And then the Overhaul of the fucking mind." In the divisive linearity of the technology the poet now discovers the corresponding cognitive function, a form of abstractive intellection whose effects are hinted at in lines that seem to recoil in horror from what is being signified, a "shrill scream / Of metal to metal across the switchyard" which lays bare the structure of empire-building as radical domination: "The scream of the Accomplished Present / A conglomerate of Ends, the scream of Parallels / All tied down with spikes These are the spines / Of the cold citizens made to run wheels upon." The ties or "sleepers" that support the road-bed are in Dorn's dark comic figure made into "cold citizens," the anonymous dead by whose killing labors the "Main Line" was originally constructed. The crews of section hands, laying rail and tamping ballast under the ties with spade or crowbar or shovel or pick, were, as Dorn knew from his 1952 foray among the gandy dancers of the Burlington line in Wyoming, usually casual workers, often drifters and tramps—a disposable work force sociologically located on the other side of the tracks from and under the thumb of the dark dreamers of empire like Vanderbilt, Harriman, Hughes. Dorn's implicit punning on "sleepers" to signal variously migrant laborers and their corpses (working "stiffs" in both senses), the ties they lay and the Pullman cars that ride over them, may ultimately derive, as the critic William J. Lockwood has suggested, from a satiric passage in Thoreau ("Did you ever think what those sleepers are that underlie the railroad? Each one is a man ... the rails are laid on them ... they are sound sleepers, I assure you. And every few years a new lot is laid down and run over"). But a similar play on railroading terminology serves as the pivot point in a mid-period Dorn occasional poem about a train journey as a coach passenger, "Parlor Car Beer," from *Geography* (1965): "They look coach, in the morning / pants wrinkled. / And I am coach, CHICAGO spelled out / across my front teeth. / Don't want to be sleeper." Here the railroad metaphor carries clear implications of a world of difference, "coach" situated in class terms as a reverse badge of honor that identifies the poet as a living resister rather than an oppressed stiff "wasted like a job" after the manner of his railroading grandfather.

"La Máquina a Houston"

Dorn's symbolic use of railroading culminates in the poem "La Máquina a Houston," which concludes the 1974 sequence *Recollections of Gran Apachería* with one of his most arresting images: the dogs of the displaced Apaches creating a wild ruckus as they follow along behind the iron horse—a pointedly genderless yet intensely mythologized "creaking," "heavy breathing," "smoking creature"— that carries away their masters from the railhead at Holbrook toward forced exile in the alien dominion of the conquering race. The train itself is an objectification of industrial capitalism's mechanistic control agenda: "A relic in its own time / Like all the manifestations of technical art / And without real gender / And hidden from direct appeal / By the particulates of the English language / Itself the agent of frag mentation." Here Dorn "reads" the divisive agency of the railroad as a metaphor for the entire control system of "white-world" cultural imperialism, an overwhelming alienating force that severs the body of the Apache nation from its heart in a devastating act of "frag mentation" that is given ironic historical accent by the verbal play on "fragging," a Vietnam-era term for the internal dissociations revealed by soldiers' assassination of their own officers.

Just as in "The Cycle" the railroad over-rides the bodies of the laborers who built it, here the prior cognitive domain of the Apache (distinguished by "the superiority of Native / over Alien Thinking") loses out to the sheer force of invasive machinery: "They had not invented Mind / and as we know / their domain was by Mind over-ridden." Dorn's analysis traces the conquest back to the work of the European scientific/historical "predictive Mind," with its dualistic logical system, a "shining double knife" that functions strictly to divide. The epistemological source of the problem, symbolically reflected by Dorn in the technology of railroading, is the same one defined by the seventeenth-century poet Andrew Marvell in "The Mower Against Gardens"; Marvell's symbolic vehicle, "civilized" man's unnatural horticultural arts of breeding and grafting, differs from Dorn's, but his point is the same: "the Pink grew then as double as his Mind."

Dorn's own mature poetics is not a naïve attempt to reproduce the decisive singularity of native thinking; rather he offers a continual unsettling multiplicity that exerts its subversive influence by borrowing a trick from the enemy, playing on the doubleness of his own words. "La Máquina a Houston" gathers much of its startling power from a series of strategic puns: consider for example the telling plays on *terminal* (railroad station / finite boundary) and on *Noos* (a Greek philosophical term for intellection / an ensnaring knot) in this summary of the Apache relocation: "And this is an important terminal moment / In the Rush Hour begun in this hemisphere.... We are too far gone on thought, and its rejections / The two actions of a Noos." The "two actions" of a double mind that splits off concrete sensation from abstract reason, body from soul, world from idea, are like sets of parallel linear tracks; as Dorn had reminded us in

"The Cycle," "Parallels are just two things / going to the same place." In this poet's hard-eyed critical analysis the duplicity of consciousness of the social/economic monolith stands revealed as a parallel-tracking control function, doubled like anything that is divided from its own nature, and designed to cut right through the heart.

III.

A Set of Circumstances and Warps of Destiny (1948–1951)

I.

A Vast Nothing

"**M**Y EARLIEST INFLUENCES," Dorn wrote in his preface to *Way West* (1993) "came from the West itself, travelling through its people and terrain when I was in high school, to L. A. on Route 66, or to work in the (then, late Forties) old growth forests of the Sierra Nevada Mountains."

Thirteen years earlier, when he published his selected essays (1980), he suggested we do a little colloquy to serve as an introduction. We talked mostly about the West, the overriding subject that pervades and organizes the occasional essays in *Views*. At one point I brought up a line from Dorn's essay on Douglas Woolf in which he'd suggested that to move West too young could sour a man's wit, and asked if he thought that had happened to him. "No I don't," he replied, "because I arrived in the West rather late. When I was in high school, my first trips were *through* the West. I was going to California, which isn't the West. That's Pacific.... When I was in high school taking my trips across the country [it was] on a Trailways bus, or in cars, in that old car pool that used to exist. You know, pay $20 and go to L. A. You'd have six people and you'd drive all the way through, to Seal Beach. I feel much more Californian than Western in that way, I always have. I was going to California when I was 16 years old. I was brought up a nomad. The West became my laboratory. And it's the subject I'm most interested in."

Dorn discriminated his memories of those early trips *through* the West, which largely featured Southern California settings and circumstances of routine penury—"semi-starvation has always been my experience of Southern California," he wrote in a 1976 notebook, "living in a garage while visiting my uncle in Pasadena"— from his recollections of his initial experiences of actual Western terrain, which did not come until a junket to the Northwest made after spring finals at the University of Illinois in 1949.

The first of Dorn's many visits to the Cascades region of the northern Sierra Nevada, this was a working trip: for some weeks he toiled on a logging crew in the woods of the valley of the South Fork of the Stillagamish and up the green slopes of Mt. Pilchuck, cutting down tall stands of fir, pine and cedar. It was strenuous duty, but work Dorn later claimed he had enjoyed. Through connections of a college roommate from Illinois, later that same summer he picked up a higher-paying job in Seattle on an airplane production assembly line and stayed on as "a college boy working at Boeing" until September, when it came time to head back to the Midwest and enroll for the fall semester at Champaign.

Back at the university in the 1949–1950 academic year things did not proceed well for student Dorn. His later reminiscences of the time were enigmatic. In the autobiographical "Driving Across the Prairie" he suggested that his only achievement in two years at Champaign (1948–1950) was getting over the prolonged emotional effects of leaving behind a lost love (this was Phyllis, his high school steady): "at [that] great university I learned to mend a broken heart by practising on my own. But the accomplishment had been condemned as un-useful and I was failed as a scholar...."

Talking about his time at the state university more casually in a 1972 interview, Dorn was not much more informative, indicating with a slight hint of self-mockery that his "big moment" (like that of Hardy's Jude the Obscure) had been his study of architecture. In reconstructing the period he implied his dissatisfaction at the university had to do with the standardized undergraduate program in which he was placed—"something called general studies ... a vast nothing." Forty years later he claimed to be able to recall only one of his instructors, an English composition teacher "who was very nice" (though Dorn could not remember his name). In a telling anecdote, he recalled his one campus brush with aesthetic modernism, something of which he'd had no prior inkling: "I first heard the name of Picasso at the University of Illinois. It completely intrigued me although I didn't have the foggiest idea who he was."

Dorn saved his most specific recollections of his life at the state university for a 1988 note on the history of his reading. "The University of Ilinois Library was my first Big Time Library—the library of Dee Brown, who later ripped off Wounded Knee.... I read Dos Passos at the Illinois library, the trilogy, *Manhattan Transfer,* between passing out Henry Wallace fliers." The Dos Passos / Wallace association provides a clue to Dorn's brief period of student political involvement in the autumn of 1948. He signed up with the campus Progressive Party and for some weeks turned out dutifully to canvas and distribute leaflets for Wallace, "the greatest presidential candidate of my lifetime, my conscious lifetime." It was Dorn's first brush with socialism. (His family had always voted democratic— "I had simply grown up with Roosevelt.") To Dorn's disappointment Wallace turned out a big loser, most of his bare million votes coming from New York state and very few from out in the corn belt where he hailed from. (Three years later, at Black Mountain, it took student Dorn a little time to pick up on Charles Olson—until Olson told a story about working with Henry Wallace, and "I was prepared to be impressed.")

The political direction of the nation caused the twenty-one-year-old Dorn some nervous private concern in his second spring at Champaign, as hostilities threatened in Korea. A federal land grant school, the University of Illinois at the time required two years' ROTC service of all male students. As tension increased in Asia student soldier Dorn found himself put to study war with some realistic prospect of practical application. Staying out of combat would be a motive for the next several years. Military studies now infiltrated his reading. "The most influential reading I did at Illinois was the ROTC manuals (a requirement then)." In compensation, as he saw it, for going through a "terrifying" ordeal of weapons drills ("I never dropped my rifle but I witnessed it a couple of times.... A mistake of ... magnitude"), he was given thorough training in close map-reading and the art of charting terrain coordinates. (This topographical instruction, coming some five years before Dorn's first exposure, via Olson, to the "areal" cultural geography of Carl Sauer, was administered by first lieutenants and majors who'd tested those mapping skills in Europe and the Pacific.) The Illinois ROTC program was, Dorn concluded, an educational "fair bargain": "for the humiliation of close drill and the robotized responses to command, you could learn the secrets of how to move regimented bodies over the surface of the earth. As it turned out, I never came into possession of an army, so that aspect has remained useless—but [later] at Black Mountain, when I was reading Woodward's biography of Grant, the Quartermaster *par excellence,* it all came in handy, plus the fact that I'd been raised in a railroad town."

His ROTC courses were among the few Dorn negotiated with any success at all. Faced with failing grades, he withdrew from the university after the 1950 spring semester. Only a few weeks later, on June 25, North Korea invaded South Korea. At this point any young American male unprotected by a student deferment entered a waiting period of generalized anxiety and risk.

2.

Wherever Intelligence and Curiosity Led

Ed Dorn was essentially self educated. Of course he attended public schools and high schools, but that was training rather than education ... his education was occurring outside the school setting.... Self reliance was ingrained in [him]. It was structural, constitutional, whether inherited or acquired.... [He entertained no] possibility of an alternative to acting in responsibility to himself, in word and deed. That is the source of [his] courage, and willingness to set off on open ended ventures with no degree of safety or comfort, safe from fear that inhibits the rest of us and keeps us constricted within systems. [He] could ... go wherever intelligence and curiosity led [him]....

    —Ray Obermayr, "Ed Dorn and My Father"

After high school, a couple of years at the University of Illinois and a period of hanging around Illinois working in factories not knowing what to do, a set of circumstances and warps of destiny took me to Black Mountain....

    — Dorn in an interview, 1993

THE ABERCROMBIE FAMILY had by this time relocated to the moderate-sized Central Illinois town of Mattoon, a light-manufacturing center situated in the broom-corn country some thirty miles southwest of Villa Grove. In the summer of 1950, back home after his two largely wasted years of attempting to acquire "higher" education, Dorn found work on the late shift at the tractor factory at Shelbyville, thirty miles west of Mattoon. He signed up for some summer classes at the state college in Charleston, ten miles to the east.

In June 1950, when Dorn enrolled in Raymond Obermayr's Color and Design class at Eastern, he was twenty-one; Obermayr, a self-described "Milwaukee socialist and ethical person" and recent U. of Wisconsin Ph.D. then in his first teaching job, just twenty-eight. Each young man recognized in the other a serious, earnest truth-seeker. Outside classes, the closeness in their ages allowed a friendly relationship that could be fairly equal. Obermayr, an Army vet and committed intellectual libertarian, had seen a little of the world and had a certain stock of formal knowledge. "He told me about things that were so exotic I couldn't believe it," Dorn would remember.

Obermayr, for his part, still recalls quite vividly the striking impression made upon him by the raw, obscure yet surprisingly gifted summer-school student: "Ed's first art work in my class was remarkable—very similar to the color work of Josef Albers, though of course I'm sure he wasn't yet aware of Albers at that time. In class he was very sensitive, very, very good. He picked things up right away; you didn't have to waste a lot of time explaining it to him. In fact I knew from the moment I met him that he was not only an unusually bright student but a really exceptional person. His intellectual acuity and sensitivity were obvious."

At the time Obermayr and his wife Lorna lived in married faculty housing on campus. "After classes Ed would just drop in. We'd talk, and we'd listen to jazz, which Ed loved to do. He was very fond of George Shearing, I remember. For a young man of that time and place, he was already quite sophisticated. You would certainly never have thought he came from a farm. I don't know where that natural sophistication of his came from; it certainly didn't appear to be coming from his mother."

Obermayr remembers the young Dorn of Charleston days as "a real loner" who seldom mingled with other students. While his factory job largely precluded campus socializing beyond his sessions with the Obermayrs, Dorn did however show a brief interest in one co-ed whom he escorted out on a few dates—a "blonde bombshell" as Obermayr recalls, "whose name, believe it or not, was Marilyn Monroe."

Dorn confided to his friend and teacher that having forfeited his student deferment, he was now eligible to be conscripted for combat in the rapidly escalating conflict in the Far East. A correspondence with the Central Committee for Conscientious Objection in Philadelphia had brought out what he "sort of already knew"— "that I was really not a C. O., I just didn't want to go to Korea." In this difficult hour, Obermayr came up with plan for him that combined immediate practicality (it promised to keep him out of Korea) with educational redemption (it offered him a second chance, a fresh start). The art teacher had connections with a small experimental arts college in the hills of North Carolina.

"I was acquainted with Black Mountain through friends," as Obermayr tells the story. "I'd gone to visit there many times, though I was never enrolled. I knew most of the faculty there. I knew what the place was about, that they gave students this unusual amount of space in which to learn. I could see quite plainly that Ed was not cut out for regular degree-mill-type higher education. He was certainly too smart, for one thing. And I'd gathered enough from what little he'd said about the time he'd spent at Champaign to know that it had been a real disaster. I never got the full details, but I think he may even have flunked out. Now here was this remarkable young man, with this exceptional mind that was very much his own. What Ed needed was not more control. He needed freedom. I knew the kind of freedom to pursue his own ends he would get at Black Mountain. I thought that might be very good for him. It turned out I was right."

Dorn lacked the lump sum necessary for the Black Mountain tuition deposit. Obermayr, though hardly a rich man, staked it to him. "I gave him the money—three hundred dollars. That doesn't sound like much now, but at the time I wasn't making a very large wage; in fact I hated that teaching job, and my wife and I were trying to save up to get out and go to Paris, so it represented a serious sum to us. But there was no way I could *not* give him that money. And you know, another thing I always admired about Ed, in addition to his self-reliance and his courage, his intelligence and his curiosity and his great nerve, was his remarkable loyalty. For my bringing his attention to Black Mountain, and giving him that three hundred dollars to go down there, he was grateful to me for the rest of his life."

For Dorn, Ray Obermayr's gift represented his rescue from the preparatory period of his imaginative life. "The first thing you're preoccupied with where I come from," he would later say of his midcentury departure from Illinois, "is how to exit. The choices were quite clear, in my part of the country, you could stay or you could go. If you stayed, you had to have a pretty specific reason for staying—you couldn't just stay. Nobody hung around. Not that it was any sort of dilemma. I was going to go, but the questions were how? Where?...."

Dorn's millennium, as he came to believe, began in 1950, the year in which the familiar binding constraints of his prairie upbringing, the old "woe of that lowly order" which had for so long stood as his "sign and weight in that land," was at last lifted from him. His lingering-time in his home place was drawing to a close. "I became that land and wandered out of it."

IV.

Nomadism
(1951–1953)

I.

The Business
of Sensibility
and Insensibility

"IT WAS ALL NEW TO ME," Dorn would say of his first season at the isolated Appalachian outpost of Black Mountain. "For one thing, I don't believe I'd ever met a person from the eastern part of the United States. A lot of people were from New York. The information they had all came into me as a flood.... They were Eastern, and my whole Midwestern experience was ... country.... I felt very country in the face of that kind of city expression and sophistication. So that shyness was mixed up with fear too but always attached to this fascination. I remember writing letters back to my friends [in Illinois] not too long after I got there full of the newly acquired wisdom of Black Mountain. That represented a big break with my past because those people were very turned off by what were then very advanced ideas of how one lives...."

Dorn spent the 1950–1951 school year at Black Mountain, studying art, writing, anthropology and other subjects. To defray living expenses he worked on the college farm, driving a tractor, tending cows and chickens, and in the college print shop, where he did the press work on Charles Olson's dance-play *Apollonius of Tyana*. He was initially both impressed and intimidated by the towering (six-foot eight-inch), polymathic, compulsively verbal Olson, who arrived in late June of 1951, direct from the Yucatán, to lecture on culture, man and history for the college's summer session. The bewildering range of reference in those lectures left young autodidact Dorn struggling to keep up: "The way I heard [Olson]," he later confessed to me, "was with a bit of strain when my powers of comprehension weren't up to it."

Lacking funds for another year's tuition, at the end of the summer session Dorn returned to Illinois. He stayed for a while with the Abercrombies in Mattoon, working at odd jobs and, now that he was no longer shielded by a student deferment, keeping an anxious eye out for mail from his draft board. While at home he re-established contact with his closest male friend from high-school days.

A year ahead of Dorn at Villa Grove High School, Gordon Taylor had played the role of a trusted, slightly older brother. Like Dorn, Taylor lacked one parent; his mother having died in giving birth to him, he had been raised by a stepmother; but in contrast to Dorn's stepfather, a hired man, Taylor's father, a dentist, was among the small town's most successful professionals. Recounting "the outcome of old friends" in the 1968 autobiographical tale "Driving Across the Prairie"—a diagnostic essay, in effect, on "the psychological principle of Illinois," written some time after he and Taylor had parted ways in life—Dorn writes of "the son of the dentist kept to the straight and narrow [who] had gone like one of the principal victims of the fifties to the University of Illinois where he learned to drink without inhibition and is now a wholesale liquor salesman on the Coast." But at high school in Villa Grove, or "The Grave"—the private nickname Dorn and Taylor applied to their home town once they'd left it—the tall, handsome, well-read, well-spoken Taylor had been a hero out of the old Frank Merriwell mold, memorialized in yearbooks as captain of the basketball team, Best Dresser, Best Looking, the "intellectual" of his class. In the school yearbook (the *Vade Mecum*) for Dorn's junior year (1947), his own notoriously lackluster scholarship earned him a jocular bequest of the graduating Taylor's superior academic aptitude ("my scholastic standing to Ed

Dorn so that he may get out"). In the same volume a Dramatic Club group photo seats club vice president Taylor front and center, while Dorn and steady girlfriend Phyllis Sprinkle (elsewhere singled out as possessor of "Most Alluring Smile") take places in the rear ranks; a shot of the Student Representative Body again centers on senior class president Taylor, with junior representative Dorn positioned directly behind him. These relationships appear to extend into Dorn's autobiographical sketch "A Troublesome Spring," wherein Taylor, as the solider figure and cooler head, is called upon by the hero to mediate in his problematic impasse with the sweetheart who seems to have chosen between them at some earlier time.

For Dorn, Taylor now represented a stabilizing point of familiarity in a time of otherwise new and often confusing experiences. They had remained close in the years after leaving school, keeping up a correspondence during Dorn's stay at Black Mountain—whence the latter, feeling both curious and out of place in the experimental-arts-community setting, had been dispensing a generous share of his "newly acquired wisdom." In Taylor Dorn had a friend with whom he shared common ground and could exchange feelings and ideas free of the embarrassment he so often felt among "East Coast" intellectual types at Black Mountain.

Currently, however, their life paths were radically diverging. Taylor, responding to the middle-class imperatives that obtained generally in their home town as well as throughout Middle America, had faced up to the specter of military service, enlisted in the Marines and was headed with some trepidation toward the legendary horrors of recruit training at Camp Pendleton, with the further likely prospect of seeing combat in Korea; Dorn, for his part, was not only assiduously avoiding the draft but would soon flee their common prairie home for shelter in southwest Arkansas with his former art teacher, the pacifist war resister Ray Obermayr (who was now teaching at a college in Arkadelphia). A continuing true believer in Dorn's creative promise as well as in the moral principle of war resistance, Obermayr was more than ever ready to aid and abet his friend in keeping himself out of harm's way. With a General Dwight D. Eisenhower presidential campaign looming, Dorn would be joined by Obermayr in a vow to "avoid the SOLID BRASS HEAD (my moniker for Eisenhower)." At the Obermayrs' in Arkadelphia Dorn was taking refuge from what he now considered a neurotic, repressed, militaristic money society and its impositions upon him as a "sensitive organism." His motive was to preserve and secure at whatever cost his freedom. Taylor's, meanwhile, was to observe the expectations of his family, his class and society in general. The Marine boot-camp recruit and the draft-dodging unknown would-be artist on the run resolved to share by letter their respective challenges. The testing grounds each would encounter would prove the mettle of their friendship, as reflected in a steady flow of correspondence from various lonely locations around the world over the next few years. Dorn's self-conscious analysis of his own trials, pains and growth during the season of nomadism that ensued for him make his letters to Taylor (1951–1955) a moving record of the birth of a poet's soul.

There is a sense of presage in a February 1952 letter from Dorn to Taylor, written from Ray and Lorna Obermayr's home in Arkadelphia. Much of the letter is taken up with Dorn's excited discovery (in Philip Horton's biography of Hart Crane) of the verse of Samuel Greenberg, a class-tortured underdog-poet in whose struggles he plainly discerns elements of his own.

> He said "The poet seeks an earth in himself." His father immigrated to N. Y. probably from Russia or Rumania, settled in a ghetto, lower east side. Born abt. 1900 worked in a factory very early, what a truly sensitive organism and what torture it must have been. Struggle, struggle, struggle. Against poverty, against ignorance, against intolerance, against ridicule, against the day by day methodological destruction of the beautiful … anyway the poetry is ineffable … no grammar, misspelling, archaic forms, inchoate ideas. But powerful and lovely poetry … that makes me damn near cry with emotion, with excitement, for its sheer beauty of sound. SOUND! This is some of the finest language I have yet to run across … goddamn it I've never read such beauty.

If Dorn as yet possessed no more than a dim inkling of the poetry he might some day actually write, the unremarked sufferings of the disadvantaged and obscure agonies of the defeated were matters of which he felt he already had some right to speak. A similar identifying sympathy now inclined him to the study of the work of another tormented "sensitive organism," Ezra Pound, who as Dorn had learned from Olson was then incarcerated by federal directive in a Washington, D.C. hospital for the insane. He linked Samuel Greenberg's poems with Pound's "Letters to a Young Poet," which he had discovered in *Poetry (Chicago)*. To Dorn, both Greenberg and Pound, in their different ways, seemed exemplary of the travails of true poetry outside—and against—the system.

But the young seeker could not exist only through books. He yearned for intimate connection and active intellectual stimulus, largely absent from his life since leaving Black Mountain. In mid-February he made his way from Arkadelphia to Knoxville, Tennessee, to rendezvous with a woman friend he'd met the previous summer at the college, Bea Faulkner Huss. Bea was the wife of Wes Huss, the Black Mountain drama teacher. The Husses had arrived at the college at the same time as student Dorn; after his departure they had stayed on to raise a family, Bea taking care of their small son and Wes eventually serving as college treasurer and business manager.

Bea Huss was to be a key Dorn connection throughout this restless, hungry time. Along with her husband Wes, a veteran of therapy with one of America's few practicing Reichian analysts (Dr. Charles Oller of Philadelphia), Bea had become conversant with the controversial theories of Wilhelm Reich, which she generously shared with Dorn. She also sent along Olson's reading lists and lecture notes, and provided news of noteworthy doings at Black Mountain. For many months when there was no other such input to encourage him, "a big letter from Bea" every few weeks kept vivid in Dorn's mind the idea of an eventual return to the college. It was for that matter Bea alone who provided reassurance that the financially-shaky institution—"more on their ass than ever," as Dorn relayed the latest news to Taylor—still remained open and functioning. "Things are furious at B[lack] M[ountain]," he reported with some envy in early

1952. "Olson is a dynamo installing a new series called 'The New Sciences of Man'.... Man this is the time to be there. Imagine what one could learn just by snooping around with one's eyes focused." He would soon learn more through his proxy source. "I will meet Bea in Knoxville (KNOXVILLE!#*) Tenn. Next Sat. or Sun. for a short week and should get then word straight from the horse's mouth." The meeting did not disappoint. Bea supplied an intriguing firsthand report on Olson's New Sciences lectures ("vital and exciting"), tutored him further in Reichianism, then drove all the way from Knoxville to Mattoon to drop him off at the Abercrombies before turning around and heading back to Black Mountain and her family.

In parting he and Bea "arrived at a definite-tentative plan" for hooking up on a less temporary basis. "We will live together for an undeterminable length of time, tentative as to where. If I can 'make good' [with fishing] in Alaska, it will be Yucatán. If not, somewhere around N. Y." His first step toward bringing the plan to fruition would involve getting to Seattle ("Don't know how exactly"), the presumed jumping-off point for Alaskan sardine boats. His route would take him "WEST," a prospect which, as he admitted to Gordon Taylor, he found daunting and "dreadful"; he reminded his friend of previous Western hitch-hiking and car-pool trials—"that trip out again into the goddamn wilderness, into I can't know what." Once in Seattle, he planned to pick up a stopgap job with a former friend from the University of Illinois who was starting a contemporary furniture merchandising venture. "The world of business"— and especially the business of "peddling modern hocus pocus"—was perhaps "not the direction one takes in order to discover the structure of reality." But it might sustain him financially until he'd had a chance to get to Alaska and make a pile as a sardine fisherman, thus paving the way to "do Mex[ico]" with Bea. They would, in the end, tour Yucatán and inspect the Mayan hieroglyphs touted by Olson: such, at any rate, was the "definite-tentative plan."

Meanwhile he was again stuck in Illinois. Back in the bustling prairie manufacturing town and agricultural center of Mattoon that spring, his mind was agitated by a series of recently-adopted enthusiasms: the language and money theories of Ezra Pound, Olson's far-reaching cultural projections, the subversive biophysics of Wilhelm Reich (which Bea Huss now had him reading up on). Reich's ideas were having a particularly potent effect. Though stranded in the Midwest, Dorn found his mind aswim in the larger flowing universe Reich had pictured, a place permeated by the primal, mass-free orgone energies in which originated all creative activity. The constraints imposed upon these energies, Reich had proposed, produced the blocks and binds that caused not only individual neuroses but also collective social disorders. Most prominent of those latter disorders in Dorn's immediate purview was the aggressive militaristic impulse, origin of his draft-board nightmares.

The only positive news of this Illinois stop was no news at all from his selective service board. "There was nothin from the draft people. No news is good news in this case." The everyday scene at his family home was now difficult for him to endure. After only three days with the Abercrombies he swore to Taylor that of all his problematic family visits of recent years, "this *last* time is *really* miserable." His new ideas and experiences did not fit a homecoming to the heartland: a bitter, barren vision appeared as he viewed old familiar patterns with a new analytic eye. "Jesus, Gordon," he lamented to Taylor, "the home life makes me sick this time. To see what is happening to destroy my potentially beautiful sister and a brother who in some respects has a native talent is a frightful thing. I can see what must have been the destructive pattern of my own disheveled life. I've known this all along intellectually but this is the first time I've felt it very plainly." He vowed to stay around no longer than "the familial formality" required: "I guess I'll give them a week of me." But in reality the dutiful weeks dragged on into a three-and-a-half-month lapse into procrastination, lassitude and doubt: a temporary triumph of the stultifying entrapment of "the psychological principle of Illinois" over the vitalizing and liberating influences of the "Essay on the Chinese Written Character," the New Sciences of Man and *The Function of the Orgasm*.

When in a plaintive May letter from boot-camp-trapped Gordon

Taylor he was charged with being unable to "fully share this choked throat," Dorn had to honestly concede his friend's point. He had no idea what it was like to be entangled within the workings of the war machine ("In fact I can't share anything on that end, removed as I am from it, and limited"). Still he insisted he was caught up in his own way in the same larger struggle, a crucial battle between freedom and conformity, "sensitivity and insensibility," waged at the level of the total organism. From the scene of his own inner searchings Dorn could offer his reality-besieged friend no better than the weak support of "an exchange of distant agonies."

> This business of sensibility and insensibility is at the same time as huge as it must seem and one that I cannot possibly help you / at least directly / with. Because I here am caught up in same struggle. It is such a constant fight, with the agents that want to [overcome] anyone who cares about the accuracy of life. They really are the same agents. In your case they are intensified, focused. In mine they are oh so subtle (as you know too) and in this way here the problem is sometimes trickier.

Dorn was forced to acknowledge one essential advantage his friend lacked—"true there is freedom of movement here." Yet he labored under constraints imposed by the same shadow forces, "agents" or systems that opposed life whether by oppressing it externally or repressing it from within. Rehearsing the Reichian message, he urged his friend to trust that whatever ills the military might bring on, the life-force in him would be able to survive them. "I personally don't think that the body can ever be wholly ruined," he argued after Reich. "The rhythmic life process can be restored to its fluid biological functioning." Taylor was advised to regard the trials of military service as an "intensification" that would inevitably result in "a restoration of ... life": "This intensification, this forcing may stir, actually, sensibilities." And when his friend countered by suggesting that military existence was indeed bearable but only through the imaginative anticipation of one's release, Dorn demanded of him an Olsonian attention to full presence in the moment: "'Looking forward' isn't useable at all in any real sense because it isn't available now. Remember this beautiful thing by Olson, 'reality ... is never more than this instant, than you on this instant, than you, figuring it out, and acting, so. If there is any absolute, it is never more than this one, you, this instant, in action....' This is big, this statement, but goddamn it is high time we thought hugely."

D ORN'S EARNEST CANON of Reichian organic intensification and Olsonian attentive instantaneity received another supplement that month from Bea Huss. For Dorn's geographical convenience they met this time in Indianapolis, a city that represented to him all the insidious agencies of Midwestern mercantilism (he deemed it a "foul place"); fortunately, as he later told Taylor, Bea "drove so we didn't have to stay there." As they took off into the vast emptiness of "the corn-west," there followed a "restoration of life." But once back in Mattoon he was quickly blaming himself for again allowing the mental excitement to dissipate. Bea had brought him "much news about B[lack] M[ountain]," he informed his friend, "and there was a lot of other talk, and I came back bursting with energy which somehow never came off, it seems like every minute was so filled, and now I can recall only faint patterns of what went on. Of course there was a lot about Reich and she says that if I write to the [Orgone] Institute I can get specifications for an accumulator. I have a couple more bulletins now and I have been reading." Discussions on the latest trip with Bea had convinced Dorn to look into constructing an orgone accumulator (or "orgone box"), a device intended by Reich as a means of restoring depleted energies. His inquiries would be frustrated; shortly to be declared fraudulent by the Food and Drug Administration, the accumulator was already unavailable, as he was disappointed to learn, to non-"professionals." Whether Dorn ever actually conferred with anyone who'd used the device remains in question. "The Reichian work I'd done was important to me and I'm sure I talked about it with Ed at one time or another at Black

Mountain," Wes Huss recalls fifty years after the fact. "But I never got enthusiastic enough about it to try to build an orgone box, or even to consider it. If Ed did, that would be just like him—wanting to carry the theory out to its extreme, to go all the way with it."

The compatibility—or lack of it—between the theories of Dorn's two current intellectual masters, Olson and Reich, had received considerable attention on the Indianapolis trip. "Bea says that, apparently, Olson doesn't know Reich," he told Taylor. "And even though I had surmised it, it still came as a surprise. She didn't get this from Charles himself but it seems that in a conversation with Connie, his wife, Connie had mentioned [to Bea] that he had some time ago decided that there was a great danger in dispersing himself and that he had better not, actually, get involved in the whole psycho-business." All the same, Olson's rumored aversion to the intellectually fashionable practice of psychoanalysis did not, in Dorn's view, constitute "a gap for him at all": instead the giant pedagogue concerned himself with the bigger picture, "the metaphysics of psychoanalysis," and "caught, independently, the spirit of the new science of the orgone." Dorn "proved" the point for Gordon Taylor and himself by citing a list of "parallels" between Reich's published opinions and those of Olson (e.g. the latter's suggestion in his "Human Universe" essay that the Mayan descendants in the Yucatán "still carry their bodies with some of the same savor and flavor that the bodies of Americans are missing"). For Dorn's purposes, Olson's thought and Reich's thought now represented complementary aspects of a single relevant perception of reality, one total, liberating, enabling source.

This enthusiastic display of evangelical fervor soon abated, however. Taylor's reply from the recruit training base was an "unbelievable, pitiful letter" which made Dorn "quite sick." He castigated himself for preaching about theories of reality to one who was actually "experiencing it—that plague, that personal and direct insult." His babblings about Olson and Reich, he admitted, must "surely sound empty to you there." He recounted an encounter in Mattoon with some local working folk who'd asked after Taylor. He had at first been moved by their show of concern: in displaying compassion "these people, who ordinarily one would take only lightly," had proved themselves "more noble, perhaps more moral" than Dorn himself. Then again, thinking further of the incident, he saw the irony in it. His first reaction had been a repetition of "my old attempt to see fundamental beauty in commonality ... isn't it strange that these same people are part of the machine that is torturing you at this instant. How many faces do we have?"

Reproaching himself for his lack of sympathy and compassion, Dorn realized it was high time he himself began to practise what he preached and seized the moment.

> Don't take this wrongly and I am not at all sure what wrongly would be / but now lately I have felt a burden-like pressure in me that says: "whereas before you were glad to be no part of that army mess and had no qualms, now that someone very close and just as deserving of freedom as you or anyone is caught up, it's a little choking if you (me) don't take full score of that freedom, if you don't at every instant make usable this precious stuff."

2.

Vagrant

THE "BURDEN-LIKE PRESSURE" to make good use of his precious civilian freedoms rendered Dorn more estranged than ever from Illinois small-town life. When a former high-school classmate from "The Grave" (i.e. Villa Grove) "had the superb gall" to call to remind him of the Memorial Day weekend alumni dance, even the harmless solicitation took him aback, reminding him of a personal past he preferred forgotten. "Does he, does this person think for even an instant...?" He toiled "sporadically" for a local farm-equipment business, but that too brought further impositions, this time in the form of "union trouble." Dorn sensed himself surrounded by a society of robots and slaves, in which one's labor belonged to everybody but oneself: grudgingly, he too submitted ("I had to join those bastards"). As for the company of his kind, he'd decided that to survive Mattoon he'd have to do without. His closest companion, a black cat, had vanished during his absence on the latest junket with Bea Huss. As a replacement he found "a very tiny kitten with very large blue eyes and a white face with large white whiskers" which sat beside him in the Abercrombie kitchen as he typed his letters to

Bea and Gordon Taylor.

By June any lingering hope of building up a nest egg in Mattoon had "pretty much petered out," defeated by "hitches like rain, the union, my own personal lethargy—just general discordance." The self-created challenge to "take full score of [his] freedom" was no longer possible to ignore. He resolved to stake his energies in the indeterminate field of action. On the afternoon of June 4, happening into the Mattoon bus depot ("a place that one would hardly visit unless one were catching a bus, events work so strangely"), he ran into a former acquaintance, as he would inform Gordon Taylor:

> Who should coincidentally be there but a Max Bectal, you remember the one-half Chippewa Indian. My condition was one of the usual indifference for the whole of the place plus an added desperation that had come as a result of a suggestion at home that I take a position as all-around man at the same place [where] my father is employed. Max paid for coffee and then announced that he was shoving [off] for Oregon that same afternoon and wouldn't it be tasty if I were to chuck all and kiss too. Mad, I said, was more the word, and why, the fuck, not. I say it as comedy now but you should understand that then I was serious.
>
> The way Max put it—and Max was borne out to be a goddamn liar—: "We'll go down here to Cowden (that's a place perhaps 30 miles south-west of Mattoon) and get a ride to K. C. with a guy who drives a load of dogs there every Wed. night, then in K. C. we'll ship out on the C. B. & Q. R. R. to Casper, Wyoming as laborers on an extra gang, jump the train and ride a freight on to Oregon, or stay there in Casper and work a week, draw up the money and get a bus from there. When we get to Oregon I have a contact that will put us to work in a saw mill at ultra wages and won't the skies be multicolored from then on out." End of Max's version.
>
> What really happened: The guy with the dogs at Cowden wasn't going that particular Wed., so I shot the only ten $ I

had for a bus ticket to K. C. ... In K. C. I had my first, actual look at where the badness, the ugliness that is manufactured and sold as product, by this society, breaks through and spills, runs out as awful yellow pus runs from a cancer which is also and by the same token, the matter of the whole thing. There men have different looks in their eyes. The stare is not so much intensely at, as it is intensely out, from their own heads. These people on 12th Street, the skid row of K. C., have mixed, conglomerate, fantastically inconsistent manners, ways. Most of them, on the one hand, have murdered or done body harm for the price of a draught beer, yet these same ones, in a tavern, which almost always reeks with their faintly puky smell, will spend their last dime for a beer for you and be insulted if you decline they are so kind with you, so concerned, they are so gentle, yet a Negro can't go into the same bar with them, these lowest of lows, and even though you may rightly say you know all this and that I should too, it isn't at all an obvious thing and when I think about it now I realize I can never say, really, how frighteningly and how close to some quality of truth I was that day, June 5. I got very drunk. Drinking all day is a new drunkenness to me. Then, and since K. C., I have found in the men I have come onto and talked with the most incredible kind of unobjectiveness. They have absolutely *no* sense of objective. And fact is completely unknown. I have largely kept my mouth shut and listened. The impulse to point out prejudice and superstition is great but I have succeeded in listening, at last, silently. Because one of the first things I learned was the uselessness, the hopelessness of argument with these people. Which brings me to a point. [What I have] said about availability and reality, excuse me for. It is so easy to intellectualize about that. And there is great danger in intelligence only. It is too easy to say, to talk, as I have heard only meaningless empty talk these past few days, about the things we should be living, but are so crippled, by now, that mere talk itself has become the objective.

One of the greatest, if not the greatest lesson to be learned from Reich is that if the intellect-body is not whole, is not a unity, then there can be nothing complete and the functioning will not be harmonic. And Olson says the same thing: When "language is separable from action," that is, if language is empty, is objective, there will be no action. Which means that I just don't know enough to try to tell you anything at all about what is and what is not available to you. All I can do is tell you what *I* do.

The Kansas City experience, with the tumultuous inner events that accompanied it, was in short "the most strange, most curious, most terrible, most ludicrous, most lewd, and at times deathly thing" that had yet happened. "I was sucked completely and wholly in," a thunderstruck Dorn summed up the momentous, confusing day. "The skid row, the bum-quarters in K. C. on Main Street [is where] I had my grand and laughable awakening as to what this human business is all about."

From Kansas City, as he later related in separate letters to Taylor, the trip unfolded in further unexpected directions. "We did get a free ride to, not Casper but, Moorcroft, Wyoming.... Max, the 1/2 Chippewa Injun turns out to be a completely neurotic s. o. b. and now the contact, through him, I had in Oregon is problematic." Dorn checked into a cheap railway hotel in Moorcroft and took stock of what appeared a rather desperate situation. "I haven't eaten for 1 1/2 days and there is no immediate prospect," he wrote Taylor on June 7. When the railroad laboring work he'd been led to expect didn't materialize, he went to work driving a truck instead. While the job lasted he stayed on in Moorcroft, sleeping in the Etheridge Hotel and taking his meals across the street at Tiny's Restaurant, between-shifts hangout of the track-laying section gangs and crews of gandy-dancers or "gandies" (so called because the work eventually induced a chronic neck-bob like a gander's from the repetitive action of tamping down ties).

3.

Sidetrip:
Wyo-Booming (1979)

T WENTY-SEVEN YEARS LATER, when we were traveling the same barren reaches of the Upper Plains on a magazine assignment to research a story about migrant energy workers, Dorn insisted on a detour to Moorcroft, where he volunteered some reflections on his long-ago experience of the nomadic laborer's condition. We cruised slowly down the vacant windblown main drag in a rented VW roadster, "one of those Noxious German Imports, not a jackrabbit but a Diesel Rabbit," Dorn peering over the wheel with his intent territorial-scout's squint as he pointed out landmarks like the fallendown old red brick hotel where he had once taken shelter from the rigors of his wanderings, and a diner located on the site of the former Tiny's Restaurant. We stopped there for lunch, and over a whitebread-and-bacon sandwich among coal and uranium miners in web-hats he recalled his errant adventures of that earlier time.

Further mementos of his days as a "windborn seed" cropped up all along our trek through that stark man-wasted landscape. Dorn detested nostalgia about the West (or about anything), and the manifest evidence, everywhere we looked, of the violation suffered in the process of extraction by the stripped, gouged and pitted earth didn't particularly surprise him—"the West just wouldn't be the West if it weren't so," he would write in introducing a chapbook of poems I produced after that trip *(A Short Guide to the High Plains)*. Still the sheer scale of the devastation was unsettling, and our tour of the Overthrust Belt—former Indian lands and grazing country now littered with a clutter of giant mantis-like pumps and drill rigs, ominous radiation-warning signposts, severed cows' heads, flocks of disused propane tanks, mountainous eroded tailings heaps, beer-can dumps, ripped-up antelope corpses, hunks of discarded plastic pipe twisted into the shape of rhinoceros tusks and mile after mile of rusted slurry-line junk—seemed to strike a certain elegiac nerve. He mourned an earlier time when a traveler in those parts "could describe a beauty which was more raw than laid open"; yet at the same time perhaps his old areal instinct drove him to want to take it all in, not only the still-raw but the newly laid-open.

After we'd poked around cracked, scorched hills honeycombed by the tracks of monster trucks, stared into canyon-sized open pits watched over by megalithic grey waste mounds, and gaped at the yellow-terraced, soda-ash-asteroid-dotted, red-orange-ore-chunked, black-coal-seam-scored remnants of what had once been grasslands, Dorn made sure we also investigated the recreational haunts of the latest wave of energy boomers. We ventured into wildcatters' watering holes where our Noxious German Import was the only parked vehicle without a rifle rack and where the rough-and-ready bar ecology of Willie-and-Waylon, Miller's-and-a-shot would likely have deterred many a sensible witness. On a Sunday afternoon in Jeffrey City—a bleak, frozen, pre-fabricated energy-frontier base camp with a uranium mill as its *raison d'être*, an atomic energy symbol decorating its water tower and a juke box the size of a pickup truck, loaded with Crash Craddock and Mel Tillis sides, powering the slow-moving entertainment of a dozen weathered web-hats in the bar Dorn picked out—we inquired of one hardy pilgrim we encountered, a sixty-year-old polyurethane insulation salesman from Wisconsin who'd just survived a record chill-factor winter in an old school bus (because, he testified, that was the best housing he could turn up), how he was enjoying Wyo-booming. "Just fine," the grizzled boomer affirmed with a kryptonite grin. "Plenty of work." "Aside from work?" Dorn pressed. There was a brief mood-breaking pause. "Aside from work? Goddamn awful." The poet's appreciative cackle betrayed a common history of similar cognizance.

4.

"C. B. & Q."

DORN'S EARLY NOMADIC VENTURE into the American unknown provided him the subject matter of "C. B. & Q.," worked up two years later at Black Mountain from his notes on the June 1952 trip. After alluding to the day of jazz, liquor and violence in Kansas City, the story establishes its main action among railway and construction workers in Moorcroft. Dorn equips an edgy, noncommital poetic realism with a sharp, laconic narrative bite, wresting from the pointless tracking of migrant workers through space the vivid, non-conceptual images of a directly-experienced confrontation with the actual. The story's terse, transitive initial sentence strikes open a vein of cold whip-lash immediacy worthy of a pulp master: "In the early morning the sun whipped against the plate glass of Tiny's restaurant...." Dorn had learned early the lesson of the Pound touchstone "Essay on the Chinese Written Character" about concrete verbs.

In the figure of the drifter Dorn inscribed an intuition born of his own history. What after all did he know better than the chronic restlessness of the migrant, going as far back as the wandering family work searches to Gary and Flint in the Depression? The errant path of the lonesome singular drifter, forever moving anxiously from

where he was not wanted to where he was not expected, never intend-
ing to linger long—a later Dorn poem, "The Sea Corner, of the Eye,"
would picture this state, "as we lie here he speeds on / like a wind-
born seed"—represented for this writer the most compelling of plots;
similarly the drifter's acutely attentive state of tense, exacerbated
vision, result of steady exposure to hard truths without the protec-
tive shields of property or status, represented the most concentrated
of observing minds. Such a state of intensified attention, Dorn would
decide, had produced his own overwhelming, unsettling Kansas City
vision, that inconclusive illumination he would devote himself to
articulating in his writing—"the grand and laughable awakening as
to what this human business is all about."

The enlightening, harrowing days in Kansas City and beyond left
also a lasting impression by way of the transitory characters that
had filled them. With "C. B. & Q." such characters would begin to
populate the written worlds of Dorn's tales as well: "nonobjective"
individuals like those whose lives he'd lately intersected, with their
raw, unintellectual ways, "how frightening and how close to some
quality of truth." In "C. B. & Q." the characters' drifting never
ceases, that indeed is the one specific thing we know about them:
their restless, rootless condition, inseparable from their otherwise
rather vague identities. Their prototype is Max, a "one half Chero-
kee" drifter drawn on the half-"injun" Max Bectal, real-life insti-
gator of Dorn's exciting and attenuating June 1952 journey. We hear
nothing of Max's inner life; it is his dimly-outlined appearance and
his words that define him (and it is Max who, at third-person remove,
defines the open trajectory of Dorn's narrative: "Max thought if he
didn't like the setup, the looks of things when they got there he might
shove on to Oregon ..."). With such "flat" characterizations Dorn
seems to be representing a quality of the itinerant's heightened
vision. "Nonobjective" yet stripped of subjectivity, these paper-thin
characters may be seen right through, revealing the naked phenom-
enology of "what this human business is all about," once the "intel-
lectualization" is stripped away. This applies equally to Dorn's alter
ego in the story, the central character, Buck.

Buck ... was in K. C. the next morning. He got drunk that day.... It was hot that day in Daddy's tavern in Kansas City. The threepiece band smiled as they sat sweating on the little band box between the two toilet doors. The heavily built man with the curly hair stood on his crutches by Buck's stool and bent his neck to hear the talk above the guitar and the drum. Max was one half Cherokee....

Max sat upright and stared all night, across the aisle from Buck, out the window. The train drove through the darkness up the Kansas line to Nebraska. In the station at Kansas City they had only given their names to the man at the gate with a list. In the car there were no white tabs on the windowshades by their seats. They rode free to the job in Wyoming....

Max must have five dollars left, unless he buys too much to eat. Buck found him in the restaurant with some of the other travelers to Wyoming. Buck ordered a cup of coffee and said to Max that they might not have to gandy if there was other work there, maybe on a ranch or road work. Max thought if he didn't like the setup, the looks of things when they got there he might shove on to Oregon....

On past Tiny's restaurant, past the hardware store and a vacant lot with an old Ford grown in the rear of it, was the New Morecroft Hotel. Buck stayed there. He had new scars right under his lower lip, and over further down on his left jaw after he had washed with strong hotel soap, more bright scars stood red and looked quite becoming. He had been three days so far without paying so that Simms the thin owner shifted his feet on the linoleum floor when Buck returned to the room in the evening....

Buck said that he had a good job down in Wichita but the goddamn foreman had it in for him because he broke three springs in the truck in one day on that bad road and he got fired. Boyd had calmed down and said that he intended to go south for the winter, maybe to Tucson or Albuquerque but he was sure as hell going to be south when the winter hit this place. And he didn't see what Buck saw in Wichita. He could go anywhere anyway because he had a car that the back seat came out of and could be used to sleep in he said.

From the 1950s into the 1970s a restless nomadism provides the prevailing structural motif of Dorn's writing. His early poems and tales provide a realistic reflection of his scattered travels as a struggling worker-writer. In more mediated symbolic fashion the same structure survives in the high comedy of the mid-period mock-epic *Gunslinger,* which proposes an image of a somewhat comparable later authorial role, that of the wandering skilled academic laborer, a singular, "impeccable" wildcatter of the energy fields of the mind; in this later lonesome drifter's unlikely comic adventures we may read Dorn's own maverick passage during the later 1960s and 1970s through the intellectual boomtowns of "Universe City." Each kind of nomadism brought its own rewards and left its own scars, but in the work the symbolic form, a migratory curve, persists and connects them. The heady virtual-reality rambling of *Gunslinger* represents Dorn's critical response to his perception of the historical fading of the older, grittier kind of worker-drifter figure. The figures of Max and Buck in "C. B. & Q." stand at the end of a historical mythic structure, a restless, pointless spinoff of that pattern of migratory movement later identified by Dorn as "the culture of westward expansion"—a culture in which, he would suggest, "the movement is connected with property." In a 1978 interview he talked about the disappearance of characters like Buck. "That character as he exists in that story is a kind of manifestation of the fifties, the mid-fifties even … to take it [farther] back, I think that the pioneer spirit is a kind of penetration into unknown territory *in a group sense*. It's a group movement—a rancher has to have cowboys, cowboys have to have cows—but it's a lot of hooves and bodies, it's not just one guy. The lonesome cowboy figure comes later, after he's already there and is riding the range. That's singular, but it doesn't represent the movement. The movement is connected with property, and it's *going to a place* and it ultimately means *settlement*. Now, there's only room for so much of that, because it takes territory, right? But then the population continues to increase, so you get all kinds of migrants, or say mobility of a work force. I think the fifties represent the last ability of this kind of Northern European to do that; and now, of course, most of that population is either unemployed or on unemployment chronically, and that function has been taken over and largely assumed by other groups—for example, the Mexicans in the Southwest. I'm talking about all the kinds of casual work you could do. So that I think Buck has disappeared, in that sense. Already he's saying well, I think I'll go back to Kansas City, and this other guy's saying, I think I'll go to Arizona before the snow flies, and so forth. So they're already thinking, where are they going to go? They can't go back to Mexico, they're not going back—they've only got themselves, in a way, they're not supporting anything, except their own mystique."

5.

On the Margin

A FTER A FEW WEEKS IN MOORCROFT in June 1952 Dorn hit the
road again, this time chasing another rumor of work on down
the Plains to Cheyenne. Once more the rumor turned out to be a
chimera, and soon he was back on the highway. Thumbing west
from Cheyenne he picked up a ride to Logan, Utah, then another
that took him all the way to Seattle. He arrived in a blur of exhaus-
tion, "miserable with lassitude," asking himself why he'd come—
"there is nothing here in Seattle that isn't in Logan." The work
prospects he'd hoped for now appeared far less certain, but he had
neither the money nor the strength to immediately resume travel-
ing. He soon learned the furniture store venture which he'd counted
on for work had not yet materialized. He checked into a hotel, where
within a few days he was joined by Bea Huss, summoned by his dis-
tress message. "Bea has been so decent in every way," a grateful
Dorn told Gordon Taylor. Bea stayed in Seattle through most of July.
The time was restorative for Dorn, who with her help conducted a
therapeutic self-analysis after the Reichian model. They explored his
personal relationships and organic sensitivities, "psycho-resistances"

and "points of intersection." "My intersecting point," he was encouraged to find, "surely exists and where it exists is in the realm of creativity. That is, it *is* creativity. And further in another way: the state of complete harmony exists as pure work (creativity). Because for the human, time and space must be worked on as a whole. This has a lot to do with the organism in flux and also with the intellect juxtaposed to the prevailing *monetary* system."

In the last week of July Bea returned to Black Mountain and her family, leaving him temporarily stricken. "This has got to be Grief, it is sad, but there are an isolated few things that are unwriteable," he told Taylor bravely. "Bea has gone back to B. M. and the best we can hope for is a reunion sometime in the coming fall, when I return East for, perhaps, good." Some weeks later Taylor would receive a calmer, more measured account of the visit: "Bea came quite easily to Seattle in July. For two or three weeks we lived our way but I couldn't find work, then. You goddamn well know that I left Mattoon in the first instance without anything to eat with. I got annoyed as hell living on her money although she was willing enough. No it wasn't exactly living on her that did it. It must have been the business of no way out in the future, nothing for the winter. Then Bea returned to Wes and B. M. for August." From Black Mountain, Dorn related, Bea was endeavoring to find a suitable place for them "for the winter in New England, for free. She knows of possibilities. I don't, if we can arrange it, plan to do anything but paint, perhaps write and the like from November to spring."

His plans kept changing aspect. An early, "vague plan to establish residence in Washington and maybe go to school there next year" warred with growing doubts "(in the light of new things) whether ... I can afford the time, there is so much to learn and so little time, and school is such a drag." The original idea of trying for an Alaskan fishing run still lingered, but the season hadn't yet begun and meanwhile he sought other work. "The Northwest [is] ok," he declared to Taylor. "The U. S. is rather large—and dumb, like men with big ears are. But I shall stay for three months maybe." In August he found work with a logging crew, and decided to "settle for at least until the later part of October ... in the West, here at the Monroe Logging Co., as a LUMBERJACK.''

He spent the late summer/early autumn season in the woods, working out of the company base camp in Monroe, twenty-five miles northeast of Seattle, and climbing daily up the slopes of the Cascades. "Don't let this scare you," he told Taylor in his first weeks on the job. "It is identically the same as all the rest of those automatic things, the ones you know too. Hard work? Jesus C., yes. Pay good and in the open. No embarrassing questions, like what is your draft class, and why? I won't give you the mechanics. It is simply logging, lumbering, in the woods. The food is bulky and things have their scale, being rather brutish, at any rate all-fingers." By mid-September the crew had worked its way up to an altitude of 4000 feet, where the air was "thin enough to make it gaspy for one to labor." On the pre-dawn climb temperatures dropped steeply, forcing Dorn to "wear long black 100% wool under deals in order not to cry out in sharp exact pain at the current point to which modern man has at this moment arrived since those first beginnings in the tidal waters of the then young earth."

His weekends were devoted to self-assigned studies. Economics, cultural anthropology and psychobiology now preoccupied him. He spent several weekends reading his way through the economic theory section of the Seattle public library. "I have concerned myself with the economics of things," he announced to Taylor. "Homo economicus, the economic man: ugly with big ears." Beginning with Adam Smith, he graduated on to Ricardo, Wells, Mill, the Adamses (Brooks and Henry), Marx ("can't help any more than the others"). An absorbing discovery was "*Ancient Society* by Lewis Morgan, the American anthropologist who knew all about consanguinity and from whom Marx and Engels got wise on early democracy and family structure." He was also following up Bea's Reichian reading tips. From the Orgone Institute in New York he obtained a number of texts and bulletins, though his order for a copy of *The Sexual Revolution: Toward a Self-Regulating Character Structure* went unfilled due to lack of "professional qualifications." Also still frustrated, as he lamented to Taylor, was his inquiry "on the availability of [the] orgone accumulator." Persistent in his quest, he enlisted Gordon and Bea to help search out clandestine Reichian materials. He was hunting also for the work of Katherine Coman, a historian of the West recommended by Olson. For light relief he was reading Pound's *Guide to Kulchur*. Like other extended pauses in his nomadism, these months were a period of earnest autodidacticism.

In the scattered studies of his Northwest isolation Dorn's intuition of a world of difference grew. Life was convincing him a painful lonely freedom would be his gift and fate: an unusual challenge, a special responsibility. Creative persons, he told Gordon Taylor, couldn't help being governed by general social rules—"you know how these economic things are." They were not, however, obliged to mindlessly concur with the forces that dominated their lives. Indeed, true freedom *required* resistance; only by resisting could one become fully aware of one's individuality, one's existence, thus one's liberty. But Dorn went further: the social body, as much as the individual a "sensitive organism," could learn to know itself only by rediscovering its creative purpose in difference; that process would take place at the sensitized body-edges and land-margins where a special kind of species-terminal beauty was now about to become available to the human race. He expanded on this in a tone of cosmic evangelism worthy of his masters Olson and Reich, but tried to make his own point about the essential relation of difference ("the marginal") to the against-the-grain quality of creative freedom ("it is only resistance that is open").

> For
> WE
> are the marginal types, dear friend, old friend. This point is delicately important. And there is really beauty, a strange extra-earth hollow beauty in it. Marginal, ever as much as those tiny hair-bearing little things that ran so carefully about early in the mesozoic were, even then! 140 million years ago having equipped themselves with blood vessels in their lungs

so as to creep further and further out of the water. And save
the day for first pithecanthropus erectus, then palaeoanthro-
pus neanderthalensis, then cro-magnards (artists),

we are

on the margin. It has *always* been these that have survived.
This is a time of great social drought. It is just possible that
through adjustment—since it is only resistance that is open,
if one is to remain hygienic—we can come out with a free-
dom of motion that is not measurable with any of the intel-
lectual instrumentation now at this early universal point
available. This is inchoate. But the terms are not too big, do
you believe.

6.

Woodshedding

ONE OF THE MEN on Dorn's logging crew became a particular friend. Bill Tindall (later dubbed "Bill Elephant" in Dorn's Seattle sketch "1st Avenue"), a half-Klikitat Indian, was a savvy veteran of the work life of the Northwest forests and shores. On days when the humidity dropped too low to allow work in the woods, this rugged "Alaskan pioneer" took the curious son of the prairie panning for gold on the banks of the Skykomish between the timberline hamlets of Sultan and Gold Bar. "He thinks he's a commie and an evolutionist," Dorn described his new friend to Gordon Taylor. "I haven't had the heart to tell him that he's really a utopian instead of a communist and a totemist instead of an evolutionist." Tindall was also a fisherman who had made sardine runs up the coast; he talked up prospects of jobs for them both on a sardine boat out of San Pedro in early October, after the logging season ended. There was "much money" to be made, and Tindall offered "a cheap ride" and "connections for work." By their agreed-upon departure date, when the boats were hiring and Tindall was putting off leaving, a restless Dorn, weary of clearcutting, told Gordon Taylor he was impatient to "leave this waste land": "my highly touted fisher friend has it in his head to work another week because we lost a work week due to low humidity (fire season) and he is short of cash. This is true and I too could use the cash. It will be another week then. And then of course if something happens to fuck the plan, I will kiss [off] regardless."

By the time Dorn reached Southern California with his friend it was mid-October. He spent his days commuting between the docks at San Pedro and the home of his mother's brother Orval Ponton in Bell, where he was staying, his nights checking out the West Coast Sound in the jazz haunts of Los Angeles ("SOUND sounds crazy in L. A."). By November, still unable despite his "connections" to land a place in one of the boats of the sardine fleet, he changed plans again and decided to head back east, hoping vaguely to make it to Philadelphia, where he had learned Bea Huss might be spending the Black Mountain winter break. He caught a ride into the desert as far as Tucson, stopping off with a contact there.

It was his first real experience of the Sonoran desert landscape, one day to figure as an important site of his poetry. (See, for example, the opening of the second book of *Gunslinger,* lyrically enspirited by a pure, heady rush of clear, dry early-morning desert air.) There was "something good about the desert," he reported to Gordon Taylor. "I don't think I have ever breathed cleaner air, seen the sky so multicolored at dusk." Never before, he told his friend, had he "been so conscious of s p a c e." Observing Olson's Herodotean injunction to find out for yourself, he ventured into the red rocks country around Tucson, keeping an eye out for signs of civilization's impact on the desert fauna, and discovered telling traces—the saguaro cacti he inspected were "all disease infected at the base and around the arms."

Apart from the fascinations of the landscape, the stay in Tucson proved "altogether trying," and after a week or two he grew restless to be on the move once more. He took out an "ad in the local sheet telling of my plan to go east," and "got 11 calls within 4 hours," as he told Taylor—"and by god if I didn't choose the worst possible one." The driver was a student ("art no less, but turned out to be artsy craftsy") whose conversation quickly rubbed Dorn the wrong way, making for a long, tense ride: "I soundly pissed him off by my colder-than-a-well-diggers-ass attitude and he wouldn't speak for the last 1000 miles and that was the biggest break of the trip." After two days of stony silence he elected to bail out in Arkansas, where he took advantage of an open invitation from Ray and Lorna Obermayr.

The rest stop in Arkadelphia with the Obermayrs turned into a stay of nearly two months, extending over into early 1953. During this "unbelievably quiet and fertile" period of self-educational woodshedding, Dorn read industriously and with the encouragement and material support of his artist friend Obermayr made a serious effort to revive his practice of drawing and painting, skills that had gone dormant since his last efforts at Black Mountain. The latter project proved humbling: "When one stops for as long as I have," he admitted to Taylor, "you must expect to spend at *least* a month just learning to see again."

Obermayr lent him a number of books on art and art history, including Ernest Fenollosa's two-volume *Epochs of Chinese and Japanese Art* ("I can say with quiet, vibrant emotion that it is Good in the wide aspect") and Henry Adams's *Mont-Saint-Michel and Chartres,* which came to him at an "especially good time" because Obermayr, recently returned from a trip to Europe, was also showing him "the many colored slides he took while in France." The religious art of the Roman Catholic tradition had been among Dorn's self-avowed cultural blind spots: "churches and church towers are things I am afraid I have rigidly ignored because of my aversion for the religion which they implicated, but this was too bad because they should be looked at not for any relationship they have to dogma but for what they were, expressions of the people and their times." The prejudices born of growing up in the cultural dead-end of "The Grave" did not die easily. Illuminated by Obermayr's slides, Adams's theories about the unifying principles of force and energy in early church art provided convincing evidence of "just how insipid the art of the Renaissance was in relation to the finer art of the Middle

Ages." After some reflection, Dorn attempted a series of woodcut prints depicting a suffering Christ in a formalized medieval style. He sent Taylor a sample—"It is my first endeavor and I will call it affectionately 'Christ relaxing after le Crucifixion.'" (He discovered in the process that he found the Christ image quite affecting: a few years later in his essay on Olson's *Maximus* the Christ figure would emerge as one of "two kinds of historic gods," an image of lowly victim-hood, "of great suffering, sympathy and tenderness," opposed to the "not resurrectable" image of Hector, standing for "unalienated beauty" and the "free ego.") "A couple of complete failures" with the hit-and-miss woodcut process notwithstanding, he kept working, trying to get the hang of it. Obermayr also lent him brushes and oils. "I have started painting and I can't tell what I'm doing yet," he told Gordon Taylor. "It is altogether possible that I will accomplish nothing at all."

Intent on the project of making something of himself as an artist, he tried to open himself up to new creative influences from every quarter. Olson's 1951 talks on the Mayans still bright in his mind, he embarked on a course of reading about the arts and culture of "the central and north-southern part of this halfsphere." From a quick study of the archeology of Copan in Honduras—an Olson-approved site—he went on to investigate "Prescott's history of the conquests of both the Mexican and Peruvian kulturs." *The History of the Conquest of Mexico* and *The Conquest of Peru* inflamed him with a strong desire to travel down the spine of the continent. "Lima would be a mighty fine place to retire to" for a sojourn of Reichian self-regulatory freedom, he decided: "you see almost nothing of it in . . . the usual travelish publications, which would mean to me that it is uninteresting to most people and so would fill the bill for hygienic living." While still frustrated in his effort to hunt down Reich's *The Sexual Revolution: Toward a Self-Regulatory Character Structure* (a text whose very unavailability argued its importance), he seemed to find hints of what he presumed to be its thesis everywhere—as in Olson's psychobiography of Melville, *Call Me Ishmael,* a copy of which he discovered in the Arkadelphia library. Each self-directed

step toward "unity" of knowledge brought new confusions and scat-
terings of urgent new questions: "I want to know where and what is
Folsom cave / mentioned by Olson [in] *Call Me Ishmael* ... the line
is: 'I take SPACE to be the central fact to man born in America from
Folsom cave to now.' And I have been unable to find Folsom cave
anywhere. [And I] still want to know more ab[ou]t [Cabeza] de Vaca.
All these things have a unity I am very sure. Even Fenollosa doesn't
seem to be discordant."

Obermayr showed him striking plates, "carried from Parree," of
"the fabrics of an African tribe called Bakuba ... these people and a
tribe known as the Bambara have so elaborated on the square as to
create the likes of which I have yet to see in any culture (at least
western)." He declared to Gordon Taylor that "these Bakuba things
are really a revelation. I'd give a purrty [penny] to find some anthro-
pology on those fellows." A parallel and concurrent inspiration came
from the art work of Obermayr's young son Eric. "I continue to be
amazed every day by the genius of Eric's drawing and painting, the
utter ease that is substantive to every area he informs," Dorn mar-
veled. "I know now what Klee was trying to do, but couldn't quite—
but what all children, if they are raised without the crippling effects
of arbitrary external authority, can and do do as a natural thing.
Which makes Klee's accomplishment all the more signal, because
his home life was typically bad."

If his own struggle perhaps resembled Paul Klee's, he could not yet
say the same of his accomplishment. Sometimes while working at
his woodcuts and paintings he paused to leaf through the newsprint
tablet containing young Eric Obermayr's designs and the plates of
the Congolese tribal fabrics "at the same time," bringing on a deflat-
ing awareness of "how puny and empty my own attempts at expres-
sion, graphic, are, and how little I've learned so far. It overwhelms me.
But my, our, problems are larger and more inextricable than theirs,
the children['s] and the Bakuba's, because anything we do that is
directed toward making something concrete of this rigmarole pre-
supposes that we have taken care of that controlling segment of our
maze of tensions and prejudices which fight so efficiently against

any insight to the pivotal center of anything." His self-analysis, a therapeutic attempt to sort out and conquer the "maze of tensions and prejudices" blocking creative flow, was a dogged struggle for clarity, conducted in the darkness of everything he still didn't know.

There were lighter moments in his learning campaign. While intellectual "ease" still eluded him, he was becoming adept at the arts of self-sufficiency. For Christmas he gave himself a haircut that was "the jazziest yet." Five weeks later he outdid himself with an even snazzier job that convinced him, he told Taylor with tongue in cheek, he'd finally found his niche as an artist: "That is the thing I am supremely fitted to do, cut my own hair."

The primary entertainment source in Arkadelphia was Ray Obermayr's record collection, generating Dorn's hipster admonition to Taylor: "Cast the flickers on that COOL edge." Jazz offered another path to personal style, self-expression and freedom, as well as a concrete insight into the new anthropology. With Obermayr he spent shades-down hours digging the latest sounds on vinyl. "Mulligan sounds completely weird," he announced. "CRRRazy from go-gone, eyes in units of thousand also coooool especially while scoffing a down scene / chopped, channeled, shaved, relieved, jet-repulsed, superaircooledluciteconditionedsonic."

By the last week of January 1953, however, Dorn's patience with the woodshed life in Arkansas was beginning to wear thin. Still working hard at his self-education, he'd finished Melville's *The Confidence Man* ("fine thing") and was nearly to the end of Veblen's *On the Nature of Peace and the Terms of Its Perpetuation* when the weather turned foul, with "much rain and chillyness." "Eric the kid is raising hell," he reported on a gloomy stuck-indoors winter day. "Tried to listen to music but futile." His painting energies lagged. Stale from too much reading and study, he joked to Taylor about the extent of his own artistic self-invention, offering the cynical suggestion that to succeed in the art world he would have to adopt a different name: "E. MERTON-DORN is my new artiste name. One has to have a [hyphen]-ated name, you know. Like Laszlo Moholy-Nagy, Pete Con-doli, Connie Con-doli. If I get to be a lap-dog, as are most fashionable artistes and all museum directors, it will be Edward Merton-Dorn."

Inevitably there rose the familiar itch to leap into the unknown. With the new year he was already "thinking of my own placement in time, space and pure form and how much of it there is left before I make my last and Big move to the northwest and subsequent riches. It will be unpleasant to bear myself away from this womb-like security, but it must be done. There is really so little time left and events are being so pushed together that I can already feel the old excitement of unpractical moves to be made indiscriminately." He plotted-out alternate short-term itineraries, one involving "going to Philly to dig Bea for a short time," the other going "home [to Mattoon] for a spell." The Bea plan, "obviously the one with more problems but the one I would rather engage in," was delayed by his lack of funds. As late as January 26 there was still "a plan afoot for Bea and I to get together (literally) before I shove west," he told Taylor. "I have no idea where it will be." But before arrangements could be finalized the demands of Bea's family at Black Mountain had made a meeting impossible. In February Dorn went instead to Mattoon for a visit he was able to dutifully prolong for "exactly 5 days." He snagged a drive-away car from Chicago to Seattle and by squeezing every last mile out of his $48 gas allowance managed to "pick up a few needed bucks" to begin modest housekeeping.

7.

Suspended

I N SEATTLE DORN FOUND WORK doing painting and remodeling on the premises of the contemporary furnishings store which his former U. of Illinois contact was finally, after a year of delays, getting ready to open. "I potch around there doing indispensable things during the day and at night I don't do a goddamn thing," he informed Gordon Taylor at the end of March 1953. "I have made a few frustrated attempts to read, write, draw, anything that would allow me to make my definition of the going reality, but the action stops, or never really starts." The job indeed comprised a litmus test for him of the "going reality" of art-as-business. He was impatient from the start with the commercial aesthetics of the establishment, and had soon concluded, as he told Taylor, that the residential architects and furniture designers who made up its management and clientele were "a vulgar lot ... the dullest lot of protoplasm that I have lately mingled with." The revulsion he felt had to do with his own current thinking on the meaning and purpose of art. Coming from a winter in the company of a practicing artist whose principles he respected (Ray Obermayr), he found the design professionals he now met and mixed with at "parties every weekend" superficial in their values and mercenary in their motives. The experience drew from him "a reevaluation of what I think is going on in the 'contemp[orary]' biz":

> When it comes to the crux of it they just simply don't know; they haven't learned anything, they are merchants, they drift along complacently on the earth shattering trends of the latest silly stick of Swedish shit, and think that the world will sink or swim on the basis of a Le Clint lampshade maintaining interest. As a matter of fact the whole business makes me ill. When I look at all this, all of it, from Eames to the lowest little prick scrounging a buck, I wonder if these idiots *really* think it's possible to isolate function. Do they believe, these many commercial travelers, that life will be made a whit clearer to the doctor's wife by this woman being able to seat her bridge party, their arses in severality on the slick contours of moulded plywood? That they are operating so much farther out on the periphery of the human mix-up than anyone else?

Dorn now decided there was "one man in the country, [Josef] Albers, who is actually painting." Against the grain of Seattle's "light-weight" commercial functionalism he proclaimed Albers's aesthetic: "aesthetics are the result, not the condition of, the cause of creation." If there was, then, only "one painter painting, really, and a handful of architects building, what"—he asked rhetorically, in considering his current workplace and the world it signified—"are all these other people doing but playing the market for all the blood that's in it?" Watching modern furnishings purveyed as products of the latest research in functional design for leisure living, he came to a formula that would apply in general to the difference between his own idiosyncratic aesthetics and those of the shop where he worked as well as of that larger "shop," the Fifties arts marketplace: "It must be remembered that research is not search, that reproduction is not production, that recreation is not creation. But the talk goes on ab[ou]t 'aht' and the sales mount and I can't find a damn soul willing to discuss the interdependencies (social) of stainless steel flatware and its price.... [Although] I like very much some of the things those people sell, I would be hard put to justifying having most of it, from a utilitarian standpoint."

In a Seattle where he lacked soul-contact, he was inevitably thrown back once again upon his own quandary of location. What was he doing there, as against anywhere else? Unable to come up with an answer to silence that nagging internal question, he couldn't help worrying it over. "I suppose I should account for my being here. The best way to describe it I suppose would be to say that I am kind of suspended between the things I desperately want and the things that have already come about that I can't completely shake off."

In his suspended state, that which was desperately wanted and that which could not be completely shaken off were categories not easily kept separate. He wanted to work at his art and writing but could not shake off his need to subsist ("you know how these economic things are"). He wanted to stay current with the new movements of the mind, especially those at Black Mountain (an installment of Olson's New Sciences of Man lecture notes sent by Bea Huss looked "exciting as hell"), but getting back to Black Mountain to actually take his degree was something he would not be able to do until he'd stuck with one job long enough to put together the requisite funds, and the chronic restlessness which kept him from doing that was another thing he could not shake off. Above all, he desperately wanted freedom, yet was beginning to fear it might be attainable only at the cost of a perpetuation of the body-and-soul loneliness that was the oldest and worst of the familiar unshakable difficulties.

At the designer parties in Seattle and its surrounding islands women now and then approached him. He took an interest in one of them, as he told Gordon Taylor. She was a member of "the tight little group" of middle-class professional artistic types, a designer for a modern furniture store around the corner from the one where he worked. "She is 23 and is married to a guy 36," he wrote to his friend. "I don't know why I tell you these particular facts except maybe that I want her pretty desperately.... She seems interested in me and we talked for over an hour in uninterrupted conversation.

I was told later that our absorption [with] each other was conspicuous. She reminds me a little of Bea, younger of course and a little more entrancing. I wonder if her husband will mind if I sleep with her, just a little."

Five days later, he offered Taylor a more detailed account of the infatuation, which had by this time cooled enough to allow him the distance to see it as a small parable of his aspiring struggles, containing elements of the comic:

> There we were, that night, sitting in D—'s apartment, many people, little groups of disjointed people, and then, in a moment, Gloria—chic, modern, contemporary, designy, talky, Built, engaging, short hair-cut-ted, bow-legged (but nice), ruminating, gestury, ahty, toothy (in an interesting way however)— came draggling her stole to my very side. Immediately there was much talk. I raved. Then she had her chance. Then there was a chorus. The emotion got, finally, to quite a pitch. I was rather keyed up. You know, the old HIGH-SCHOOL BOY'S DREAM: slick, young (23) tomato hanging, sticking to your every word like flies to a day sucker. With the added incentive of her husband glaring jarringly, shamelessly at we two.

Critical thinking had then set in, as the now-doubtful lover went on to relate.

> At that moment I could have enjoyably gone to bed with her and that would have been conveniently that. And I think that she, stirred up as she was by the intensity, the directness of our correspondence, could have loved me a great deal for those few, nervous moments. But then you know how difficult it is to sustain something like that with a person who, really, at base, at inception, is an idiot. She really didn't, doesn't, know much, in that she, partly at the suggestion of her husband I suspect, is led to believe that she really can't get to the center, *know* a thing, read, understand. ACT.

Dorn pursued the abortive romance half-heartedly, but after a week announced to Taylor that though he still saw the woman nearly every day, he now talked to her only "of light things, like the structural possibilities of pressed shit for casual dinner-ware this season." The prospective affair was "already passé, dead, dropped."

The psychic backlash of the minor expenditure of misplaced emotion included a fresh wave of disgust with both self and scene and a corollary access of the restlessness that so often plagued him. "Events are breaking apart here very rapidly," he told Taylor on April 2, his twenty-fourth birthday. "Immediately, I must force my energy in the direction of Alaska. Everything has failed thus far. I assure you my only reason for being here in the present context is that I can free-load off these people with the added comfort (or annoyance) of their being quite decorous while I do it."

Despite his frustrations, the state-of-his-soul assessment he supplied his friend indicated he felt the moment still held hints of some better auspice:

> I write from today, my birthday, 4/2/53. 24 y[ea]rs. 24 garbled, mystifying years. What gets me, after all this, is that I have not made a *complete* hash of things. There is a kind of dispersed, rambling awareness of what it is that composes reality; that is I can at least think about the structure of certainty, the relativity that goes on. But things happen
>   like
>   today when I had so goddamn much energy I almost went nuts, and all I did was jump around and arch my back. I tried to talk to these miserably lifeless people, got nothing but a few platitudes ab[ou]t something being nice, and went out and bought a few bananas and that settled things considerably. After that I looked at a Life mag[azine] that just happened to be there and could feel it coming on again. And out of the corner of my eye I catch faint beginnings of what must happen to me in time to come.

V.

A Light From the North
(1953–1954)

I.

Young Poet in Love

BACK IN ARKADELPHIA, Ray Obermayr, Dorn's first and most faithful enabler in the creative arts, received an elated letter from Seattle. "He said he'd just met and fallen in love with the most beautiful woman he'd ever laid eyes on," Obermayr remembers. "He'd never mentioned to me having a serious interest in any woman before that time." The woman was Helene Katherine Helmers Buck, a tall, slender, delicate-featured, honey-haired twenty-six-year-old from Duluth, Minnesota. Daughter of a Norwegian sea captain who'd been stranded in New Orleans by a measles quarantine and ended up plying his trade in Duluth, where he'd married the daughter of a judge, Helene had left college in 1947 to marry David Buck, a banker's son and World War II combat veteran. Their son Fred had been born in 1948 in Michigan, where Buck was in school on the G. I. Bill. In 1949 the family moved to Seattle, where Buck took up a school teaching job. A second child, Chansonette, was born in 1952. In 1953 Helene's brother Fred was also living in Seattle, working on his masters at the university, and, as Helene recalls, "doing oddball jobs like painting to help with the tuition." Dorn, who by now had his own small apartment on the same hill as Fred Helmers,

recruited him to help with the painting of the contemporary fur-
nishing store that spring. "How they met I don't know but it was
through the university somehow," Helene says. "And I first met Ed
at a party my brother had. I was struck by his face, and wanted to
draw it and asked him if he'd pose for me. I laugh now thinking it
must have sounded like a 'come-on,' but I was sincere. After that he
and my brother came often to our house. 'What was he like?' That's
hard to answer. For me he was a brand new world. He was full of the
exuberance of Black Mountain and shared his excitement with me."
Helene, gifted at drawing and affected like Dorn by a hunger for the
creative life, responded to his ideas and views with ideas and views
of her own. She returned his visits, climbing the hill to his tiny
"sparse" apartment, where "the toilet was filthy but the sink was
scrupulously clean. We sat for long hours at the small table, talk-
ing." By early summer, she was bringing her kids along "to visit her
friend," as her son Fred, then five, recalls.

The modest Seattle apartment was far from the worst living cir-
cumstance the young drifter Dorn had endured in the course of his
footloose ramblings. Though the pangs of his lonely quest for self-
knowledge and knowledge of "the structure of reality" remained as
active as ever, the example of his 80-year-old landlady, a devoutly
religious widow who toiled in the garden all day, working "like a
dawg" at pulling weeds, held a philosophical lesson for him, as he told
Gordon Taylor. "The very things she is trying to preserve are killing
her, destroying her: the flowers. And that's the way with myself,
largely. It's this beating one's head against the wall that is so killing,
if that's all it is. It's the way it's been for the past few years—when
all the while I never seem to solve, to bring to fruition, anything for
myself." The spectacle of the landlady, a living portrait in persever-
ing futility, reminded Dorn that at least he did not inhabit oblivion
alone; indeed, in many respects the landlady, whose vulnerable, strug-
gling decrepitude canceled out her minimal propertied status, was
his neighbor at the social margins, where human struggle was not
heroic but commonplace. On those frontiers the virtue of heroic per-
sistence and the assent to numb survival dissolved into a single uni-

versal will to continue living, an act of indiscriminate volition which indicated stupidity as much as courage. "I think I'll forget it, the whole human business (mess) and go on."

In fact his present situation could be painted to seem relatively comfortable. There was even a view of sorts: a huge flowering laurel bush outside his kitchen window which he enjoyed watching change colors in the shifting lights of the long midsummer northern-curve dusk, studying the subtle differences in its darkening shades of green. The painting job with Fred Helmers was covering his small rent and meager expenses, and after a few paydays he had even managed to salt away $100, for him a staggering sum. "There's no more money problem, immediately," he told Taylor, "and the cheap apartment I have is really the best place, for my feeling, I've ever lived [in]. I have Vermont cheese and bad Sauterne and generally enough to eat, without the possibility of over-eating."

His inevitable contacts with "the human business (mess)" were changing as subtly as the appearance of the leafy laurel bush outside his kitchen window. Having gradually drifted out of the social ambiance of the "contemporary" designer crowd, he was now "traveling in much different circles." There was a brief reunion with his half-brother, David Abercrombie, who'd come out to the Northwest on a summer visit, and was working as a logger ("We spent every weekend together and had some very good times," David recalls). And through Fred Helmers and other grad-student contacts he'd become conversant with the social life around the University of Washington and had made the acquaintance of a few prominent "names"—the aesthetician Susanne Langer ("an awfully perceptive, intense, old lady"), the "sometimes excellent" poet Theodore Roethke—and was in "fairly frequent contact" with several up-and-coming campus poets, including Kenneth Pitchford, a young graduate student who'd studied with Allen Tate at the U. of Minnesota, and Kenneth Hanson, a poet-instructor "who knows Charles Olson and Pound, reads the ideogram and is, I feel, a significant person." At least as significant, given the realistic urgencies of lack and need, was the fact that he was also now the object of some surprising female attention. There was at least one carryover in his life from the now-passé furniture-store phase, the "chic, modern, contemporary, designy, talky" twenty-three-year-old married "tomato," who had proven his pessimistic estimate of their chances for an affair over-hasty. Then at Helmers' party he was approached by another proposition altogether: his painting partner's fair, clear-eyed, open-faced, honey-headed sister.

At this stage in Dorn's alienation-vexed self-drama, falling in love was an unlikely stroke of fate that at first had him feeling a little miscast. "I don't take intimacy with other people that easily or quickly," he would one day admit to an interviewer. Announcing the news to Taylor in June, he suggested he'd suddenly experienced an epiphanic brush with reality—and that it had shocked him by the dreamlike sense of unreality it carried with it. In such a shocked state it was difficult to keep up a "normal" impression of self-possession. The familiar everyday routines which he like other people confidently took for reality, he'd now decided, were nothing more than a convenient construct. "It's so often an artificial structure, we rehearse patterns to apply to things we can't possibly know about. Proust says (somewhere) we play certain favorite roles so often before an audience and rehearse them so constantly when alone that we are more likely to refer ourselves to their fictitious evidence than to an almost completely forgotten reality." The fictitious evidence of his own former favorite roles notwithstanding, Dorn had had an inkling of a third possibility, a form of validating company that skirted Proust's dilemma of inauthenticity by being neither solitary self nor skeptical audience—that ideal someone with whom it was not necessary to play any role at all. He would one day speak of his ingrained disposition to seek "a woman as reference" in any human situation. Now, pleased and relieved yet bemused, he told Gordon Taylor, "I have a woman at last, which I very much need. God damn it I don't want to be insensitive about this but I might as well out with it. I have two women, actually. Both married. Isn't that strange? I'm doomed." But his attempt at containing such heavy matters in a few light sentences quickly led to a qualification of conscience. "Pardon the utter, fantastic falseness of this," Dorn begged. "It's as if I have a tight biological knot in my guts. I'm trying to dissolve it, in rather weird ways." Within a few weeks of waiting and biding his time, the field of possibilities would be reduced to that ideal yet still problematic third one, the tight internal knot concentrated to a fine tension that would cause him to feel alternately apprehensive and weightless.

By midsummer Helene's marriage—in her son Fred's words, "rocky anyway"—was foundering. She moved into digs of her own, a small apartment "way up on a hill" on North 36th. Perched atop a steep flight of stairs scaling the hillside, the place had, as Helene recalls, a "nifty view" out over the many neighborhoods of Seattle. By night as she and the poet-drifter sat talking "the little red lights / in the water of the bays" blinked out ambiguous messages about the fate of their fugitive love. "I'd settled myself after leaving my husband and my two children to do what I felt I had to do. Ed kept climbing the many steps up to my apartment, and I don't really remember how it happened, it was such a gradual thing, we were living together." In Dorn's own refraction of the time as suggested in the enigmatic *Hands Up!*-period lyric "Time Blonde," his love is figured as a delicate "figurine," perhaps echoing his first advertisements of Helene to Gordon Taylor as a finely attuned creative soul ("she draws delicately"). (And one recall's Helene's portrait in words as drawn by an old friend, Lucia Berlin: "Helene is fine; that I'm sure was one of her main attractions for Ed. Fine in the best sense, well bred, a lady. She has a graciousness; not elegance—quality. Ed loved quality in poetry, fabric, cars; he treated her like fragile china.")

> She was a figurine moving
> among the hills of seattle
> experimentally clothed
> she drove an experimental car
> to the stores
>
> What was life then?

It was wandering between
the planted trees of a climate
of light red rain, it was
just the going to and fro
in a light cold climate
hoping to meet, but nothing said,
to bed, if she had the time.

By which I mean didn't we
wait much of the time staring out
at the various parts of the city
and during those nights
of waiting
the little red lights
in the water of the bays
did they not say no use?

"Conditions have changed, somewhat," Dorn explained in noti-fying Gordon Taylor of his new address c/o Helene that August. He was, he declared rather momentously, "living avec a woman, Helene's the name, an unusual woman whom I met with her husband one day and immediately fell in love with, with the slender reed grace of her." She was a promising artist in her own right, he said, and "no dummy" ("I think there's stuff to her"). The only major draw-back in the situation had to do with the complications of her attempts to both gain her freedom and keep custody of her children. "There was a mess attached to their split and the impending divorce and it's kinda hard to keep going without being inconvenienced by the forces and pressures of the people who thought there was something to their miserable marriage [and by] every one of their ... petty reme-dies." To Dorn the constraints imposed upon his beloved by her hus-band and relatives were a "damn outrage." Against and in despite of such resistances, love would conquer. "We're living together and that's a fact, first fact, and I love this woman, this most beautiful woman ... and we're in love, together."

Poetry began for Dorn in this first summer of his love, a time he would within a few short months determinedly look back upon as "those wonderful days, wonderful summer days in Seattle." As might be expected of a young poet in love, an early effect was the ability to notice fresh facets of language. When the lovers went on their first trip together, a ferry voyage to the San Juan Islands, the inlet-carved land forms of the islands, glimpsed by Dorn through eyes washed clean by his love, took on a fjord-like, "faint, Norwegian touch." The lightening touch of love upon language now illuminated for him also lines of poetry that had once left him unmoved; he suddenly "got," for example—as though the ferry had navigated among water spirits—the resonance of Olson's epigraph to *In Cold Hell, In Thicket*, "yr eyes, yr naiad arms."

He had now embarked on an earnest poetic voyage of his own. "I've been working right along [in poems] now," he told Gordon Taylor on August 14. "I think I see some glimmer of light about what it is I'm doing." The stage of his tentative first starts was the love affair, though the main romantic action remained largely concealed off in the wings. A lyric beginning "The bleat of time" caught a fleeting moment in "a room wet / with the enchantment / of decayed passion," where a lover discovers a "fragmentary note" bespeaking love's "concurrent mistakes." Another, titled simply "5", replayed a small relationship drama, balancing an anticipated reunion— "when you return to me down those / wooden steps"—with "an account of obvious differences"; as late as mid-October Dorn still considered this piece his "best yet." The strongest testament to "those wonderful summer days," however, was "Grasses," the first of his poems to be selected by guest-editor Denise Levertov for a Dorn debut set the following year in *Origin*. Apart from the unnerving moment created by a single honest dissonant note—the "broken minds" of the lovers—this poem offers the most promising figurative picture of the affair. The lovers are placed in tall grasses beneath madrona trees "on the unguarded area" at the "uncultivated" margins of a park, with the madronas that "roamed variously / in the creeping darkness" subtly figuring an unstated movement of expressive feeling toward freedom and escape.

The impulsive direction of his life obeying a similar tendency, he persuaded Helene to take flight with him into the unknown. "I don't know what will happen," he told Taylor, "where, that is, we will go." In September, carrying only single suitcases, they boarded a bus bound for San Francisco, where Dorn proposed to find work to support them. He told Taylor Helene would be getting a divorce and regaining her children in a few months; "we'll be getting married sometime after that."

2.

Love Chaos

THE GETAWAY VENTURE WAS MARKED by bad signs from the out-
set. The bus ride south was "a strenuous one": the heat was
"devastating," over 100 degrees in Sacramento, and Helene was ill
by the time they reached San Francisco. A plague of "enormous bugs
which were impossible to destroy so armored were they" drove the
couple out of the Hotel Dante. After five days of "searching in the
hills" they finally found an apartment—no bugs, clean, with one
room "freshly painted white"—at 14 Bannan Place in North Beach.
Once they'd moved in Helene went back to Seattle, as Dorn told
Taylor, to see her kids, "clean up odds and ends, pack the remainder
of our gear, and settle the hash of a remnant few who still don't
believe we do love, have, will." He would stay on "to get a job and
try life in S. F. till it bores too much."

No sooner had she gone, however, than he was stricken by an
attack of self-doubt, brought on by the "pressures" that assailed the
couple from all sides—emotional, economic, legal. Before Helene
could return to "settle our nerves," his own had almost got the bet-
ter of him. Stuck on his lonesome in the strange city, he walked the
streets, observing the various floating-island ethnic populations, "Ital-

ians, Chinese, Japanese"—"they all look so stranded, or perhaps it's me [that's] stranded." The neighborhood bars and hotels likewise seemed to exude "some desperate quality," again likely a projection of his own inner state. At night in his bare white-walled flat he conducted an uneasy soul-"purge" in his poetry, hounding his alienated state back into the mysteries of private history and "the disaster of a / too barren beginning." The results were not so much poems as blurts of filtered retrieved-memory confessional, like these lines associating sex with exposure, darkness, and ominous punishments:

> But do not cast me into the dark
> closet again or
> beat me for running nude down
> the black oil road that first time
> of passion.

His fugitive cast of mind and downward-tending spirits meanwhile did little to help his job-search. A satiric fragment titled "Rotund" in honor of one particularly insincere personnel director—who was pictured "smiling [with] molten regularity ... in his swively / chair"—made light of what his later assessments portray as a wrenching defeat, the inevitable toll of his folly in attempting to live by impulse. "It has taken me two years to learn a very sorry lesson," he would write in the chastened aftermath of the trip, "that I am no longer at Black Mountain, [n]or in any remotely Black Mountain-tinged context. And even if that is oversimplifying it, or mixing realities, it has still been my basic mistake. And not, absolutely not getting work in San Francisco, which I just didn't, is the common example. Not that I didn't try, Christ, every day, [but] what came out as 'try' was an organic sickness that turned every color of the intellectual rainbow, including self-pity."

Helene returned from Seattle, and they shared a few stolen weeks together in what the poet called the "Bridged city under fog-white hills"; but as Dorn would write in the same post-tryst sonnet, "San F," "The weeks were love and ended, our eyes turning / Away." His beloved's return had brought fateful news that enhanced the pressures upon them both: she was carrying Dorn's child. Once again Helene went back north—"returned to Seattle because I wanted my kids," as she now remembers. This time Dorn tumbled into a "completely death-impelled frame of mind." His inner dialogue spilled over to his Marine confidant in Korea:

> Why do I want, so unnaturally, for me, to get married? Answer: because Helene and I are heavy with a tiny, new, forming baby, the idea of which excites me almost beyond my tears, tears I can hardly keep off this page. And I am stuffy enough within the context to want it to have a name. God, do you think "marriage" means anything to us beyond the relationship two people can build in, to, for, around, by ... one another? No— having the baby would be just fine if it weren't for the fact that she has two already (she's 26 they are 2 1/2 and 5) which won't be given up by her husband.... So the kids couldn't be gotten and that's too bad because they're beautiful kids and it breaks my heart as much as Helene's to think of the expression on little Freddie's face as she told him she was leaving. It just rips your guts right out.

Now, as in a few earlier moments of trial, Dorn appealed to his old high-school friend for understanding on grounds of their special empathy, a singular and common "vibrant field of force [which] is defined [as] our *roots*."

> All I want from you at this point is some understanding, maybe sympathy is a better word. You know we used to talk in our barren years back in the Grove about finding "the" person, woman, the one, the true matrix? I found, I have found it in Helene. It's the only absolute thing I've seen as long as I've lived. And even if you disagree on absolutes (as I do too) I still can't find a more apt term to frame it. I have never had an experience as intensely deep as my loving Helene, and that's

with a constancy of wonder which is beyond, completely beyond me. I took her to the plane Friday and she flew back to Seattle to see what could be arranged about the kids with David. If nothing else works she will stay with him to be near them in order to give them the love they are lacking without her, and I will go back to Seattle to be near her, because, simply, I'm powerless to do anything else if that happens. And the big problem is going to be [finding] a realizable arrangement for having our baby which should arrive in April sometime, as nearly as we can determine. I want that baby very much with, I think, the same urgency that I want Helene. But the divorce hasn't come through and won't until Nov. 5. Not far off. I don't give a shit about trivia like whose name [the child] has, it isn't that, but I do want to *have* it. There is obviously a missing sense to all this, eh? For instance the details of *why* Helene is being plagued by nightmares about the happiness of the children are too fantastically myriad for me to hope to make you comprehend in the time I have. It could be described as a mushrooming, a mushroom that has injected itself into the best parts of our life and so has made it dangerous to not seek a solution as straight as possible to this thing that leaves me with pure misery, the only I've known, in my whole trunk, starting at the bottom of the pit of my stomach and going into and lasting in my chest, lodged like phlegm.

The "missing sense" which remained to be identified had to do with deeper psychic disturbances, an "emotional nightmareing" that now brought Dorn's already shaky nerves to the brink of a "crack." "Shortly after [Helene] left S. F.," he would later tell Gordon Taylor, "I am awfully sure I was an apprentice to death." Held motionless in a state of "wakeless suspension," he sensed, as his poem of the crisis would relate, "Her absence an agent of fever" sweeping over him. Out of the ache of pain "Silently plaguing like a dream I can't remember / As I held back love with a gripped fist," he realized belatedly—as the poem "San F" also disclosed—a further truth about the dangers of living on impulse: "The mental move must precede suitcases packed." For a week he lay twisting with sickness, gazing up through a lingering fog of "two memories," before following Helene back to Seattle.

"Give time the time to rewind cells," he would conclude his sonnet on this unsettling episode, "Another meeting will arrange new hells." Back in Seattle in late October he was still battling the psychobiological effects of the trip ("mental nausea, the flu of some sort, watery bowels, etc.") when "another meeting" revealed that the outcome he most dreaded appeared to have come about: "Helene is back with her husband, and the baby will be born a Buck." This latest news held little in the way of consolation. "She is apparently happy, and this is important to me. I love her more than, literally, I love life." Dorn's own pain overflowed into a long, desperate letter to Helene that was (he decided soon after giving it to her) "maybe too much of a confessional." He told Gordon Taylor he intended some day to retrieve the letter and send it on to his friend, "and it will give you some notion of my malady. But now things are too raw."

3.

Vocation

DORN BEGAN A DESULTORY work-search and found a cheap place to live: "two very large rooms" in the former Belgian consulate building at 1205 E. Prospect, across from Volunteer Park. The low rent ("$30 for everything") freed him from the immediate necessity of finding a job, in turn allowing him time to proceed with the writing which was now absorbing him. The uncertain relationship with Helene kept him "strung in suspension, caught, still in the love chaos that fills in some odd way most of my day"; the concurrent intensity of creative chaos within him kept him steadily at his typewriter, a $5 second-hand-shop 1910 model Royal, at a table by the window of the erstwhile consulate library, with a leafy "prospect" over the park—"so much a natural place for me," as he told Gordon Taylor in early November, "I usually don't leave it for any reason other than to get food or information that I might consider vital to going on. And when I do leave I don't want to, because as far as I know there isn't a better place. I am finding it for the first time in my lazy life easy, in fact necessary, to WORK. To write Poetry, of which I think I am capable, a certain kind, without illusions about my intellectual potential. And to know all about the craft I can learn, the bungling way I do learn." Chronically self-critical and "without illusions" about his "intellectual potential," Dorn had found relief and permission in a Robert Duncan broadside ("The Artist's View") he'd picked up at City Lights Books in San Francisco: the poet Duncan's half-playful message concerned the hard lesson of giving up the idea of greatness when one was not capable of it. Following Duncan, Dorn would pursue not greatness but his own intuitive daemon; he would strive to write not great poetry but a poetry of "a certain kind"—i.e., *his own,* crafted as best he was able, bungling or no. With steady work on poems came a new sense of vocation. His recognition that poetry was his calling was arrived at through an instinctive process of elimination, "after realizing that painting was never my medium, and couldn't be—language having been my first impulse but dropped for some untraceable reason except to account for the switch to painting by some sequential ornamental construct."

He was giving some thought to enrolling at U. W. as an English major, so as to hone his craft-sense—and also to gain a degree, "since I don't deceive myself about making a living by writing." But the mere thought of academia still brought on phobic reactions. On the one hand, he rationalized, "a plunge into that insanity might even be revealing." On the other hand, was not the whole idea of going back to school simply a "self-justification to avoid the real work of writing (it will consume lots of precious time)?" In his dialogue with himself the counter-arguments against academia inevitably prevailed. In a time when others were paid by the government to go to school, he himself would have to get a job in order to manage it. "I don't and won't ever have a G. I. Bill. And that means certain things." His present writer's economy was the product of a natural self-sufficiency trained in long experience of survivalism and autodidactisim. He had come to know poverty with the familiarity of an intimate companion. "I'm not bitching," he told Gordon Taylor after detailing his acquisition of the antiquated thrift-shop typewriter. "I accept it as my lot and what the hell do I care anyway. I can learn anywhere. And besides I am weary, sick to death of moving. I won't be budged from this place till I create some of the substance I see all about me." On Prospect Ave. he had "a safe ... going existence" in "the cheap best place I have ever had, and the will to work, no a need, and not too many friends and those I have are selected with minute care. I know Helene and she comes over often enough and (I love her) this is almost enough humanity."

Other options were weighed and rejected. His recent San Francisco experience had left him in no hurry to return there, nor did he feel the longing for New York which seemed to affect other poets he'd met (in the latter regard his early disinclination would prove permanent). "To me right now it's enough to be inspired without getting into the political mess that would be inevitable in New York, I can't afford that right now because I don't, simply, have enough larnin. My ignorance is shameful. For instance I am just now reading Shakespeare with insight. That's a big lag—to try to write poetry without a knowledge of the craft would end in the same goddamn way the painting ordeal did. And I refuse to let it happen.... I'm not trying to protect myself but I need time.... 'Time isn't money but it's everything else' (Pound?)."

To his skeptical friend Taylor Dorn began to defend Seattle with a new vigor. "Seattle, in spite of your raised-eye doubt, is not entirely the stix." He listed local poets Pitchford, Hanson (who'd lately "written some of the best stuff I have read"), and a vague cast of "at least 1/2 dozen good poets" around the university. And while, again, there were no local artistic big names—"it isn't New York"—he believed there to be "some of the best painting in the land going on." Altogether, the quiet, misty corner-pocket town was currently a right fit for him. "I like it here and I will say it. I like the landscapes in the fall, I like the mist-rinsed hills, the rain doesn't annoy me, and I like the fact that you can buy a coat for fifty cents at St. Vincent de Paul or Goodwill, as I must, my poverty is so complete. It isn't only Helene that keeps me here. I think life will be a lot less of a struggle here than it would be in New York, and the more I can lessen the bitterness of keeping alive the more ease I shall have in doing what I must do, write living poetry."

4.

A Serious Business

F AR FROM A CASUAL MATTER, for committed apprentice Dorn the writing of poems was a serious business that required a progressive struggle as much moral as literary, entailing a continual effort toward self-transformation. He told Gordon Taylor of daily battles with his bad habits of the years, "this laziness & the escapism I was taught at a too tender age," the residue of "our common, struggling, picayune, ridiculous, wasted, bewildered, morose past." Life itself demanded this intensity of him: "as long as you are [alive] you still carry the single moral responsibility, living: for if you don't you ... ignore the prime pulsations that total life." The struggle to "create some of the substance I see all about me" was a labor of instant-to-instant attention. From his watchful Seattle prospect his carefully-framed poems, exacting, self-conscious exercises in perception, scoped out a long land-and-water view as backdrop for quiet moments of aerial epiphany. In "Several Gulls" and "Decorum for a Grey Day" the wanderings of his attention followed the flight of seagulls he saw shearing in over the hills, driven by storms to "dupe gravity with no force" in a "dance ... abrupt as dawn on the moon," or reeling back out toward bay and Sound in "languid circles" through a grey "weightless light" that appeared "source-less" but for "luminous holes in the horizon." Sending these along to Taylor he apologized for "toying with" such studies (they "might be taken for exercises," he admitted), citing by way of justification a local painting master: "There is a statement about here that says if you're stuck for an idea you can always throw in a gull: *vide* Morris Graves." (It was, of course, "no observation [which] anyone might not come to," given any susceptibility to such space-drenched landscapes.)

Another master, Olson, lay behind the poetics of instant attention Dorn propounded to Taylor. "The moment any of us get on to anything is right now, what any moment is, is instant, caught, onto, grey sky, dirty gulls high, high as clouds are in some pressures here. Yes *dirty gulls* in spite of M[orris] G[raves]. . . ." Practitioners of verse might well "try with . . . exercises" about gulls—as he'd done—but such studies could qualify as poetry only if (as another master, Pound, preached) the discrimination of attention was absolutely precise. A gull closely observed might in the moment appear dirty; it was the poet's particular moral responsibility not to miss such nuances of reality.

An application of this demanding moral aesthetic was Dorn's working principle in a poem called "Litany for Yellow Lamp."

> Outdoor lamps that light more
> Than themselves are a burden
> And destroy night where night
> Is most local. Where night
> Lays surely on pine needles
> There is inevitable care.
>
> Stop and go lights the importance
> Of asphalt for those whose wild
> Intentions are motor driven,
> The intent is less endurable,
> But there are left here and there those

Who can't categorize the moon,
Yellow, like some older street
Lamp, whose sanity brings no
Rape over sleeping leaves and
Whose light marks time, ambitious
Only in its own composition,
Awaiting its periodic heir.

A poet, as both Pound and Olson taught, could not afford logical categorization's easy abstractive way around direct confrontation with reality—whether that of the locally-clichéd seagull, or of poetry's oldest object, the moon, or even of the most familiar and therefore most challenging subject matter, people. Human contact indeed became the subject of one of his most effective poems of the period, "Store Scene" (it would accompany "Grasses," "Litany for Yellow Lamp" and "Relics from a Polar Cairn" in *Origin*).

Some woman stood there, in the aisle, waiting.
The child clutched roundly the coat, in handfuls,
The woman of whom I speak, sat, juxtaposed, on
The stair,
                and felt the vibration, across,
                of seeking fingers.

What made this not a linear event was
The difference of, a multiple humanity in,
The act, participating the way we independently
Were.

                I mean that the woman, that the child,
                are engaged with their intent.
                The stair held a point of wonder and
                I get my connection at the bottom

                                step on which she, the woman
                                of whom I speak, sat.

Most recent mother, the pangs still caught
In the breast, so lately assertive of more
Than motherhood, yet stiff with unweened attention.
When she spoke of the child, it was from the sloughed
Context, a woman that fell into tomorrow without
Taking off her clothes.

Another non-linear moment of particularized attention snatched
from the routine everyday order, the "point of wonder" caught in
this poem is no more imposing a matter than the witnessed touch
of a mother and child, a "vibration ... of seeking fingers" that
momentarily conjoins a moved poet-observer and his unselfcon-
scious living subjects through a "multiple humanity in / The act, par-
ticipating the way we independently / Were." For the poem's madonna
with child, her look of experience disclosing recent "pangs ... of
more than motherhood," Dorn had at hand a possible model in the
woman he loved. In such a poem, his act of attention—the kind of
"impatient, quickening, blood-circulating, catch-now construction ...
that's new" which he'd advertised to Gordon Taylor—was a way
of breaking down the constraining wall of distance between subject
and object, self and other, thought and world.

5.

A Light from the North ("Relics from a Polar Cairn")

THE MOST AMBITIOUS EFFORT of Dorn's first year of composition was his first poem about history, in which attention to life on the "northern curve" led—by way of one of his most ardent autodidactic quests, on the early record of Arctic exploration—to the discovery of a poetic light from the North. "Relics from a Polar Cairn," Dorn told Gordon Taylor in sending a draft typescript of the poem in mid-December 1953, was his "latest," "a dip into my excitement over [Vilhjalmur] Stefansson and the Arctic." This taut, compressed sixty-one-line historical metanarrative tackled Dorn's determinate sector of space and time as boldly as Olson's historical pieces did his, with a similar urgency; unable to challenge his polymathic master's range of referential resources, however, the earnest apprentice here turned his lack of "larnin" to his expedient advantage, gaining in the process of staging a single critical insight what his mentor sometimes lacked, an edgy singularity of focus. Cid Corman, general editor of *Origin*, where "Cairn" would appear, would find in the poem a predictable "clear influence of Olson," but some identifiable signature of Dorn's as well—"an edge of his own already." Dorn's dry, ironic distances were already audible in an emerging tonal acerbity. Honing that edge on his first big poem, he made an early assertion of the authority that would claim a public ground for discriminating private judgment. His audacious aim in "Relics from a Polar Cairn" was nothing less than to illuminate by an act of critical distancing what he now termed, with a sweeping certainty bred of many an industrious public library reading-room hour, "the whole cultural absurdity as emblematized in Arctic anything before 1900, say."

Dorn began work on the poem in the late summer of 1953 while staying in Helene's "nifty view" hillside apartment on N. 36th. "He was engrossed in that whole Nordic bit," she recalls. Dorn had his true love, too, looking into Stefansson's arguments for the virtues of the all-meat diet. "He was ecstatic about that man, and of course I, then, after reading him, was too. We ate his diet. I remember that very well because I cooked the fat back, or whatever it was, in my little apartment way up on a hill in Seattle."

Like many of Dorn's early research missions this one bore the originating stamp of Olson: he had first encountered Stefansson's challenging and invigorating cultural proposals through the Black Mountain teacher's reading lists. Olson, son of a Swedish immigrant, projected in his pedagogy a sense of personal affinity with the intrepid Arctic expert: the son of Icelandic immigrants to Manitoba, Stefansson was like Olson a self-made authority with a reputation for independent thinking and iconoclastic views. After his years of active exploration in the far north he had established the world's largest collection of Polar Literature at Dartmouth College, object of dutiful Olson pilgrimages during the latter's preparatory studies for a mythological verse epic in the late 1940s. Though the verse epic never came to pass, Olson succeeded in transmitting the excitements of Stefansson's discoveries to student Dorn, who in later years would recall that legacy as the seed of the poetry he submitted for his Black Mountain degree qualification exam in 1955; "Cairn" would be its first fruit.

"I'm certain, aside from the man's great individualist/survivalist skill and knowledge, Olson was totally attracted to Stefansson's northernness," Dorn wrote to me when I was at work on writing Olson's life in 1986. "He tied Stefansson in with Hooten, the great anatomist, on the study of tooth decay in medieval Icelandic grave sites: this was part of the evidence for a 100% meat diet being the best for physical maintenance. Stefansson's ideas of that are summarized in a book called *Not By Bread Alone.* All this was not purely disinterested, I thought when I learned that V. S. was a paid consultant to the Hormel Company in Chicago. Still, the ideas are rather compelling as he writes of them; he was a fanatic meat-diet proponent in any case. All this had to do with a life of great physical activity, of course—he wasn't talking to people sprawled in front of TV." While Olson's interest in Stefansson's dietary theories remained strictly academic, Dorn actually tried them out on himself during his Seattle stay of 1953–1954; as he explained to me, he had for some time thereafter been a hard-core red-meat-diet devotee, persuaded by Stefansson's writings that "if you didn't keep to an all meat diet, you'd turn into a creep in soft shoes, your hair would fall out, your teeth would rot, your energy reserves would drop and you'd have bad, awful-smelling stools. Stefansson made it sound like life on anything but pure meat wasn't worth living. You know, for a long time I believed it, it just rang true."

Dorn's immediate subject matter in "Cairn" was the ill-fated polar expedition of the nineteenth-century explorer Sir John Franklin, whose traveling party of 129 Englishmen had been sacrificed for lack of earth-knowledge to the "cultural absurdity" of death through malnutrition amid regions Stefansson had later shown to be teeming with life-sustaining edible fauna. In one of his poem's most striking images Dorn imagines a young English officer whose "religious papers" have been found in the burial cairn, carrying his Bible to his early grave "like a blooded hound / with his leash in his own mouth, ringing / in the articulate air a cultural error." The lines that follow, in the December draft sent Taylor, somewhat awkwardly spell out the poem's message—"There was no other reason than mental for not knowing / the keyword: / FRESH." By the time Helene, now Dorn's typist, re-typed the poem for *Origin* a few months later,

Dorn had revised his abstract summary statement to a resonant, located physical image: "Their mentality fogged like breath not knowing / the keyword: / FRESH." "Fresh," in the poet's double-saying, refers to both fresh meat and fresh thinking. The "tin kiss / to tradition" that in the poem's closing lines has sent the culturally-unknowing Englishmen to their deaths "in a calamine expanse ... where / even Eros would be well-dressed" represents an ultimate embrace of the cultural past, at once poignant and blind, honorable and terminal.

Dorn's version of the story of the Franklin party closely follows the account given by Stefansson in *Unsolved Mysteries of the Arctic* (1938), a volume he had turned up in the Seattle public library. At the time of Dorn's writing, the Stefansson thesis remained a matter of some controversy among historians of polar exploration; an independent corroboration of Dorn's poetic judgments in "Cairn" is provided by one of them, Richard Cyriax, in a 1939 study *(Sir John Franklin's Last Expedition: A Chapter in the History of the Royal Navy)*:

> The Arctic explorer Dr. Vilhjalmur Stefansson has proved that animal life is fairly plentiful in nearly the whole of the Arctic Sea and on some of the land, and that it is quite possible to live entirely on the food that is procurable locally. His conclusions are that the absence of animal life formerly believed to prevail in many parts of the Arctic regions was apparent only; that failure to procure fresh meat, especially seal meat, was due to lack of knowledge rather than actual scarcity of animal life; and that, if explorers had possessed this knowledge and had understood where and how to find the game, they would seldom have had any real difficulty in living on the local fauna. If Sir John Franklin's officers and men had known these facts, they would not have suffered from scurvy, since plenty of fresh meat is an effective preventive, and, furthermore, they would not have died of starvation if they had divided themselves into small hunting parties.

Dorn's ironic deployment of historical materials in "Relics from a Polar Cairn," like his choice of the cultural and spiritual discontinuity between "white world" and native as theme, foreshadows important developments in his later writing. "Cairn" is the antecedent of such major works of cultural distancing as "The Land Below," *The Shoshoneans, Recollections of Gran Apachería*. Like "Cairn," such works would address through ironic means the shock of contact between New World natives and European arrivistes, and derive strong oppositional tensions from the collision of values therein implied.

In Dorn's application of the figure of contact-shock, here and later, the radical cultural discontinuity that separates native inhabitant and European interloper signals a deeper gap between different kinds of "mentality." This is a devolutionary "difference," moreover, dividing the earth-wise pre-logical origins of human consciousness from the degraded, alienated "predictive mind" of white-world history ("their mentality fogged like breath").

At the opening of "Cairn," Dorn poises his reader at the brink of a concrete inscription of history, spelled out in the objects that are all that remains of the Franklin party:

> Regard the open grave: iron &
> brass implements, copper
> kettles, cookstoves & brass buttons, dead
>   cold like early ideograms
>   on the crisp ice.

The exegesis of this objective "text" takes place in the form of the imaginative development of Dorn's poem, a critical re-modeling of history by images staged to expose and interpret "in the articulate air a cultural error." Dorn's achronological narrative of contact unfolds on the frozen edges of the Arctic Sea, where the men of Franklin's ships *Erebus* and *Terror* were lost in 1847–1848. The whole area, as Stefansson's later voyaging had proved, was rich with seal, caribou, walrus and other animals whose meat would have provided protection against the fatal malnutritional disease scurvy. The point of Dorn's poem is the failure of Franklin's party to recognize that fact. Stranded "here in this cadmium north / twenty thousand years after the first lesson," the oblivious Englishmen of "Cairn" waste their energies "scouring the brittle hills" in search of the ineffective European-prescribed antiscorbutic rock-lichen, trek exhaustedly after "ptarmigans & willow partridges" (a "delicacy in england," but of trivial nutritional value) and expend critical resources on a hunt for small game which they manage to over-cook, thus squandering its precious vital juices: "the leanest hare is scorched to death (burned / in the flames of its own oil...." In a more prosaic early draft of the poem, the symbolic futility of the moment is brought out in greater detail: "they / had used as fuel the very thing that would have saved / them, the oil from tissue." As a contrasting picture of successful survivalism in the same frozen landscape, Dorn presents a local Eskimo hunting party having no trouble felling a walrus "with crude tools": a "single clue" to the "final equilibrium" of man and nature, this instructive tableau goes ignored by the doomed, pathetic Englishmen, "valiant skeletons" who, sporting to the end, "play a game of football for encouragement, / ... on the way to their final cairn."

Perhaps the crowning irony in Dorn's poetic application of the Stefansson thesis comes in his representation of the expeditionary party's single substantial success at large-game hunting, the capture of a polar bear. Children of the Enlightenment, the white-world explorers overlook the animal's potential food value and concentrate on it strictly as an object of scientific observation: their rationalist mentality exposed in its practical uselessness, they are noted to have "measured it every conceivable way / but there is not a sign that they ate any of it." Dorn's focus on the "educated" but inflexible minds of the young English officers reveals the organic limitations and faulty compensatory adjustments of Western science in adapting to alien mindsets which are more attuned to nature, a subject the poet would pursue in the later cultural tragedy of *Gran Apachería* (1974). In the later work, the scientific mentality is seen to come to

material dominance through sheer force of its technology—the sol-
diers' directive shotguns, the railroads that carry off the last Apache
warriors, even, ironically, the recording instrument in the
poet's/observer's/reader's hands ("we are the man with the camera").
While in the prophetic New World fable of "Cairn" enlightenment
science fails and nature and the earth-wisdom of the Eskimo pre-
vail, in *Gran Apachería* the balance shifts and the technological "pre-
dictive mind" finally overpowers a native mind that is "devoted to
pure observation" and is "no mechanic of the future."

Together with his tortuously compressed syntax, Dorn's stub-
born omission of explanatory and connective narrative elements ren-
ders "Cairn" difficult in many passages. Like his master Olson's,
Dorn's use of undisclosed sources occasionally causes an odd deflec-
tion of meaning and motive; there is at times a sense we are being
asked to know something more about the matters at hand than the
poet has a right to expect of us. To appreciate such poetry it is per-
haps helpful if not necessary to pursue the poem back to its sources.
Turning to Dorn's chief sources for the history and cultural anthro-
pology in "Cairn," Stefansson's *Unsolved Mysteries of the Arctic*
and *The Friendly Arctic*, we find some of his poem's more difficult
passages clarified and its message usefully glossed. Stefansson's par-
ticular criticism of the English as explorers of the Far North, for
example, sheds much light on Dorn's generally contemptuous attitude
toward the lost men in "Cairn." Non-English members of Franklin's
party, hired Indians and French-Canadian voyageurs, had, as Ste-
fansson pointed out, proved far more adept as hunters of caribou:
"Why were the Englishmen, in self-help, a complete dead weight on
the party? Was it beneath their dignity to co-operate in securing
food? Was helping the workers, in their minds, detrimental to dis-
cipline? ... We are already beginning to talk about the ability which
British explorers of a hundred years ago demonstrated for not learn-
ing from their own experience, the experience of fellow explorers
or from the native people, the Eskimos." Dorn's poem treats that
tragedy as culturally symptomatic: the proud and persistent failure
of generations of "enlightened" British explorers to comprehend the

actual lay of the land in the Arctic is shown to parallel the failure of the scientific mind to cope with the actual complexity of nature. The reader of "Cairn" is compelled to admit that Sir John Franklin was not, as Tennyson's laudatory verses on his monument in Westminster Abbey had suggested, an "Heroic Sailor Soul," but the unwitting agent, as well as the eventual victim, of a deeply entrenched state of cultural endarkenment. In the words of Stefansson, Dorn's trusted source on the North, the physical cause of the demise of Franklin's men may have been scurvy, but "an antecedent cause of the scurvy was the failure to adapt themselves to local conditions which derived from the mental environment of their country, social class and time." That cultural insight finds its poetic statement in the effective symbolic parable of "Cairn."

Over the course of the year following his completion of "Relics from a Polar Cairn," Dorn's poetic *modus operandi* would undergo a further sea-change, largely consequent upon his return to Black Mountain; the eccentric "edge" which Corman had noticed in the poem would come to seem to Dorn not sharp enough to qualify as distinctly his own. In the kind of harsh self-critical re-assessment that would accompany more than one of his purposeful transitions as a poet, he would decide the poem's formal restraint and "objectivity" neutralized his idiosyncratic sound, drowning it in his argument and materials. To Kenneth Hanson, who had complimented him upon its appearance in *Origin,* he wrote from Mexico City in February 1955 that he had grown unsure about it: "I have mixed feelings now, mostly bad, about ... 'Cairn.' Can't tell what it is exactly, but something to do with it not being a measure of what *I* do to what that [material] is. Maybe a bit corny to say 'it isn't me.' Anyway the Arctic is so much more, you know it's as stupid as writing a poem to roses with a big bottle of cheap perfume in y[ou]r hand. (But that might be interesting.)" Like all of his poems of the first three years of his serious commitment to the art, "Cairn" would be withheld from publication in any of his subsequent collections. For Dorn, the cost of being oneself continually necessitated the shedding of past selves, and their telling evidences. (In a later stage of self-revisionism Dorn's creaturely sympathy with the edible fauna of a mechanized food economy—as well as his neo-"Protestant" moral fury against the excesses of the eaters—would bring him to qualify the poem's substantive point as well. Implicitly retracting his former advocacy of the Stefansson all-meat diet, in his late comic epic *Hi Plane / Westward Haut,* he offered a pointed moral satire of the national carnivorousness represented by the feedlots and slaughter-houses of the banks of the South Platte, an assembly-line abattoir-complex built to supply mammal protein not to polar survivalists but to a dangerously proliferating technological society's addictive meat-consumers who "just can't stay away from it, it's the smell of growth.")

6.

A Sense of Kinship

THE WINTER OF 1953–1954 was a time of creative turbulence in Dorn's soul. Against the quandaries and confusions of "love chaos" his search for form in poetry served as a kind of shoring-up action, a redemptive therapy; meanwhile in his personal life new hells and new heavens continued to succeed one another with the bewildering variability of black storm clouds and blue clearing passages racing in rapid alternation over the mist-rinsed Seattle hills. Within a few weeks of the devastated late-October retreat from San Francisco, his swirling emotions—and relations with Helene—had again begun to stabilize. "Except for the destruction of my confidence which seems to have been going on all my life," he informed Gordon Taylor in an characteristically paradoxical November message, "I am happier than I have been."

When the date he'd projected for a wedding that month came around, he was still a bachelor, his love anguish now significantly complicated by his dwelling upon the coming child—a potential key, as he now surmised, to the unlocking of the oldest riddles of his alienated private history. "No, I ain't married, I won't be," he told his friend anticlimactically as the anticipated nuptial time passed.

I would marry only one living woman and that isn't very fore-
seeable. But I did WANT that baby.... Goddamn it, Gordon,
we've known each other a long time now and it must have
passed between us in some sense that I am, have been all my
life, in an anguish, the struggle has been largely repressed,
over a lack of kinship. I don't know articulately what I mean
by that but it has something to do with having had all the
years of my goddamn empty life an emptiness, a non-love
from any source that was equal to mine. From my family I
got nothing but misery which has ended in complete disin-
terest on my part. Before I wrote stock letters home, now I
don't write at all. And it's a relief. I am sure I killed a beauti-
ful part of Helene's love by a too complete consumption of it
by my own. And oddly enough things are better now that the
pressures of San Francisco are off and we have no worry about
things like food, shelter, the coming baby, etc.

In the ensuing weeks, as he told Taylor, "matters improved dra-
matically." A new understanding with Helene brought renewed trust
in love and a corresponding lift in morale. "For the first time in a
long time," he reported, 'I have a heartfelt direction and I'm happy
as hell, and not blasé about many things." By December the "emo-
tional nightmareing" he had been through over Helene was coming
to seem a necessary trial of passage, the psychic purgative required
to cleanse him of excessive and destructive emotional needs. The
"reduction," he announced, was "almost complete." By the alchemy
of love he had escaped his hells and started life anew. Daily meet-
ings brought long talks and a calm sense of gathering resources for
a shared future. "Things between Helene and me are better, in many
ways, than they have ever been, the love is if possible more lovely,"
he wrote on December 11. "And I think [it was] because I had the
sense to lose my head so totally that I was able to see myself in
enough new relationships to wait peacefully until she got herself
clear of a couple of basic things."

By the new year plans were settling into place. Dorn happily notified Taylor on January 19, 1954 that "Helene and I are living together again, things are all worked out and for the first time since last summer it looks as if life might be possible, if we're cunning." She had taken a place of her own, as he explained, "on the west side of Queen Anne Hill, with several windows toward the mountains, Olympic." At the end of January he gave up his place across from the park and "move[d] completely in with H[elene]." He was deeply affected by the tenacity of her love for him, which he now saw holding up bravely in the face of "a dramatic flood of letters blasting [her] for not going through with the 2nd try with David, all presupposing to pin the red A on her breast and send her through the streets complete with shaved head, and ghost dogs yelping thinly at her ankles." Once Helene's children joined them, due precautions with mail had to be taken to conceal the fact of his presence in the household until her divorce could be finalized. He carefully instructed Taylor, "This is legal in case a question should arise about her fitness to have the babes." Keeping the family intact was now a paramount aim, love and "a sense of kinship" having become inextricable aspects of the single emotional objective and fact.

7.

The Difference

THE IDEA OF GOING BACK TO SCHOOL continued to tempt Dorn, but his proximity to the University of Washington did little to simplify the decision. In January 1954 he enrolled in a university extension night-school course in elementary Latin, a "first brush with an inflected language" which he found "real enjoyable." "Next quarter I will be a full time student maybe," he told Gordon Taylor. But to pursue classic languages he would first need an undergraduate degree, and his earlier interest in signing up as an English major so as to study poetry was rapidly waning. He had no taste for being turned into a cog in an academic assembly-line, and the U. W. English department, "supposedly one of the hottest" in the nation, was appearing on closer inspection more "like monotony."

At least part of the problem derived from his association with U. W. poets, particularly those of the graduate-instructor echelon. An object lesson for Dorn in the stalemate a "literary" grad school might be for a poet was provided by Kenneth Pitchford, a "very bright ... poet with potential" who appeared to lack the life-knowledge "to recognize his own experience and cope with that, not with what he knows so many of, four bit words." Campus poet Pitchford, just

twenty-three, had in the opinion of the twenty-four-year-old out-
sider Dorn "thought about too many things for his years ... and so
the caught art in him lags too terribly behind what it is he does know,
which makes him very often academic." For Dorn the catch-all term
"academic" now signified a concentrated distillation of life-nega-
tives: it was a moribund, purely cerebral state that missed the beat of
"the vibration," ignored the urgent throb of "the prime-pulsation,"
disregarded the plasmic flow of "the quickening blood." The cul-
turally boxed-in "mentality fogged like breath" which Dorn had
diagnosed in his poetry as deadly seemed in the end all that aca-
demics had to go on. True creativity demanded so much more. "You
must trust the fluid along with the mentality," the fledgling poet
preached from his epistolary soap-box to his Marine friend in far-
off Korea.

In obvious contrast to the academic mind-set stood the ethos of
Black Mountain, as much as ever Dorn's benchmark of "the differ-
ence," "something I can get nowhere else," the encouragement of
creative freedom and the nurturing of a vibrant individuality. A liv-
ing reminder was coincidentally at hand in Mark Hedden, a U. W.
grad student in English whom he had met three years earlier when
both were students at Black Mountain. After a straight dose of the
academic grind, Hedden was—as Dorn told Gordon Taylor—"fed
up and ... having a tooth-gritting time of it." A musician/composer
as well as a poet, Hedden possessed a breadth and flexibility of mind
that distinguished him, in his fellow ex-Black Mountaineer's eyes,
from the U. W. poets—he was, Dorn reported, not stiff and guarded
like others in academia but "willing & spontaneous in parting with
what he knows & feels, which is considerable."

It was their common hill-fort-privileged vantage on things that
made Hedden the only artist Dorn knew in Seattle with whom he
would consider collaborating. They traded ideas on composing an
Olson-style dance-score to be performed by "a piano dancer here-
about, name of Nishitani." Brought along to a coffee-bar where
Hedden was serving as the dancer's accompanist, Dorn quickly dis-
cerned "She's a beauty" (but then self-consciously crossed out that

assessment, lest Taylor get the wrong idea). The two Black Mountain alumni agreed to attune their words with Nishitani's vibration, "if she becomes sufficiently interested in poetry as dance." A rapt Dorn composed a lyric about her, "A derelict air," which illustrated his latest dictum to Gordon Taylor on the peculiar characteristic that separated poetry from prose, a subtle "difference" which echoed that between mere mentality and creative vitality. "I think the difference between prose & poetry is often one of vibration, the length of vibration as one goes along perceiving, the impatient, blood-circulating, catch-now construction ... that's new: NOW."

> A sharp green counter
> was where she sat
> & her color was
> velvet it darkened
> just right, like love
>
> The blues, so slowly chant
> a memorial counter-charm
> keyed with coffee odors
> yellowed during 78 whirls
> of revealed lacquer.
>
> Still her dark hips
> shift for cloth necessities
> with no hints of malediction
> for the blues demand space
> as temporal as a snowman,
> or marimba sounds.

8.

Ice Cream & a Movie

THE TIME IN SEATTLE rewarded Dorn's attention to its moments doubly: even as his poetry began, there came a welcome end to the anguished, "largely repressed ... struggle ... over a lack of a sense of kinship" which, as he'd told Gordon Taylor, had haunted him all his life. On April 18, 1954 Helene gave birth to a boy, Paul Dorn. On June 29 her divorce was finalized. On July 1 Ed and Helene were married by a justice of the peace in Seattle. "I held Paul on my lap while the j. p. did the deed," Fred Buck remembers. "Afterwards we went out for ice cream & a movie."

As part of the divorce settlement David Buck pledged substantial financial assistance to his former family. In the actual event, through their subsequent travels and travails Buck's provision for them proved generous beyond the letter of the law. To Dorn, his new wife's ex-husband became in effect a partial patron, investing in a "secondary stake in what I do"; it was an arrangement to which he seems to have accommodated himself with no more sacrifice of his pride than absolutely necessary. "We could never have done the things we did without David Buck's friendship and support," Helene testifies. "He paid Ed's tuition at Black Mountain and would have backed his getting a master's. No matter where we went or what we did, we knew his child support $200 would always be there."

The questing nomad-poet and his bride packed their belongings into the Morris Minor convertible that came to Helene from Buck in the settlement and embarked with their three children on a cross-country honeymoon sojourn in the general direction of Black Mountain, where Dorn intended that fall to resume his wandering progress toward an "acceptable structure of reality."

9.

A History of Yearning

That lingering light and ceaseless rain which filters down from
the northern curve....
   —"1st Avenue"

I N 1971, on a trip to Seattle for a poetry reading, Dorn took me
on a small tour of the city which included recollections of several
prolonged stays he'd made there in his early wandering years. He
led me down into the complicated lower-level underworld of the old
Pike Street market, where it wasn't too hard to imagine him prowl-
ing as a restless, obscurely driven young seeker in the lonesome days
of 1952 or 1953. We came up again out of bright subterranean illu-
mination into soft luminous-gray daylight underneath a low, thinly
weeping sky. A superstructure of ramps passed down over the mar-
ket to a waterfront of big docked ships. We strolled through blue
mist-soaked streets Dorn had rambled with the half-Russian, half-
Klikitat "totemist" fisherman-lumberjack called Bill Elephant in his
writings. Later he conducted me around the university district, another
site of early adventure and trial. From neighborhoods of import

stores and red cedar totems, brambles and hemlocks, dark brown houses and black Norway Spruce, we watched dim pale lights of evening come on in the surrounding hills, and through heavy ever-green canopy purple clouds opened to let a far-up northern sky shine out for a moment clear as a history of yearning from that alien world.

VI.

Crossing Over
(1954–1956)

I.

Indian Country
(Seattle to Illinois)

IN EARLY JULY 1954 Dorn departed from Seattle with his new family in Helene's Morris Minor convertible, headed across country. The world of difference that was to become a kind of home greeted them at their first stop, at Wakema Mound, an archeological dig on Indian grounds along the Columbia River near The Dalles, Oregon, where Dorn's friend Mark Hedden was working. "We were at the Dalles 2 days trying to make it thru the road to Mark and the dig," Helene reported in the first of her regular dutiful postings from their far-flung travels to her ex-husband and their current provider David Buck. "The Indians were really hostile—each gave us a different direction & none got us there.... Fred's saying 'me paleface' didn't help much either. We really felt Chief Seattle's wrath coming thru that country." Dorn himself sensed a brooding immanence about the place, "wild pasts jutting mysteriously into the present." But his own account revealed him no less comfortable in the encounter than his new wife: "the Indian country along the Columbia River, where you can smell the hostile dead, see them dancing in the forbidding black rocks, does something definite to the white blood."

Their first venture across the West instilled a "cowboy & Indian" theme in Dorn family mythology, later source of many hours of imaginative play among the children. "We did see some true cowboys, but most of the booted men were sod busters," Helene told David Buck. "Fred & Chan went wild coming thru [the] West—clung to us & stared with awe at anyone who slightly resembled cowboys." Dorn family Western treks would often resemble small pioneer sagas of adventure and endurance. On this trip the sturdy "mini" sustained an emergency stop at a foreign-car dealership in Denver for wheel re-balancing, but withstood 125 degree temperatures in Kansas ("which we weren't sure we'd survive") to safely deliver the traveling party of five to the Abercrombie home in Mattoon.

2.

Little Differences
(Mattoon)

THE NEWLYWEDS' FIRST VISIT to the Illinois in-laws was perhaps predictably not without strain. The unusual circumstances of the union had heightened family sensitivities all around; there had been a "ruckus ... way up there in Minnesota" over the birth of baby Paul, and now Helene found that her new husband's mother and stepfather "talked down Ed, feel he & I not fit for parenthood." Ed's fourteen-year-old half-sister Nonna, "who smokes & buries dead birds (has coffin silk cloth etc.)" took charge of Fred; while Ed and Helene were out of the house, Louise and Nonna sheared the six-year-old towhead's copious unkempt locks. Helene was horrified. "I wish you could see what they did to our beautiful boy's head of hair! They snuck the sizzers on him when we were out erranding—I wept & Ed fumed, but the damage was done. I couldn't bear to even look at him for a couple of days! They told him he looked like a girl, etc... it is all these little differences in us & them that gave them the idea we were no good parents ... which they got through to Fred."

Fred Buck recalls the visit from a child's perspective. "It was hot and sticky. There was nothing to do. Meals were large, with iced tea. The Abercrombie house had a canal at the rear of the back yard and I found little stick crosses on the bank here and there, dug underneath and uncovered tissue paper but nothing inside, no pets or body parts. I watched Liberace with Grandma on the little TV. Nonna took me to see *River of No Return* with Marilyn Monroe and Robert Mitchum at the movies."

The haircut episode, with its obvious symbolic overtones, perhaps reminded Dorn, the exogamous son, of incidents in his own youth; he would later comment that as a young man he had "saved himself" from "the psychological principle of Illinois ... by letting my hair grow and establishing a ritual of my own person which even the slightest reflection will reveal as a dangerous thing to do." Under pressure throughout the Mattoon stay, he even quarreled with old friend Gordon Taylor on their first meeting in over two years. An argument developed over cultural attitudes, Dorn "shot [his] mouth off" and found himself lecturing Taylor on "how to live," a subject, he later ruefully admitted to his friend, that was "any man's own business." The argument had been bred of the tensions at his overcrowded family home. After a week of mutually felt "little differences" with the in-laws, exacerbated by having nine people packed into "one-and-a-half" bedrooms of "a small builder house" in the middle of a sweltering prairie summer, the Dorns took off from Mattoon for Chicago, Helene declaring "this Illinois is the most stultifying country of my experience."

3.

A Traumatic Enlightenment (Chicago)

LITTLE DIFFERENCES CONTINUED to haunt them in the big city. Neither Ed nor Helene knew their way around Chicago: Helene had previously seen only the railway stations and the Outer Drive, while Ed possessed but slightly more experience, having once attended a Duke Ellington concert at a downtown theater before retreating to stay the night with his mother's brother in Gary. Arriving in "this hostile burg" at the beginning of August with a month to kill before going on to Black Mountain, they immediately launched into a search for housing. Stopping in for coffee and baby-bottle-warming at a restaurant in a "rough neighborhood" near the cheap hotel where they'd spent their first night, they "found it Puerto Rican—totally," and "took ten minutes of frantic arm waving to get the man to understand we wanted a bottle filled with milk & heated." The owner of the place finally "came in and rescued us, gave the kids some balloons & sent a customer to his landlady to see if she had an apt. available. No, but her friend did." The restaurant owner conducted them by taxi to 477 Deming Place on the North Side near Lincoln Park. The $16-a-week two-room apartment was, Helene supposed, "in the middle class bracket," a fact that did little to help country

boy Ed feel at home ('I was never middle class"). In their new sur-
roundings they encountered "nothing but hostility," and were soon
wishing they'd "found something in the P[uerto] R[ican] section"
instead. Ed, who not only lacked proper business clothes but had
begun growing a beard, discovered he looked out of place in the
middle-class neighborhood. "I've never seen so many dumpy peo-
ple," Helene reported to David Buck. "And how they all stare at us!
It could be Ed's beard, but he never caused that much sensation any-
where else!" The apartment itself, while relatively inexpensive, was
cramped and "awful." A "sidewalk-width" third-floor back porch
was shared with another couple who kept their side fenced off; the
neighbors' little boy was "very rude to F[red] and C[han] ... told
them his status was higher than ours so they couldn't come on his
part of the porch." To provide the kids an outing Ed and Helene
took them by streetcar to inspect the Loop, attend a Danny Kaye
movie ("which stunk") and visit the fossil room at the Field Museum
("Fred was really impressed with the dinosaur"). As they rode the
crowded streetcar an "oldish woman while pushing her way out of
the car stuffed one whole dollar into Chan's hand." The windfall
represented a token counter to big-city inflation. Before Buck's sup-
port check arrived, the Dorns were "down to 15 bucks."

By mid-August they had moved out of "that n[orth] side horror"
and found a new apartment at the other end of the city, at 1326 E.
53rd in the Hyde Park district near the University of Chicago. "Two
cubicles" three flights above an alley in a tenement in a largely black
neighborhood, the place was once again woefully small for five peo-
ple, four of them sleeping "stuffed in a tiny room." Their first nights
in the place came during a "smothering" heat wave, when the atmos-
phere in the airless rooms became "thick and wet and obscene."
"It's just a godamn fight to stay alive," Helene told David Buck from
the urban inferno. "To expect any energy left for doing anything
creative is absurd."

Their consolation was having escaped both the middle-class neigh-
borhood and "the status quo," a power that "binds with brick and
concrete and envelopes you like the heat tenaciously and stubbornly."

Despite the oppressive heat, as the weeks went by there came signs of cultural relief. "Chicago isn't so bad," Helene decided after they'd made a pilgrimage to the Art Institute. "Whistler and Manet, Picasso and Seurat, Lautrec Van Gogh o god, so exciting!" The colors in the paintings were enough to make them ready to "live thru most anything." And their new neighborhood was much more to their liking. The intrepid Fred established cowboy and Indian games in the alley, as his mother announced. "No more hostility ... kids play madly with the little Puerto Ricans a complete language barrier but they play together down there in the dirty yard all day and into the night."

For the adults their "second place in Shy [Chicago]" supplied an education in urban life and as such "a traumatic enlightenment." Inventorying their circumstances for Buck at the end of August Helene admitted many "discomforts"—"it's hot, it's dirty (do all the washing by hand), it's cramped, it's 3 flights up, a dingy foul smelling hall, it overlooks an alley"—then suggested all the difficulty was more than compensated for by what they were learning about life. "For all its heat concrete & screaming cars, I would not trade a day. ... I think I've imbibed some of Chicago's violence in my veins." Particularly revelatory was the family's first close acquaintance with inner-city sociology. Writing about the view from their tenement porch over the all-night parking-garage across the alley, Helene tried to summon something of the paradoxical authority of that otherness to which they had become witness; her letter became as well an impassioned apology for the precarious kind of life they'd chosen.

> But the alley has the Kimbark Garage, comfortingly lighted all nite—especially when one gets up at 3 A. M. & has to go out into the dark hall to the bathroom—there is always one of the Negro parkers sitting out on that funny straight-backed chair with its uneven legs there in the alley on the cement, in front of the garage and underneath the almost bright neon KIMBARK. It's the alley, I guess, that keeps the neon from being bright and the round overhanging ad for lubricating oil,

further down, from being nothing more [than] slightly rusted tin. It's the Negro too, that bares the sign to what it really is. Because somehow, he's managed to keep himself despite the city. And the alley is his, dammit, and he knows it & is so goddamn much more comfortable in it than we are with the false fronts we've kept for ourselves. We've lost ourselves so completely in the loot that we clutch tight with our whiteness ... that we carry the mute tone of steel and concrete in our dress, attempt the posture of a skyscraper, and laugh only now & then so as not to disturb the straight up & down of things. Stick to the gray rectangular plan! We gave the blacks their alleys and the Indians their reservations. And they've got us, both of them. I would like to think they *knew* they've got us ... but I'm not sure, not sure except for those red men at the Dalles. They know. And they show they know ... whether the University digs up their dead or not. They know. And they look you in the eye with their knowing. And then *you* know, and you retreat. This trying to get at the Negro goes much harder—it is so new to me ... & to feel his place, to get in touch with him, is much more complex. It's here especially that I feel so miserably lost in my need for some of the present anthropological knowledge ... & here that I become even more of a voyeur than usual! Discomfort, David—sure; but, as I see it, not to be applied to how one *faces* things in the future, but rather, how one SEES—the problem one of *being* and thus expressing—the whole of it. That's my gripe: there is so much of the people who face things; lost is the ability, desire, to *look at* things. Like the curve the blacks make, with their alleys, flaming clothes and laughter.

"Interracialism of the intellectual poor is a good index of their rebellion," sociologist Michael Harrington wrote in *The Other America*, his 1961 study of the largely invisible culture of poverty then existing within the so-called Affluent Society. "Like most of the educated middle class in America outside the South, they share the rhetoric of equality. But, unlike most people, their life has led them to an interracial world."

Dorn's search for work in Chicago intensified by mid-August with the prospect of running out of money looming. Jobs were "scarce to begin with," Helene reported to Buck, "but Ed is really a dead duck anyway. His speech and face aren't that of a laborer & those who hire know it ... and he hasn't any of the clothing required for a white collar job, too much education for a laboring job, too little for anything else! & no pull, no references in Chi., too many [previous] jobs, on it goes!" With an audacity bred of desperation Dorn finally "got sick of it," lied about his background, saying he'd been employed since high school at the plant where his father worked in Mattoon, and quickly landed a $42.50-a-week stock-boy job on the three-to-midnight shift at Krogers supermarket on E. 79th. He would be no stranger to night-shift and swing-shift work in coming years. "Anybody's led a lot of lives," he'd one day say. "My own ... was once extremely shift-ridden." He trimmed vegetables, stocked shelves, put purchased groceries into large bags and carried them out to purchasers' cars, weighed produce, and unloaded cases of foodstuffs from large trucks. At the end of two weeks he collected his first and last paycheck. "He will smile as they have told him to smile and then say goodbye to the Kroger Team because he doesn't aspire to 20-years-without-one-day-missed buttons," Helene reported on quitting-day.

4.

Difference as a Sign of Freedom (Black Mountain)

A T BLACK MOUNTAIN one's difference could be worn not as a badge of shame but as a sign of freedom. When the Dorns arrived in September for the opening of the fall quarter the "brand new world" Helene had anticipated upon meeting Ed began to materialize in full ragged, disorderly creative detail. Few places could have been farther away in physical feeling or in spirit from the "concrete & screaming cars" world of inner-city Chicago. The Dorns now found themselves setting up house, as Helene told David Buck, "right in the forest." They occupied one wing of a ramshackle lodge nestled on the wooded flank of the mountain (the other wing was occupied by three student painters). Helene was faced with "cooking for a family of five on a two-burner hotplate." Fred entered the first grade at a local school "from which he drags home hymns," as Dorn noted, "some very nice"; the curriculum included Baptist fundamentals, Bible-reading and stories of the life of Jesus; one of the boy's classmates was the daughter of evangelist Billy Graham. (Dorn adjudged the school "very interesting.") On college grounds, meanwhile, mountain-country fundamentalist schooling gave way to unlikely scenes of freestyle communal upbringing, regarded by Helene with some initial interested bemusement. Immediate-neighbor children included small offspring of faculty couples Bea and Wes Huss and Connie and Charles Olson. Two-year-old Chansonette spent her days in the scrub woods around the lodge playing on makeshift swings or "throwing stones with Davey [Huss] and Kate [Olson] at the bears lions & tigers off in the trees ... and telling Olson he can't take down her pants for her (he was swinging them one afternoon) to go to the bathroom ... 'you don't know how' ... & she has trouble learning that nobody cares around here if she wee wees outside, I think that was why she didn't want him to help her! But she has discovered that she can go about the campus nude ... and does so quite often." Within a few months, however, the obstreperous behavior of some of freedom's more "obnoxious" products was enough to convince the single-minded mother—as she'd tell Buck the week before Thanksgiving—that "Reichian child care is shit!"

Further down the hill on the kudzu-vine-choked old lower campus closer to the highway, wild nature was taking over even more dramatically. The financially struggling college was slowly dying from the bottom up, with lower lodges, "quiet house," dining hall, gatehouse, music cubicle and other buildings now "unused with the jungle growth slowly taking them over," as Helene discovered. "It is a weird sight & easy to understand how large settlements can be buried alive by the jungle. There is not enuff money, you see, to keep them up nor to heat any of them." In this epoch of semi-respectable decline the shoestring faculty was being paid in "milk eggs butter and some produce from the farm plus a steer now and then, and 29 bucks a month food allowance." To fetch their own fresh consumables every evening the Dorns threaded their way down the path through the gully beyond the upper lodges, crossed a bridge, climbed some distance, and came into a clearing—"suddenly you are out from under the trees & vines and to see the sky in such expanse never fails to be a shock.... The cleared land is startling. And then the farm house comes into view." Terence Burns, a student worker and lodge neighbor to the Dorns, doled out the milk and eggs which had been produced by Black Mountain cows and chickens. For Ed the experience was of course not entirely unfamiliar, but for the rest of the family it was quite new, as Helene noted. "It is the kids' and my first real farm experience and it is wonderful.... The kids go wild over the animals, and actually so do I." Terence Burns told Helene that young farm volunteer Fred had "got terribly upset ... the first time he saw the mother of the new calf in the milk house. 'She's leaking!!!'" (These were in fact to be the final days of the college farm, which would fail over the coming winter.)

A certain defensive survivalism was imposed by the physical isolation of the college, which maintained little social contact with the surrounding rural population. A local reputation for, if not the reality of, rampant radicalism and bohemianism set off the college community by a culture gap steep as the overgrown ravine that skirted the Dorns' hillside lodge. Ed, whose way was to differ, was one of a very slim minority of Black Mountaineers with a rural background, unapologetically viewing "the dullness of all radicalism in the same old worn & boring light as, say, bohemianism." Still he and Helene thought of themselves along with their college colleagues as "working artists," joined in fellowship, if only a fellowship of common alienation and isolation. When one wandered off college grounds to the small towns and back roads of the Swannanoa Mountains one entered, as Helene felt, "another foreign country."

Black Mountain was a foreign country of its own. Outside lay the rural South—"a section that here at the college we are so set off from." Though it was in fact but five miles to the nearest town, at night the thickly wooded slopes of the place could get to feel "remote from everything in the blackness. And does it get black! The moon does not seem to have much of a chance thru the trees." Helene, in her first trip to the South, spent many long dark nights alone thanks to a largely nocturnal classroom schedule that involved Ed in repeated late sessions. Foremost in exacting such extensive time demands was Dorn's main mentor Olson. Olson's writing class, for which Dorn was working up his Moorcroft drifter notes into "C. B. & Q.," met one night a week. "It got started in the evening, maybe eight, nine o'clock, and would go on till it finished," Dorn would later recall.

"Sometimes that would be around midnight, sometimes one, two in the morning. And then sometimes the thing would keep going all night in a strange way, not necessarily with him but just because it started ... a lot of things did that at Black Mountain.... It was really a night place."

While Ed strove to keep up with Olson's nocturnal pedagogy, Helene, stranded in the woods with the kids, often fought to shake off "that same uneasy feeling" of difference. Her letters from those nights show another side of living at Black Mountain. To David Buck, who was paying Ed's $385 tuition, she made dutiful efforts to convey something of the atmosphere of the place. Describing Black Mountain, she said, was "not an easy task." The difficulty began with trying to describe "the land itself":

> It is like the dog chasing its tail.... I sometimes think I have caught it and then suddenly it is gone. The South is foreign land. Truly. It has been so many times described [as] the sleepy South—but it's true dammit! Its hills—mountains—sit as tho formed from a quiet graceful bubbling of the earth. They are so green and round and rolling. And the towns among them just seem to be resting. I cannot imagine them during the Civil War. I cannot imagine the South ever exciting itself enuff! The people are impossible after the first few days. I've been sug no no shiugahr'd enuff to last me a lifetime! There can be no mixing with the man on the street ... our northern blood is too thin and runs too fast. Like with the Indian, there is this line that can't be crossed ... tho with the Indian I feel a respect, with the Southerner I just want to laugh.

Ed, for his part, gave Buck occasional reports of progress in his studies. He touched on Olson's writing course and a tutorial study with Olson on Shakespeare "with papers on certain plays plus general supplementary reading of Elizabethans." At least one of the Shakespeare papers survives, a brisk, diagrammatic essay on *King Lear* done in an assertive propositional style reminiscent of Olson's;

with corrections in Olson's hand, the evidence of the paper demonstrates enough about the close labors of both teacher and student to confirm that David Buck's investment was not being wasted. That quarter Dorn also took a music tutorial with composer Stefan Wolpe, whose recordings ("a crazy new long play out on Esoteric") he recommended to Buck. He elected to study French. The college, however, no longer had a French teacher, so he and Helene took lessons from a fellow student who was "about to graduate in French."

In November 1954 the first severe cold spell of the season at Black Mountain had the whole Dorn brood along with the other remaining inhabitants "wrapped in blankets all day." The college faculty, weighing dwindled enrollment and recent fundraising failures against cold weather operating costs, moved to cancel the winter quarter. The Dorns considered prospects—and costs—of wintering in New York, then opted for "hibernation" at the college. It was not merely the economics of the thing, Helene indicated to Buck; Ed was "really in deep now" with Olson. After a long talk with Olson he had settled on a plan for shaping his studies toward graduation; the work would be concentrated on the American West, by common interest and mutual agreement of student and teacher.

The Dorn family's first Christmas together was spent in the beleaguered little mountain citadel. Ed and Helene stayed up all night on Christmas Eve, drinking wine. After a "lovely" family Christmas Day, the kids were put to bed "with aspirins but smiles," and on a Christmas night of "Bright moon and brisk air" above the pines, Ed and Helene climbed the hill to join Wes and Bea Huss for a "quiet last wine." While the Dorns were at the Huss's, painting teacher Joe Fiore and his wife Mary came around caroling.

Ed went on a road trip with friends to New York over New Year's. When he returned he found himself the sole actual student left on a skeleton campus. Faculty members still remained, they only because "nobody has enuff money to get out right now." On a windy January night "midst screaming children," Helene's New Year's letter to David Buck bravely reaffirmed the "working artist" ethos to which she and Ed were committed. Whatever its trials, they preferred their present rigorous life to the complacent nihilism of the urban bohemian crowd, "that lost crowd of pretenders."

5.

Life as If It's Just Started (Mexico)

DORN HAD LONGED TO SEE Mexico ever since hearing Olson talk about the archeological expeditions of Prescott at Black Mountain in 1951. At the end of January 1955 he and Helene decided to make the trip. They would find a place in Mexico, she would paint, he would work on a manuscript to present as his degree qualification. "This place was really getting me down and our life was going to pot," Helene told David Buck. Dead of winter at the hill-fort had brought longings for light and movement.

The voyage began with a frantic race to Asheville to secure a vehicle license before a state-office closing time. The travelers headed southwest through the mountains on U. S. 64. A hundred miles down the Blue Ridge the Morris developed valve trouble. At Murphy, North Carolina they made a garage stop, then drove "off from the main street—and [left] all the baby things smack in the middle of it." It was, Dorn told Olson in a note from their next stop, "about the cleanest mistake I've made so far."

A similarly harried stay at Ray and Lorna Obermayrs' place in Arkadelphia, with "5 children and 5 adults under one roof," provided amateur culture morphologist Dorn the opportunity for "rummaging in a couple of Caddo mounds" while waiting for the whole family to get vaccinations for traveling in Mexico. They also needed birth certificates to prove the citizenship of the children, but their application was held up because Ed had failed to enclose a dollar as prescribed. In the second week of February a "state of funk" induced him to move on anyway, toward the border.

In East Texas the shot valve in the Morris gave out completely and the sojourners got stuck in the big oil town of Houston over a weekend, awaiting repairs. "What an awful place—so modern and plastic-wrapped it's nauseating." Yet they'd never seen a sky so magnificent or experienced air so clear. "It is a shame those damn Texans had to wreck the place with their big everything new everything—bosh!" At Brownsville they discovered a local festival going on. Unable to get either birth certificates or beds, they forged on across the Rio Grande. The great river, Helene reported in her account of the expedition to David Buck, was "not grand but puny there—more like a creek."

They were held up in Matamoros awaiting the kids' birth certificates. The backward border town smacked of color, life, the vivid structure of reality—everything "plastic-wrapped" Houston lacked. "Matamoros is really Mexico—*very* different." After two days of waiting for the birth certificates it dawned on the Dorns they were apparently the only ones interested in such technicalities: "what a difference across the Rio Grande." They survived a two-hundred-mile stretch of "the worst road we've ever traveled—but oh so fine for the places it passed through" to reach the Pan American Highway junction at Cuidad Victoria, where they made a stop. On the town plaza a local photographer captured a pensive Fred and a doubtful Chan in serapes and sombreros on the saddle of a mockup cowboy pony. Dorn himself appears to have been regarding everything with the close eye of a student suddenly confronting the palpable incarnation of the object of his studies. His notes on the hotel where they spent the night—a hotel "which was also a kind of wicker chair factory"—led to a narrative poem of some sixty lines. The largest poem included in the "bundle" of his writings presented that summer for his Black Mountain graduation, this lost work was also perhaps his earliest trial-run at the border-country material that would one day ground the narrative of *Gunslinger.*

Continuing south on the Pan Am the Dorns found "fine Indian villages" dotting even the "heavily touristed route." In the market town on Tamazunchale, at the foot of the Sierra Madre, they attended a local Saturday morning market. "Market day & our first" appeared to Helene "a fantastic thing": "The Indians' colored clothes in the streets for about 3 blocks around their market buildings, which are mostly *large* open structures somewhat like our farmers' markets only five times more open and *stuffed* with people & their wares. Fred spent the morning helping one Indian put [out] his stuff on the cloth in the street. It happened to be flash lites, jack knives & the like. And they *use* flash lites."

Many of the villages through which they'd passed had no electricity; they'd several times had their gas tank filled by candle light. In one village they had eaten soup in a restaurant that had the only electricity within miles: they'd looked around in a ceramic shop "with the friendly old Spanish gal showing us her pots by oil lamp." Here were signs of those older, more authentic human patterns of life which Olson had found in Yucatán, and which the Dorns too had escaped America to seek. This first leg of their journey would remain the high point of the quest, as Dorn indicated to Gordon Taylor in a letter written a month later in the transcontinental trip's exhausted final stage:

> Central & Eastern M[exico], with the Indian, has more go, rhythm, guts, jingle, more *eye,* ah, the life is crazy there, seems as if it's just started.... I am sure the lighter the skin gets in Mexico, the more unalive, dead. The dead Castillano—the Indian is always alive—alert—interesting, the Mexican is always interesting, [but] the Castillano is nearly dead, the only pity being that he isn't, then they could get on with a very promising way of life.

With the ascent of the Sierra Madre the voyage posed its first serious challenges. "You ain't done *no* mountain driving," Helene declared after the fact to Buck, "till you done it from Tamazunchale to Mexico [City]." The endless switchbacks brought on acute carsickness, complicated by a gastrointestinal bug. "Poor Chan was so bad she lost lunch and dinner!!" Twenty-two-month-old Paul was "on fire with fever" by the time they reached Mexico City. A recommended hotel proved to be surprisingly expensive. The management, while friendly, couldn't comprehend the Dorns' instruction-manual Spanish. A doctor who was finally rounded up to examine the sick child prescribed, through an interpreter, a course of rest and daily injections. "Mexico City makes me sick literally," Dorn wrote to his Seattle poet friend Kenneth Hanson. "I got the 'touristas,' which is a highly advanced case of diarrhea. Fred has it too, so Chansonette; Helene escapes [but] Paul is in terrible shape."

After four days Paul's condition seemed improved enough to allow the journey to go on. Mexico City was too costly for the Dorns' already compromised budget; they pressed on westward over the mountains. By the time they crawled into Guadalajara "Paul was like dead" from diarrhea and dehydration, and had to spend a day and a night receiving intravenous feeding in a local children's clinic. After the three-day stop in Guadalajara the travelers had "to boil *everything* for him."

They set out again, headed northwest, back into the mountains, bound for the sea and Mazatlán. Both Helene and Ed wrote accounts of this part of the trip. Helene recorded a "stop at Acaponeta (a wonderful happy little poblado—music, loud music & laughing everywhere & hot as hell!!) ... had to take Fred to D[octor]—he too burning with fever—a huge shot fixed him and we continued." Dorn expanded on these details in an unpublished story, "A Romantic Old Sea-Port," about the latter stages of the "endless trip from Guadalajara down to the sea and Mazatlán." The tale is a subtle study in separation and distance, with two extensively developed scenes. The first is a "stop for lunch in a small poblado" where a raucous Mexican wedding is going on.

The boy had to be taken on the man's back down the main street to the doctor. The doctor was eating lunch with his family. He brought his napkin into his office and sat down with the standard pronouncements in fragment English. The ailment was altogether ordinary and the shot in the arm and the payment pure consequence. The doctor returned to his lunch and the boy and the man, this time holding hands, walked slowly down the street. The woman had kept the other two children and was ordering food in the outer patio of a restaurant not far from the car. The man was still holding the boy's arm and waiting for the line of one-way traffic to break and then they would run across to the restaurant. As they entered, a loud blast of guitars and brass instruments flushed through the patio and on into the emptiness of the inner garden. They sat down with the rest.

Dorn's carefully restrained narrative encloses his weary travelers in an exhausted silence intermittently broken by the noisy jubilation of the wedding. They linger in the café over cigarettes as the sun slowly descends over surrounding hills. While the couple is described only by their few words and gestures, the precisely composed or "placed" landscape backdrop draws our attention away from them, so that we seem to look off into the distance as they talk—toward those sharply focused "hills cut here and there by rocky ravines, in some places green with shrubs and trees, in clumps, or singly, placed with a sense of age."

The dim shades of yellow tiled floor formed that tranquility over which glided the preoccupied musicians coming in and out of the café, at intervals, to attend the marriage celebration. The cool blocks of white white stucco walls running out into the arches of the garden, peaceful and silent, were aloof, fading, untouched in the creeping, arousing city, in the fastidious glaring march and rising, smiling crescendos of the music in the inner room.

"My God," he said turning his glance in a slow arc from the garden, across the faces of the children, then taking in her whole figure in the chair opposite him, and then resting on the street, and the ultimate half-gaze of the total geography of the world behind her, through the door, My God, what does it take, for something to happen?

"How do you feel now?"

"About the same" she replied.

"I suppose when we get to Mazatlán things will be different," he went on. "At least that is the end of something. At least the end of the road, in a certain sense, even if it isn't that, for everyone."

"I am anxious to find out what the sea is like," she told him, putting out her cigarette, and then making an effort to go.

He ignored her impulse and continued as if leaving were a threat to the futility of going anywhere else....

The voyagers of Dorn's tale seem to have spent themselves completely simply in getting this far. "They were exhausted, tired of straining all their faculties on one given object." The tale's climactic scene occurs when it is learned that the highway bridge over the Rio del Presidio into Mazatlán is actually a road-map fiction, "in the last stages of construction but not yet open to traffic." With "the idiotic, half-finished bridge" looming off to one side as "a mocking possibility, a merciless baiting to the futility of their existence," Dorn's determined-driver hero reaches a critical point of decision. He elects to risk following in the muddy tracks of a line of other vehicles fording the river. Almost as soon as the car rolls into the water, he realizes he is helpless.

From the instant they entered the water they were in trouble. Driving very slowly, he strained to catch some hint as to where the shallowest path lay, and how far up on the cars ahead the water came. But with the illusion of the car going almost perceptibly downstream he gradually, with much hesitation, with the rhythm of a dream, got into deeper water.

His "anxiety" causes Dorn's distracted hero to attempt to drive "a trifle too fast," and he loses all control. As the travelers, stranded in the flood, drift slowly downstream, the car is surrounded by a gang of brazenly smiling, vaguely menacing "muchachos."

> "Oh," she said. "We are to give them some money." He took out his billfold ... one bill, 100 pesos. This is all I have, he said. She frowned, But our money may not be in Mazatlán, you know, it very possibly isn't; we can't give them our last money. We can't, he said, but that seems difficult to explain. The men were patiently extending their hands.... There was no hint of a way past these men. There were 15 or so, surrounding the car. Estudiantes, she began, no somos touristas, nosotros somos estudiantes.... There was no outward sign of recognition, and now those on the outer edge were straining to see what the delay was. In his uneasiness he read their unspoken replies, and to avoid the looks of the men at the sides of the car peered straight ahead into still other men arranged in front of the windshield. They continued to refuse to see the difference.

In cultural difference Dorn locates the ironic point of his tale. These travelers may define themselves as students not tourists, but they appear to the stubborn "muchachos" very much tourists nonetheless. The ineradicable signs of cultural identity emerge as fates.

By the time the Dorns finally reached Mazatlán Helene had a high fever. Ed spent hours getting a doctor. "We all thought I was dying of typhoid or malaria," Helene later told David Buck. "The D[octor] finally came, pronounced it food poisoning, and through his gum chewing English ordered a lurid group of pills & 4 shots—1 a day." Dorn prowled the waterfront, "once the collecting point for pirates and brigands." At the end of Helene's therapy they "left Mazatlán desperate ... our money gone for D[octo]rs and drugs." "Two more shots and a fortune in pills" were required in Tepic, "a clean city ... more Americano than pablum and ... full of that strange

Dupont sanitation." Ed wrote Gordon Taylor that Helene's intestinal infection was "pretty bad" and would terminate the trip "before we expected." Fleeing north, the Dorns reached the border at Nuevo Laredo with $5 to their names, $3 of which they immediately spent on a room and food for the kids. The family had been living on one meal a day since Mexico City. At Nuevo Laredo Buck's support check was late; "frantic," they managed to persuade the hotel manager to extend their credit. Finally Helene put in a collect call to her mother in Minnesota, who wired fifty dollars. They drove straight through to Black Mountain with only a single stop in New Orleans. Back at the college after 36 hours behind the wheel, Ed gave in to the tenacious "touristas" and was forced to bed with a fever. Along with the two younger children, he had to be treated for the lingering effects of the Mexican illness by a North Carolina doctor armed with "some new wonder drug."

Dorn would evoke the last days of the precarious 1955 adventure in the 1966 poem written in England, "An Idle Visitation." The lines there spoken by a visionary gun-toting stranger who arrives (like Dorn himself at Black Mountain in March 1955) worn out after a harrowing trip across "the enormous space / between here and formerly" (a desert, or a life) would recur not long afterward in the opening of the heroic western romance of the first book of *Gunslinger.*

> Then you will no doubt know where we can have
> a cold drink before sunset and then a bed
> will be my desire if you can find one
> for me, I have no wish to continue
> my debate with men,
> my mare lathers with tedium
> her hooves are dry
> Look they are covered with the alkali
> of the enormous space

(Photo courtesy of Nonna Abercrombie Lytle)

Dorn's maternal grandmother, Bessie Ponton, with Ed, seven,
David Abercrombie, two, and cousin Bill Ponton, Summer 1936.

(Photo courtesy of Nonna Abercrombie Lytle)

Ed with stepfather Glen Abercrombie, Windsor, Illinois, circa 1945.

Dorn as underclassman,
Villa Grove High School.

(Photo courtesy of Nonna Abercrombie Lytle)

(Photo courtesy of Nonna Abercrombie Lytle)

Graduation photo, Villa Grove High School, 1947.

Phyllis Sprinkle, 1948.

*"her eyes were
as dark as agates /
in 1948 ..."*

(Photo courtesy of Jennifer Dunbar Dorn)

(Photo from the 1947 *Vade Mecum*, courtesy of Jennifer Dunbar Dorn)

Villa Grove High School Dramatic Club: Gordon Taylor, front row, fifth from left; Phyllis Sprinkle, fourth row, second from left; Ed Dorn, last row, third from left.

(Photo courtesy of Fred Buck)

David Buck with son Fred, Seattle, 1949.

"We could never have done the things we did without David Buck's friendship and support."

(Photo courtesy of Fred Buck)

With Bill Tindall ("Bill Elephant"), Seattle, 1952.

"he's really a utopian ... and a totemist."

(Photo courtesy of Fred Buck)

Seattle,
Summer
1954.

(Photo courtesy of Fred Buck)

Seattle,
1954.

(Photo by Paul Leser, courtesy of Jennifer Dunbar Dorn)

With fellow students Joan Heller and Dan Rice, Black Mountain College, 1951.

"I felt very country in the face of that kind of city expression and sophistication."

(Photos courtesy of Fred Buck)

With son Paul at Black Mountain,
Fall 1954.

*"I would just as leaf take an aspirin
as a degree."*

Helene Helmers Dorn, with son Paul,
Black Mountain, 1954.

*"An unusual woman whom I ... immediately fell in
love with, with the slender reed grace of her."*

(Photo courtesy of Jennifer Dunbar Dorn)

With Charles Olson, Black Mountain, 1955.

"The way I heard him was with a bit of strain when my powers of comprehension weren't up to it."

(Photo courtesy of Fred Buck)

Stepson Fred Buck in Ciudad Victoria, Mexico, Spring 1955.

"life is crazy there, seems as if it's just started."

(Photo courtesy of Fred Buck)

Dorn residence at Lake Mattoon, Illinois, Winter 1955–1956.

"Our 4 room delightfully mad, storybook cottage ... "

(Photo courtesy of Fred Buck)

500 Anacortes Street, Burlington, Washington: the Dorns' residence, 1956–1959.

"Red house. Green tree in mist ... "

(Photo courtesy of Fred Buck)

Ed's mother, Louise Abercrombie, on a visit to Burlington, February 1957.

"my mother / never knew about the world ... "

(Photo courtesy of Fred Buck)

With step-daughter Chansonette and son Paul, Burlington, July 1957.

"That tall grass. / Toggenburg goat stood in, looking, chewing. / Time was its cud."

(Photos courtesy of Fred Buck)

Ed (above) Helene (below)
in the "secret garden," 500 Anacortes
Street, August 1957.

*"Rising above the secret garden
(that's what they named it)
was a sheer wall of black rock 75 ft.
high. It was a very secret enclosure."*

(Photo courtesy of Fred Buck)

With Fred, Chansonette, Paul, a neighborhood friend,
and Laddie the collie, in the "secret garden," 1957.

Fred and Ed, Burlington, 1957.

"a 'cocked eye'"

(Photo courtesy of Fred Buck)

(Photo courtesy Fred Buck)

Burlington, 1958.

"Hasten to your own kind, to your own dream, to your own land / Hurry while there is still someone to go with you ... "

(Photo courtesy of Fred Buck)

Burlington, 1958.

"my wife is lovely / my children are fair ... "

(Courtesy of Helene Dorn)

Helene's portrait of Ed, 1959.

(Photo by Fred Buck)

Ed and Helene Dorn, Santa Fe, 1959.

"my desire is to be / a classical poet / my gods have been men ... / and women."

(Photo courtesy of Fred Buck)

Helene and "gunslinger" Paul,
Santa Fe, 1959.

(Photo courtesy of Fred Buck)

Acequia Madre, Santa Fe, 1959.

(Photo courtesy of Fred Buck)

Acequia Madre, Santa Fe, 1959.

(Photo courtesy of Fred Buck)

With Robert Creeley, Gael Turnbull and Paul, Lawrence Ranch, Taos, July 1960.

(Photo courtesy of Fred Buck)

Ed's father, William Dorn, Indianapolis, 1960.

"Thirty years, and I don't even know what he looks like."

(Photo courtesy of Fred Buck)

Ed at Camino Sin Nombre, Santa Fe, Fall 1960.

(Photo courtesy of Fred Buck)

Helene at Camino Sin Nombre, Santa Fe, Fall 1960.

(Photos courtesy of Lucia Berlin)

Lucia Berlin, New York City, February 1961.

"Then I turned and I saw Beauty."

In New York for publication party / reading for *The Newly Fallen*, February 1961.

" ... the only time you scream is when you get your head caught in a subway train door ... which I did. Although I didn't scream, not wanting to appear a hick."

(Photo courtesy of Fred Buck)

Camino Sin Nombre, Summer 1961: Ed in white linen jacket hand-sewn for him by Helene.

(Photo courtesy of Fred Buck)

With Paul, Camino Sin Nombre, 1961.

"Here ... the air stays bright all winter ... "

(Photo by Gordon Clark, courtesy of Jennifer Dunbar Dorn)

Robert Creeley at Camino Sin Nombre, Santa Fe, September 1961.

"I hated to see them go ... "

(Photo courtesy of Fred Buck)

Obermayr ranch, Pocatello, Idaho.

"Are we needed? On this mountain ... "

(Photo courtesy of Lucia Berlin)

At Obermayr ranch, May 1962.

"Few people / are as lost as I am ... "

(Photo courtesy of Fred Buck)

Pocatello, 1962.

"Reflecting today, and laughing at myself in this exile ... "

(Photo courtesy of Fred Buck)

Helene in the Dorns' home,
Obermayr ranch, Spring 1962.

*"How you loved me / through all
travesty / how you kept those
lovely eyes / clear ... "*

(Photo courtesy of Fred Buck)

Pocatello, early 1963.

*"I'll miss this time, sometime, /
these old cold mountains / these
cold blue hills ... "*

(Photo courtesy of Jennifer Dunbar Dorn)

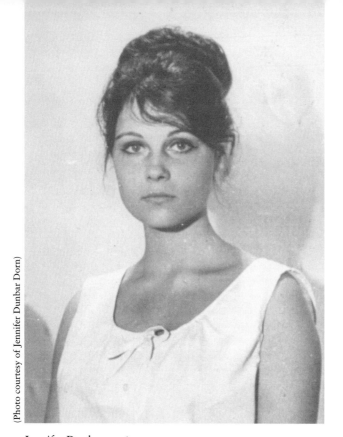

Jennifer Dunbar, 1964.

"Jenny ... is lovely, like a fine day."

(Photo courtesy of Jennifer Dunbar Dorn)

Jenny, Maya, Ed, and Kidd Dorn, Vancouver, 1971.

(Photo by Ellen Mann, courtesy of Jennifer Dunbar Dorn)

North Beach, San Francisco, 1978.

(Photo from author's collection)

Poetry reading, early 1970s.

(Photo from author's collection)

Ed Dorn and Tom Clark, Boulder, Colorado, Winter 1979.

(Photo by Georgia Donovan, courtesy of Jennifer Dunbar Dorn)

Jenny, Maya, Kidd, and Ed Dorn, with Brad Donovan
and Richard Brautigan, Paradise Valley, Montana, 1982.

(Photo courtesy of Jennifer Dunbar Dorn)

With Nonna Abercrombie Lytle and David Abercrombie, Illinois, 1983.

(Photo by John Rudiak, courtesy of Liz Hiebner)

At the Taos Poetry Circus, June 1997.

"Reading useful to sort out where to go ... "

(Photo from author's collection)

Denver, Summer 1997.

(Photo from author's collection)

The Dorns with Desmond Tutu, Denver, 1998.
"Tutu, model & corpse" (Ed's inscription)

(Photo by Jennifer Dunbar Dorn)

At Keats's grave, the Protestant Cemetery, Rome.

(Photo by Jennifer Dunbar Dorn)

On the Spanish Steps, Rome, December 1998.

(Photo by Jennifer Dunbar Dorn)

Below the window of the room where John Keats died.

"I took some pretty good notes at the Spanish Steps and the Keats house. Keats's room is very haunting ... "

(Photos by Jennifer Dunbar Dorn)

"Garden of Knowledge," Green Mountain Cemetery, Boulder, Colorado.

"Some distant starre flashes even him / an indiscriminate salute."

between here and formerly.
Need I repeat, we have come
without sleep from Nuevo Laredo....

6.

Finding Out for Oneself
(Black Mountain)

"**B**LACK MOUNTAIN HAS THE RIGHT FEELING for me again and we come back quite different people," Helene Dorn declared to David Buck a week after the family's bedraggled early-March return from the border. "The college hasn't folded yet. Things don't look good; but there will be a Spring quarter & Ed will finish with Charles no matter." What Dorn had underway with Olson was a private tutorial mapped out before the Mexican trip intended to "organize [his] studies of the West."

This was the field of interest that would provide Dorn's "laboratory," as he would tell me in a prefatory interview for his essay collection *Views* (1980), "the subject I'm most interested in." He'd been traveling the West since 1947 and reading about it more and more intensively as his association with Olson grew; by 1955 he already possessed a view of New World history that went back to Prescott and Cabeza de Vaca. His reading inspired him because it reflected an intuition as old as his prairie longings for distant horizons. "The thing to do is to look West," he had told Gordon Taylor in a reflective pause during his nomadic travels of late 1952.

Olson's remarkable tutorial reading list, a provocative statement on historical methodology (as well as a classic specimen of the master's slash-and-burn scholarship at its most decisive and opinionated), later to be published as *A Bibliography on America for Ed Dorn,* had been hand-delivered in installments to the Dorns' lodge late on two January nights when everybody in the family was asleep, so that—as the student recipient of this prodigious piece of pedagogical largesse would later put it—"it came to me for breakfast." The tutorial now began to involve Dorn in long, late talks, the matter of which ranged from "how to read the land" to "how to live, by Charles Olson." At 1:30 on a March morning, Helene, lodgebound with two children still suffering the lingering *touristas,* lamented "that goddamn poet" was still "up chatting with Charles" an hour past his "wonder-drug-taking time" ("Men are bad enuff, but poets stink!"). Dorn was being advised by Olson, a "generous and enthusiastic" guide, to follow the model of history set down by Herodotus—"*istorin,* to find out for oneself"; to absorb himself intensely and entirely in his subject, "*to dig one thing*" in a "saturation job" that might require a "lifetime of assiduity." Carl Sauer was an example here: "to *dig one thing or place or man*" until the subject was exhausted, as Sauer had done with his early studies of the land and culture of the prairie, was to be "in forever."

If the personal meanings of Dorn's interest in the West went far back, as suggested, studying with Olson was the challenge that released them into action. "My curiosity, the questing after what will identify the West in some big conceptual sense," he would acknowledge, "certainly comes from there. I was ready for it ... if you grew up on the plains, you're already on a geography. I mean it's such an overwhelming geographic term. The social basis of the central Illinois farmer is extremely thin and it's also characterized by a kind of skepticism—a social skepticism. You know farmers tend to be skeptical about both weather and people.... On the prairie there's a certain evasion—a linguistic evasion—of words as such." Looking at the land with an eye trained by an Olson or a Sauer, Dorn learned to see its crucial role in determining cultural and individual fates; how, say, in Olson's paraphrase of Sauer, a "prairie village called Chicago is still, despite itself, a prairie village."

In the months leading up to his end-of-summer graduation exams, with Olson now "in charge of [his] reading," Dorn applied himself to his studies with a singular concentration. Compelled by his master's grand bibliographic challenge, he forsook the modest college library ("a wartime barracks building, and in substance no more than a shelter") for the venerable Sondley Library in the market square of Asheville—once "the home library of Thomas Wolfe," who was locally reputed to have "read the whole thing," and the "first fine collection" Dorn had ever seen. On expeditions to the Sondley he began working his way through his tutor's daunting list of recommended readings, starting, as Olson had prescribed, with "Carl O. Sauer, from 'Environment & Culture in the Deglaciation' all the way through 'Road to Cibola' back to his first job, for the State of Illinois handbook (1915?) on the new State Park at Starved Rock." For Dorn the Sauer highlight was "The Morphology of Landscape," that key text on the areal method of culture-reading. There were other inspirations as well among Olson's recommended readings on the West. Dorn would eventually draw from items in the *Bibliography on America* a number of important poems, including two 1959 pieces provoked by Katherine Coman's *Economic Beginnings of the Far West*: "Death While Journeying" and "Ledyard: The Exhaustion of Pure Distance."

From his newly-organized studies of the West Dorn moved on— and back—in a second tutorial with Olson. It was devised in part as a replacement for a summer-quarter degree-requisite class: Dorn felt he could no longer gain much from classrooms, and told Olson "I want to leave your spring classes [on Shakespeare and the Elizabethans] just what they meant to me, not an overload on my illiteracy, but a confusion for me to untangle, which I like." The project was designed to explore the back-story of Westward Expansion in the culture and thought of those first "western" voyagers, the Greeks. The tutorial discoveries, again, would reverberate in Dorn's own narrations. Beginning with his final shaping-up of "C. B. & Q.," a "Greek" pattern would appear in renditions of his own migratory odysseys,

as well as in his accounts of those of fellow writers—like novelist
Douglas Woolf, in whose Western road plots Dorn would make out
a Homeric "geometry" ("The American West is the place men of
our local civilization travel into in wide arcs to reconstruct the pres-
ent version of the Greek experience"). With Olson again at the bib-
liographic helm, the young intellectual explorer roamed out on the
find-out-for-yourself trail of the Greeks as far as "Nietzsche's work
on the pre-Socratics" ("one of the books that had a great influence
on me ... one of the great books that I know of"), by way of the
several volumes of ethical, literary and historical dialogues in
Plutarch's *Moralia* and Athenaeus' compendious anthology of man-
ners and customs, the *Deipnosophists* (in which his demanding
teacher had instructed him to at least browse, so as "to survey 'a
vast discrimination'"). Olson also suggested he learn classical Greek
(a case of "do as I say, not as I've done"). Autodidact Dorn obedi-
ently applied himself, obtaining a classical grammar and struggling
through several chapters before giving in to a stubborn impatience
with the sheer scholasticism of it all ("the verb is a bitch").

7.

Testing and Self-Testing
(Black Mountain)

APPROACHING THE ACQUISITION of a college degree at the advanced age of twenty-six, Dorn addressed the occasion with all due—if not overdue, or even undue—seriousness. Also with a certain general sense of anxiety. Attacks of scruple over his "illiteracy" were an unavoidable side effect of having a teacher whose learning was so intimidatingly extensive. In a letter to Olson about his graduation preparations the pressure Dorn was placing on himself shows up as a nervous assertiveness that shades into expressions of acute self-doubt. He assumes a pose of disdain for the very object of his pursuit: "I would just as leaf take an aspirin as a degree." In his next breath honesty makes him contradict himself: "I want it badly." He reproaches himself for his "lazyness" and "insufficiencies," laments his intellectual scatteredness and the "vague, half-thought, self-conscious" disorder of his mind, admits his "tangled" confusions of scholarship; yet a moment later announces he has his sails set on a postgraduate fellowship at Harvard ("to fit their lie to mine"). He acknowledges his "peculiarity" of acting-out a compulsive resistance to authority: "imposition is not what I grow under." On the other hand he acknowledges the conflicting factor of his practical desperation: "Sooner or later have to have a Jahb, 3 kids etc." Concluding this semi-formal request for a meeting with Olson to discuss his graduation plans, Dorn made his need clear with a handwritten plea inscribed in bold two-inch characters:

Help!

Olson however was now largely preoccupied; in the teacher's life, suddenly, there were "particular pressures driving," as Dorn put the matter delicately in one letter. Olson's private pressures had to do with marital difficulties (he'd become the father of an illegitimate child by one of his students, Betty Kaiser) that were causing him to become increasingly withdrawn and inaccessible. He conducted communication with his charges, including Dorn, by brief notes. The late-night talks ceased. In the final stages of his degree preparation Dorn was, perhaps appropriately, thrown back upon the rituals of his own relentless self-testing.

He was attending to the issue of his graduation a good deal more particularly than anyone else at the college. By August, he was growing impatient. He determined himself ready for immediate graduation. It was his responsibility and prerogative to decide on the proper moment, he declared in a letter to Olson and the Black Mountain faculty. He spelled out the conditions under which he intended to take his degree—the most rigorous and "formal." He wanted no "coziness," no "familiarity," no "lazy solution." He sought to obtain not simply qualification but validation, an acknowledgement that would help him to keep his distances intact, to "stay discrete." "I am a lump, I am a lump of shit, I have nothing to show that I'm not, I have [only] a little to show where I've been." He was aware, he said, that without a degree he would remain "in danger of finding myself in G[rand] C[entral] Station [without] a ticket." Still he insisted that the sign of acceptance not be a hollow one: "What I want isn't a ticket so much as to stand outside the gate and have somebody say one time he believes I am going somewhere, but not [tell me he knows] where, I will be damned if *anyone* knows that." It was up to Black Mountain to decide whether he would receive a degree; what he was demanding as his right was the degree of difficulty.

The first part of the graduation exam would be oral, conducted by any remaining members of the faculty who could be rounded up, with Olson presiding. There was also a requirement of written material. As the outside examiner to inspect his submitted manuscripts Dorn chose poet, short-story writer and *Black Mountain Review* editor Robert Creeley, who had arrived at the college that July. He had admired Creeley's poetry since coming across the chapbook *Le Fou* in City Lights Books store in September 1953. As Olson's elected right-hand-man, the newcomer appeared a natural choice. Creeley "alone [is] trustworthy," Dorn suggested in making his request. The ground of the connection would be provided "not [by] any sympathy coming from my own writing to him, but from my own reading of his nature, of his writing."

Creeley, like Olson, was a Massachusetts native with Harvard among his prestigious disaffections. Dorn, who'd so far dropped out of nowhere better than the U. of Illinois, was facing an inverted form of the old class disadvantage, aggravated by an incident that had marred his relations with Creeley in their the first meeting. As Creeley recalls the episode: "Ed and I had at the beginning—an evening party outside just after I'd driven in—got off on the proverbial wrong foot, just that I met Helene first and thought she was great, so was hanging around her while Ed kept his distance and surmised my state of interest in his wife, who I did not yet know was his wife. Emotionally, like they say, that took a long time to straighten out." Dorn, suggests Creeley, wore his edges very openly in those days, and "wasn't that comfortable with the bulk of people." "[He was] 'up against it' characteristically—at that time at least his wariness and displacement were characteristic. I recall thinking of him as 'Malvolio' in Jonson's *The Malcontent*—he favored, if that's the right word—the outside track."

Notified in August 1955 of his assignment to "test" Dorn, Creeley wrote to Robert Duncan in San Francisco about it:

I'm also to be an examiner it seems.... I begin with ms/ of poems, among same: "To Robert Creeley, a plea to his put out eye..." "... When your fury / is a hymn what is my simple fury? / Like sitting? On what? Is this like / dreading? Your single eye on me..." It seems I disturb this young man, etc. Actually the poor devil (Ed Dorn) is eaten badly with guilt, and pride—and the situation of having married a very lovely and decent (so it seems) woman, with two kids by a former marriage, and now another by their own—and no money, etc., etc. Anyhow that will keep me occupied god knows. And he's no fool, and the line is sometimes tight enough, not this quick tale of the self-disgust, etc. When one of these men breaks through it is a pleasure, and a help at the moment—yet I have no wish to get involved with this thing too completely. Anyhow it's a Real Problem—like they say.

"I would guess the feeling I have here in writing Duncan," Creeley comments in looking back on the letter, "is part of the same business—I am wary of [Dorn's] wanting to 'qualify' all from his side, which he certainly did and could—he was testing the 'testers' very intently. My 'fury' was at loss of a family (and eye), so Ed as I read him is asking, ironically, 'Can I have some chance for some "anger" too, Bob?'"

"I have a long and consistent record of flunked 'tests,'" Dorn wrote Olson shortly before the graduation exam. The oral exam took place in late August at the college, with Olson and Creeley representing the faculty. "I remember Ed coming back tired," Helene Dorn recalls, "and saying it was really just a talk session." Clearly, after all the self-demanding buildup, the reality of the exam had proved deflating.

"I was just enough older than Ed for that to be a problem," Creeley says. "And now he's graduating. He wanted a validation. He wanted at that point to weigh in with us, with Charles and me. But the exam was far less *testing* than Ed would have wanted. It had more the sense of a welcome—not so much being welcomed into a club, as simply, 'Ed, we don't intend to *test* you.' How would *I* expect to test *Ed* in the particularity of his information? And Charles likewise certainly wasn't interested. But Ed seemingly wanted to be *quizzed* in some particular way that would equate with his intention and his preparation and his need. He wanted to be made equal with us, i.e., wanted more out of the occasion than it could possibly provide."

Creeley also evaluated Dorn's writings. Dorn later claimed Creeley had given him a letter recommending graduation "with reservations." The letter, including Creeley's critical reservations, was for some time preserved by Dorn as his only paper evidence that he held a degree. This somewhat unusual "certificate," Dorn recalled, was "crazy actually"; Creeley had volunteered "long range speculations about me as a writer." Had those speculations proved accurate? Dorn was asked. He hedged: they were "perfectly fair and justified in the circumstance of that function."

8.

Outlandish Introductions (Black Mountain)

D ORN HAD BEGUN TO QUESTION the practical value of the Black Mountain degree even before he'd received it: such a credential, he suggested in a late June letter to David Buck, would "distinguish" him by its uselessness, "since no one recognizes this degree"; to qualify for teaching work he'd have to parlay it at least into an M. A. He proposed graduate school as a kind of transitional enterprise which would enable him to take over as his family's provider. "I must do graduate work, because I just wouldn't make it, once I assume responsibility for this outfit, in a high school." (High-school teaching, he explained, "would only be tolerable to me if I taught Greek.") Buck had offered to help out with costs at any graduate school Dorn chose. Weighing himself self-critically—like Morton Draker—against the quality of competition, the ambitious young man had made up his mind he should no longer accept second place. "I somehow want to get to Harvard, to which I am sending outlandish letters of introduction," he told Buck, "to somehow get myself a fellowship, which they undoubtedly won't hear of but I wouldn't feel right if I didn't try."

The hopefulness of "somehow" was of course a key to the young writer's singular aspirations. The Harvard project represented a pure long shot, in which he had the backing of Olson alone. It was generally known at Black Mountain that Olson had once been "a minor big man at H[arvard]"; less well known that he had departed that institution under a cloud, a stress-induced nervous breakdown having terminated his Ph.D. candidacy in 1939. Olson's actual current influence at Harvard was little less tenuous than Black Mountain's academic standing. Not that academics could be presented as Dorn's long suit in any case: "They will have to take me, ultimately, as a writer," he understood, "which they will be delighted to do, if I am uneeeeque enough." Still he had no illusions about long-term security within academia for his kind of singularity: "on the other side of it, if I am unique enough, they, on the other hand, can't tolerate me either, so I will end up a 'migrant' which will suit me fine." Here Dorn was seeing into his own nature—and his employment future—with uncanny accuracy. ("It never occurred to me," he would tell me twenty-five years later, "that I couldn't sell my mind to keep going in order to write.")

By July he had sent off self-introductory letters, sample manuscripts, and requests for fall semester fellowship money to Harvard graduate school and to his backup choice, the Writer's Workshop of the University of Iowa. Target of his first "outlandish" introduction-letter was one of Olson's former American Studies professors at Harvard, Kenneth O. Murdock, who was presently chairing the university's General Education Committee. Murdock wrote back promptly, "very favorably, most encouragingly, as well as indefinitely." Dorn was to await further word. Odds remained steep, but the courteous reply confirmed that Harvard, with its "more certain civilization," was where he belonged. "Whatever they have of the imbecility of other institooshuns, they are still the place that doesn't castrate one for the sin of talent," he reported to Buck. "I inquired of this to Murdock and he said, no, they absolutely do not."

Discussions with Black Mountain drama teacher Robert Hellman, a veteran of the Writer's Workshop, induced Dorn to put in for money at Iowa as a fallback. Notifying his patron Buck, he cited three reasons: the Workshop was "enjoying a season of great prestige in the field right now" ("significant if I had difficulty getting a job"); at Iowa, unlike other programs, "one offers 'creative' work for one's thesis"; the school's out-of-the-way location would afford "a singularly decent chance to save money by living on hominy." When his letter of overture to Workshop director Paul Engle went unanswered for a month, however, Dorn began to have misgivings. Engle, who'd been teaching at Harvard for the summer, finally wrote back, apologizing for the delay and offering a mixed response to Dorn's "Pound-like poems"—"not wholly to my taste," but "interesting, often more than that." Overall, Engle's response was positive: "Iowa would be a congenial place for you," he assured Dorn. The Workshop director proposed admission with a fee-remission waiver, and made a conditional offer of fellowship money, contingent on availability. A wary Dorn was left to ponder the variables, surmising the director to be "no more or less reliable as to his word than any others, that is, culture mongering poets who have become pimps for universities."

Dorn spent the remainder of the summer wavering in his mind between "one place vague but more desired" (Harvard) and "the other more concrete but so so" (Iowa). The outside chance of a Harvard fellowship kept preying at his mind ("things could jell") but by mid-August there was still no further word from Murdock. The end of Black Mountain's summer term (September 5) and the opening of Iowa's fall semester (two weeks after that) were now bearing down. "There is a sharp edge of about a week here," an anxious Dorn told Buck. "This still hangs."

Finally word came from Harvard: he would be admitted to the graduate school, but would not be eligible for a first-year teaching fellowship. The defeat of the fellowship plan stung Dorn's pride sufficiently to cause him to react angrily against Harvard in specific and academics in general: "Horseshit! You can't trust the whole bloody lot of 'em anyway." There was "no reason why" he shouldn't have been given a teaching position. "It galls me, that Murdock & Harvard don't make an exception on the basis of my work and give it a chance. So much it galls me I couldn't morally 'pay' Harvard $700 for the privilege of waiting a year to give them my talent, let alone ask you. So I think I must go to Iowa. It is a question of certain personal demand (in a sense 'moral') on my part that I have this responsibility. Christ I can remember at the U. of I[llinois] I would have to beg, borrow and usually steal $40 for a semester of that hogwash. Anyway [I] can't stand it. Makes me sick. And the superior encouragement of Iowa pulls me that way."

The Dorns resolved to drive to Mattoon, leave the children with the Abercrombies, go on to Iowa to find housing, then double back to retrieve the kids. "The upshot is this," Dorn notified Buck: "we will, to get our brood there intact, need extra money this month.... I mean, it would give us a psychological strength, like they say, to plan with the money in hand and pay on the spot, old chap, for our going away." Buck, who as Dorn acknowledged now had "a secondary fate in what I do at this point," complied.

9.

Star-Crossed
(Iowa City)

ORN'S ATTEMPT TO BEGIN a graduate-school career back in the "corn-west"—as he'd once termed the prairie in a letter to Gordon Taylor—appeared star-crossed from the outset. The day before the family's September 1955 departure from Black Mountain, Helene, given to noticing omens, was crossing the footbridge outside their lodge when a "great black branch" fell and crashed into the ravine below. At getaway hour the dark sign was fulfilled. "As we were leaving our just closed up house preparatory to climbing in the car and saying the last goodbyes," Ed later told David Buck, "Master Fred the incredible incredulator runs onto the bridge and slips through the railing to the rocky stream 20–25 feet below where he sits screaming with a bump on his head that looks, like Mike Hammer would say, a ticket to a concussion." Like a resilient hero in a Mickey Spillane potboiler, the indomitable Fred survived, but only after a frantic rush to the local doctor (who reported the precocious seven-year-old second-grader "shocked but not stopped"). Shy of injections after Mexico, the stoic youth "lied about pain in certain joints fearing a shot was in order"; they were allowed to travel, and made a brief return to the college to regroup. A small get-together with sentimental farewells and ham sandwiches was put on by Bea Huss, and then the Dorns, approximately after the manner of Ezra Pound's Greeks, "took Chan's cat, kitten really, down to the car, dried our eyes as best we could and set forth on the godly highway."

The first coffee stop came seventy-five miles into the voyage. Dorn had become accustomed to shepherding the group through such intervals in the family treks: "when we stop for coffee it's like a Melanesian trading party." This time there was an unlucky variation. As the little nomadic band was "piling back into the car ... the cat slipped out and under a Greyhound bus on to the highway. H[elene] got out and went around to look and the wretched thing had been smashed like that by a car. Well, it was a dear cat, dear to the kids and it seemed like too much."

The jinxed trip continued, with Helene now at the wheel. Along the road another "great black branch fell ... 'for no reason whatever.'" The corn-west seemed to be spooked. They reached Mattoon, deposited the kids with the Abercrombies, and drove on to Iowa. In an Iowa City coffee shop they pored over the classified section of the local paper and found only one listing for an apartment of suitable size, and that at $90, twice what they were able to pay; so much for the idea of living cheap "on hominy" in corn country. A further detail in the listing stipulated—as Dorn noted in mock amazement—"no children, whatever that means, I can't imagine." A graduate-student contact from the Writer's Workshop ("the supposed friend of a dear friend") showed up at the coffee shop to greet them. When the contact first nonchalantly suggested they solve their housing problem by taking the listed apartment "and do[ing] something else with the children," then later had "the gall to suggest we 'buy a trailer, lots do it,'" Dorn knew he had come to the wrong place. As if to underline the realization, while they sat in the coffee shop yet another omen startled Helene: "a huge black wolf spider ran out from under the booth and bit her."

In one of his most decisive impulsive exits, the wary wayfarer fled Iowa City and was back on the corn-west highway "within the hour": admitting the whole trip had been a major "blunder," he later professed not to know how he'd managed even that extended a stay. "It took us a full half hour to realize we'd been there too long. What took us so long? Can't say. Probably I wanted to make it work. Get something over with, find a place, get some rest, etc. But in five minutes any alert human being could see by the look, the people on the street, and the people who were recommended [to us], that Iowa City is absolutely nowhere and not a place I could learn anything I don't already know with ease."

They headed north toward St. Paul, improvising a new plan—a visit to Helene's parents. For forty miles the relieved pioneers consoled themselves over the Iowa City debacle by agreeing they'd at least avoided the even worse mistake of lingering. "It was so *wrong* and we were so *elated* at having recognized for perhaps the first time in our joint lives how accurate we were in our appraisal." Then the ill fates of the trip reclaimed control, a tail-light blew on the Morris, "chilled our mood, and eventually turned us, back, toward the reality of Mattoon."

IO.

Stranded in
the Antenna Forest
(Mattoon)

IT WAS MID-SEPTEMBER when the Dorns repaired to the Abercrombies', forced back on the somewhat strained hospitality of the in-laws for the rest of the month. A chastened Ed was put in the unenviable position of having to explain to David Buck why the following month's support check should be sent on to Illinois, not to Iowa as planned. He asked Buck (who was now back in graduate school himself, in a Ph.D. program in Education at Stanford) to "'spot' a new 'graduate' at least one blunder," self-consciously (and class-consciously) explaining that "spot" was "a billiard term I don't know the equivalent of but [it's] like the French you know, so left untranslated." Then he came to the bitter, ten-cent point: "You know, give me Iowa, forget it. I should have known and didn't. I promise to be good."

He'd learned by his mistake, he told Buck. He had not lost his drive to make something of his mind, he'd only got the location wrong on his first try. "If I go on to school, it *has* to be Harvard, where I will at least have some peers. Because I want, after all, going to school to be of 'value' and not just a dry pursuit of a higher degree." He would shoot for temporary work as a laborer in Mattoon, while researching jobs as a school teacher back East, meanwhile preparing for an entry to Harvard as early as the spring semester ("if I can make it money-wise"). Still the admission that he was in retreat after a demoralizing rout remained implicit in his earnest attempts to assure Buck he would be getting the brood "out of this situation as soon as possible."

"This situation" meant a cramped sharing of four small rooms among eight people by the canal in Mattoon. "There is no hostility at my home," Dorn reported with the tact of a dutiful son, "but there is no easy ease." He found work driving a laundry truck around the south end of Mattoon. The job entailed long hours, beginning before dawn, of driving and slinging laundry sacks. Armed with his first paycheck he and Helene started looking for a house of their own to rent. Once he'd given his mother $10 of the check for food, however, the money they were left with could qualify them for a deposit on nothing better than a shack. After inspecting a two-room hovel that lacked stove, sink or toilet, had a fallen-down outhouse, a pump a half-block away, and a view across an alley upon a warehouse and a junkyard, Helene put her foot down. "Well, hell, we've been through a lot, but the kids have never been put into anything that horrible.... I *refused* to let a goddamn booming factory town do it to us." They stayed another week at the Abercrombies' instead.

At the start of October there were signs the initial "rough" period in Mattoon might soon be easing. With Buck's monthly check in hand, the Dorns found a seeming haven—or "heaven," as Helene called it—in a little four-room house, located six miles out of town on Lake Mattoon. The place was vacant of furnishings and had no electricity, but with a couple of cats borrowed from the Abercrombies for housewarming purposes and their sleeping "sacks," the Dorns moved in right away. The lake was a relatively secluded spot; there were woods where Ed and Fred could go hiking and "camping," frontier-style, and fish could be caught along the shores. Helene, still having trouble adjusting to small-town attitudes, was happy to be getting at least this far out of Mattoon; she was still bristling over the way Illinoisans appeared to regard them as destitute or reprobate, "underprivileged or irresponsible." People smugly assumed that they were "doing without," but just the opposite was true. "When we sit here, in the middle of a 'boom' rich small town, with a damn beautiful kerosene lamp because we can't & won't pay $12.50 down to the elec[tric] co[mpany] for lights ... we're not 'doing without,' we're doing!"

By mid-October the modest paradise by the lake seemed in danger of slipping away. The expense of making the house livable ate into their slender budget, and then a day's absence brought on by the strain of toting heavy laundry sacks cost Dorn his job—a devastating blow to the fragile family economy. "The bind came when this usurious, plastic-alloy-hearted bloodsucker of a fucking laundry owner I was driving a truck for for $45 a week replaced me in the route because I was sick one day from bleeding piles, and then, after I had worked 1 1/2 weeks ... neatly deleted my two days' wages I still had coming by claiming shortages." The short-change termination was a kind of experience that was not without precedent in Dorn's work history, but this time, with a large family to be concerned about, the stakes were proportionally greater. For a few days he drove around Mattoon seeking work. On the day he ran out of money for gas (October 14) he swallowed his pride and dispatched an urgent solicitation by wire to David Buck in Menlo Park.

AT THIS POINT HELENE NOT THE ONLY FLAT BUSTED MEMBER OF THE FAMILY. WE ALL ARE. HOUSE FOR TWENTY DOLLARS BY LAKE. FRED CAUGHT TWO CARP. SICK ONE DAY. HEMORRHOIDS FROM 75 POUND LAUNDRY BUNDLES. TREACHEROUS BOSS HAD REPLACEMENT NEXT DAY. RENT FOOD SICKNESS THREAT OF WINTER BRING TOTAL DEPRESSION TO OUR FINANCES IF GOD WILLS IT TODAY PLEASE = ERNEST DORN

The Dorns received the answering crisis-relief letter, containing a month's rent in cash, on the 17th. That morning in the lakeside shelter the mercury dipped to 40 degrees. "EVERYONE down to Paul" was suffering from chilblains. There was no money left for heating oil. Ed was getting ready for the six-mile walk into Mattoon to resume his work search. "Your double-sawbuck," he notified Buck after the special-delivery envelope was delivered, "was a line cast in the well for us, we were (10:00 A.M.) just going under."

He vowed to his benefactor he would step up efforts to "land a job toot sweet," promising it would be something "responsible" this time. The end in sight remained "finally going to Harvard and it not costing you too much." He was seeking connections through New York painter Franz Kline (whom he'd met and befriended during a late-summer visit by Kline to Black Mountain) for a teaching post "in a 'private' school in or around N. Y." He wrote Kline a "wonderful letter, in which I extol myself (in absence of anyone else to do it)." The painter wrote back saying he'd taken up the Dorns' cause and would "explain [their] plight" to a possible contact at the Cedar Bar. The efforts of Kline, however, turned up prospects only "for painters." It took another fifty-dollar advance from Buck to carry them to the end of October. Dorn cast out further work-search lines to Olson and others back East. Ill with flu, he hit the streets in a dogged and fruitless circuit of the hiring offices of Mattoon. There were openings in town, but he repeatedly seemed wrong for the part. "These g[od] d[amn] factory employment persons just don't approve his face or speech I guess," Helene observed. When Halloween came around, Dorn was still unemployed.

LIFE BY "THE LAKE OF THE MATTOONS" was extremely basic, but the Dorns, equipped by nature or necessity with a fiercely determined self-belief, were developing a knack for accepting inconvenience as an expedient ally in the quest for freedom. A subsistence austerity, undergone out of commitment to principle, could take on the aspect of a simple, genuine "reality"; in the midst of a Land of Plenty, poverty and deprivation could be made into the moral proving-grounds of a defiant if threadbare independence.

Even with Ed out of work and their future in doubt, a pallid "drizzly chilly" early-November day took on a warm glow like that of the old-fashioned wood stove in Helene's resolutely sanguine account: "The Victory Morning sends off heat from the living room, across the 'Waverly' floor to all parts of our 4 room delightfully mad, storybook cottage here on the shore of Lake Mattoon ... the *only* place around here that we can really feel at home in. I've told you before, I'm sure, of Mattoon & what a truly horrible place it is; but somehow here in our wonderful termite-ridden cottage we feel *out* of the mechanics of Mattoon and *on* the prairie. We heat with wood fires in our V. M., look out the windows to the ducks going by on the water, and the trees on the other shore, ochers & vermilions—it's really beautiful & a great pleasure to be out of the lush green easy growth of the mountains...." The "lake-dwellers" had ample time for "being thorough at playing house." Starting up housekeeping from scratch, they toured the second-hand stores of Mattoon to find serviceable "cheap enuff stuff" (e.g. four kitchen chairs for $1). To cover the bare floors, a family rug-making project was launched, Ed braiding and Helene sewing. A living-room-sized rug made of pieced-together scraps kept growing beyond their original modest design: "God! What a tremendous job but it is so exciting we keep letting ourselves keep right on," Helene reported, "every time we walk by or look into the living room [we] can scarcely believe we've made such a wonderful thing!" With their new thrift-store "shiny red rocker" and recently acquired black kitten, the bleak, empty front room was transformed into a sea of color.

Helene baked bread and did the family laundry on a washboard. Similarly defying Fifties cultural mythology of Progress, Ed chopped wood for the stove: "it costs us nothing; this is very suspicious." For the kids he "hung a swing from a *very* high branch of a tree by the side of the house so that it was a wonderful *long* arc." Improvising with materials at hand, he devised some ingenious toys: for Fred, a "hilarious little 'car' out of moldy wood he found in the garage, old buggy-wheels & a cat food can"; for Chan, "a hilarious 'horse' out of same moldy lumber & two large buttons for eyes." A vacant, unheated "play room," furnished with a $2 rug to combat drafts, became the kids' designated activity-area; its central fixture, an old abandoned sewing machine, served variously as "everything from a pinto pony to a kayak" for cowboy and Indian games in which Dorn perceived a trace of makeshift animistic magic. "The forms it takes seem to be endless. I found an old faucet one day and put it on the spindle and didn't know what it was but it was taken for granted, yes it belongs there to be sure."

Adjusting to the sociology of the place still posed challenges, though, not least for the kids. The neighborhood's middle-class denizens seemed disposed to judge people's worth on the basis of possession of the latest appliances, central heating, television. Educating the children in a less materialistic view took conscious vigilance, as Dorn was learning. Fred in particular was old enough to be exposed to the hypnotic influence of the one-eyed beast of the monoculture in visits to the households of neighbors. "When he comes home from 3 hours of the cycloptic plague (home is still possible?) to dinner we feel like shits because our table has legs of wood instead of vertical rockets waiting for zero [and] the roof of our bungalow has a low Mach number.... It is very damned tough trying to maintain reality that says a wood stove actually burns and gives heat in the midst of the antenna forest."

11.

Like Ulysses, Troubled but Unvanquished (Mattoon to San Francisco)

D ORN'S QUEST FOR WORK continued into the prairie winter unabated. December began with a check from Buck accompanied by a sobering warning of "a broke month" ahead. Dorn was in a bitter frame of mind when he wrote back. "I got to feeling no-account this morning after we got the 100 with the note," he said. "And terribly sad that I am so despicably caught here in this damnable God-shunning place. No work. Perhaps I should resort to the expediency of psychoanalysis. Or trade off my psycho-resistances. Or get a new suit with pleats in the pants. Or get a new tongue with clichés on the tip. Or what? . . . It's so difficult being no-'count these days. In the 1860s a man who had a no-'count son ignored him and the son spat into the apple barrel (or cracker) and strummed. If he happened to be 'intellectual' nobody considered it dangerous, he was just no-'count. And that was no more a thing to get excited about than not taking a bath. Now, of course everybody takes a bath and you can tell those that don't immediately."

He had run out of ideas. In a thriving heartland industrial center, where shoes, road graders and light bulbs were produced, where broom corn was harvested, oil was pumped and fish teemed in commercial hatcheries, there was no job for him. "Maybe I can pick up corn, Monday. Or they want help in the kitchen of the Knowles cafeteria. Anything. I get the cold door everywhere here. Couldn't even carry thru a frustrated attempt to cash in on the recent hail damage in Mattoon by lying that I was an old roofer because I didn't know what a 'butt-bundle' was when the prick asked me how many I could lay, say." By letting himself get stuck in Mattoon over the winter he'd placed the whole family in "an overly ridiculous situation." The only way out he could see was to get to the East Coast and find "a job I can do," which meant "peddle my wits.... I have enough naivete to think I still have several left. But here, where the concentration of 'useful' people is extraordinary in a society that's damn near 100% useful, I, man, don't make it."

He hung on in Illinois until the third week of January 1956. By then the only work he'd discovered was free-lance taxi-driving. His few fares and fewer tips were too little and too late to keep the rent and fuel bills from piling up—as Helene recalls—"to the extent we had to split 'in the middle of the night.'" The "saving grace" of a $200 support check from Buck provided the wherewithal for making their exit. Helene, after all her brave efforts to keep their life "storybook pure" in "the gingerbread house on Lake Mattoon," was not sorry to be saying goodbye to what she had never ceased to regard as a hard-headed, small-minded part of the country.

They left under cover of darkness, headed southwest across the continent into the teeth of ferocious midwinter weather—"the WORST," as Helene would write on a blizzard-white night atop the Continental Divide of New Mexico, four days out of Mattoon: "This is our 2nd blinding snow, fog in Okla[homa] so that we had to pull over for the night, wind across the desert—oh me! To say nothing of ice, etc. & our car conking out after what we thought was a *complete* overhaul (at a pretty price) in Champaign, Ill[inois]...." The car breakdown necessitated a three-hour pause for $15 in repairs in Oklahoma City to get them back on the road, only to find the latest mechanic too had failed them. To keep the Morris running Ed had to insert "a match stick to hold where the fool didn't replace a nut."

"Laughing thru it all," they drove west. In New Mexico "snow coming down so furiously" that they were slowed to a five-mile-per-hour crawl forced them to hole up in a motel at the top of the Divide. They waited out the blizzard in the motel bar over beers, watching Lawrence Welk on television, while Fred sat by with a 7-up. Helene sensed another turning point in their winding road. "Just think— the 3 of us the only ones in this bar, drinking beer here at this bar & the rivers all of them flowing in opposite directions on either side of us! The wildest! And we don't give much of a damn about much of anything after Mattoon for how many? months.... It's great to be in the vast West again ... we feel like Ulysses—troubled but unvanquished...." They momentarily considered turning south toward Juarez but instead drove straight through to Los Angeles, where, as the latest plan had it, Ed would earn enough money to get them on to San Francisco.

12.

The Common Lot
(San Francisco)

D ORN TARRIED NO LONGER than a few days in Los Angeles before
concluding that work was not immediately to be found and
that he had otherwise neither means nor reason to be staying. They
drove north, stopping in Menlo Park for a visit with David Buck
and his new wife and stepchild. In early February they moved on to
San Francisco, taking a four-room furnished flat at 184 States Street
in Corona Heights. The place was not cheap but had one important
qualification: "They allowed CHILDREN! Wow!" There were trees,
a hillside out back, a playground next door, and, in a neighborhood
Dorn determined to be "the geographical center of San Francisco,"
diverse social opportunities for the children with playmates of all
colors and persuasions. Across the alley behind their house a dis-
used parking lot was given over to kids' games. "Fred, natch, he &
7 others, have a great fort built in the vacant parking lot across the
alley," Helene noted. Fred Buck still recalls that vacant lot, "where
my mates and I dug a hole (for a trap or clubhouse or something)
and covered it over with a cruddy piece of pink carpet from the same
lot. I think I remember trying to get my sister and her friend to try to
walk across it (à la catching heffalump)." The vacant lot supplied

Dorn the location for a poem:

> Trees standing in the vacant lot
> again today, a masterful forbearance.
>
> A masterful forbearance, the children
> too, playing on the sidewalk,
>
> and in the vacant lot, that
> they don't all go away, one by one,
>
> one could love them both, the trees
> and the children.
>
> 1 playing with a white ball, 2 in a frail tree
> climbing for the crown. My daughter alone
>
> on the mound of rubbish sand disappears
> into a cave of pink rug.
>
> > Certain screams
>
> then a sense of patience.
>
> Her, my daughter's well of forbearance.
> The playmate she wades across the sand to
>
> is dark black, a color.
> Nearby the process, a game of ball.
>
> Ah. The vacant lot is vast, I can speak of love
> only at the edge.

He called the poem "The Common Site," then later changed the title to "The Common Lot" when including it in his first chapbook

(*The Newly Fallen*, 1961). It represents for the poet a thoughtful self-situating within the value-sets that define the moral world of his poetry. The language reverberates with the abiding terms of those values—*common, forbearance, love, patience, speak,* hopefully but tenuously counterposed against all that is implied by *vacant.* The central paradox underlying Dorn's early lyric premise is here stated: to speak of love is possible only at the alienated margins of the social vacancy. Only by way of absence is utopian presence imaginable. The poet, while acknowledging his inevitable sharing in the common "lot" or condition, is reminded by his attendance upon the common site (the vacant lot) that his position will always be that of the speaker at its edge.

"The Common Site" was one of three Dorn poems written that spring in San Francisco to appear in the journal *Ark II / Moby I,* of which he served informally as a contributing editor. (Only "The Common Site" would be preserved by Dorn, and he would withhold even that from later collections.) All three poems seem to emanate from states of exclusion, stymie or constraint. In "The Common Lot," the poet's self-imposed detachment keeps him on the sidelines as life's otherwise involving game of "process" unfolds; in his very withdrawal lies his paradoxical participation, as mediator, through his observation of the children at play, between the white-world values from which he seems to have turned away, and the otherness of everything contained in "dark black, a color." In a second contribution, "The Revival," the former poem's stabilizing "sense / of patience" gives way to a restless irritability ("Today I am impatient with small horrors ... Today I am a fast dirge, my shoulders quake"). In his third poem, an edgy comic monologue titled "Lines from a Sitting Position," the speaker of the lines seems tormented by the dehumanization of his own artistic impersonations: "Extraordinary / Illuminating / & Inspiring, / otherwise / why do I have my hands above my head / QUACK QUACK QUACK QUACK / I am perched far out / with the back of my head / rather botched / inspiringly! / Extraordinary! / A man banging on my door doesn't seem to be / illuminating, / he wants me to come down / oink oink oink oink /

How excruciating!" Together the three poems reflect a watchful, uneasy, self-conscious state of mind, its cynical defenses undermined by a nagging self-dissatisfaction: "Today I have not flown, like a great tired vulture / to pick the dried crust / plastered around the body of Hope" ("The Revival").

Self-esteem problems came with a bitter failure to find work. Pressing himself to establish his independence by assuming financial support for his family, the young writer was discouraged and humiliated by the negative results of his first weeks of looking for jobs in San Francisco. "There seem to be jobs, i.e. so many have them, but one needs to be naïve, a quality I begin to think the gods denied me, for their own damned reasons, at birth." He studied the daily *Examiner* want ads and spent many futile hours chasing down supposed prospects, increasingly frustrated with "the g[od] d[amn] rain" inexorably coming down, "wet streets, and the crease gone from my pants." Interviews went badly—"I need more intimacy than is possible across the counter, so to speak"—and sometimes proved painfully brief. He showed up in person to apply for a white-collar job advertised by United Airlines and found himself rejected on general appearances, "so startling to them in my Goodwill coat they had to stammer a bit before 'correcting' the newspaper ad where you really did, need experience. My, they even tabulate their collars." The lesson was twofold: first, he would need a makeover ("I look pretty tacky, I'll try to get a godamn haircut, maybe a coat"); second, he'd be better off "eliminating the 'pretty clothes' sorts of occupations." He struggled to maintain his self-respect: "At least *I* am not embarrassed, who the hell, after all, is it that is right anyway?" He decided to shift the focus of his search to work of a different "class": "I want a job in a warehouse. I want a job on a tanker." Finally he resolved to follow the way of the world and concentrate less on "looking" than on "contacts." "I do get a little impatient looking," he told David Buck after two-and-a-half weeks. "In fact, it wastes so much time, I am not going to look any more. I shall look for contacts only."

Buck was able to supply one "contact": a fellow Stanford graduate student who required ghost-writing. The "contact" had a day job and little time for his school work. Dorn was not in a position to be choosy. "Did you say he was a merchant seaman or an insurance broker?" he inquired. "The main thing, as I see, is that he isn't broke. But that is hope." Soon he had taken on the work. "I haven't found a job yet," he reported in a letter to Olson at the end of February, "but have made my first money from 'writing.' From some papers on the 'philosophy of education' for a graduate student at Stanford. An insurance man, by main interest." The papers were "in the president's English," and written strictly for the "buck," but despite the circumstances of duress he "fooled with a writing in which it is possible to have the cake too," finding ways to subtly undersell "the goods" ("they do want the goods so bad they'll listen to it even if you tell them what it is you're saying when you say it"). He discovered he could turn them out without much trouble "in ab[ou]t 1 1/2 hours" each. The pay was $7.50 a crack. Soon, however, even this token "writing" income had dried up. In the first week of March he found a temporary factory-laboring job. "I have made some 'money,' believe it or not," he was able to declare to Buck upon the strength of a single paycheck. "I was a gunny sack turner. The job was, of course, in a sack factory. I turned 6000 on the machine but damn near was blind at the end of the day and had stood in one spot so long that, on walking away for lunch, I nearly fell lame. C'est la vie, we save ourselves as best we can."

After the trying first six weeks, in mid-March, as during earlier straits of unemployment in Illinois, he took a shot at taxi driving— "did that taxi bit," Helene recalls, "and ended up as chauffeur to [a] Mafia man." Fred Buck, at the time a second-grader at Andrew Jackson elementary school, dimly remembers his stepfather's unusual private passenger, "some gangster who wanted to protégé the college kid into the club." With the taxi-driving job the Dorns could afford "to be blasphemous and get the phone connected" in their new, cheaper apartment at 1478 Grove Street in the Panhandle. The new place, Helene reported, cost $15 less per month yet was "larger, much larger," "so much better than the one on States Street & so much more to the point for us that it makes everything seem possible again." The place was unfurnished and needed plenty of "scrubbing" and "fixing," but the Dorns were accustomed to such reclamation projects: "We're out of the recent black period and it is good to feel clean again, and clear." To keep up with the bills, by late spring Ed was supplementing his part-time taxi-driving with a second job, as a baggage handler on the night shift at the Greyhound depot (his early morning swing-shift partner was another young writer sojourning in San Francisco, Allen Ginsberg). Throughout their four months in San Francisco, the struggle to make a living remained a steady preoccupation.

Here such obscure struggles felt more isolating than ever. San Francisco was the first "town of Culture" Dorn had ever lived in, as he admitted to Olson: a place where "masses of people" were "fans of first one art then another," and the consuming bustle of "so much so called activity" on the arts scene could not conceal a general greedy "predisposition toward money."

Early encounters with the San Francisco poetry scene evoked dry reports to Olson on taking part in a journal-editing project ("a thing to be called 'Moby,' a child of Mike McClure's") and on visits to the court of local master Kenneth Rexroth, who was "lively and a fair talker" but seemed to lack "historical sense": Rexroth talked about "Reich not as the Anti-Christ arising at the end of an epoch to further the detention of a clearly asserted cultural 'ideal,' but as the man who said, 'All those who can come will be done thereafter with capitalism.' ... I had never witnessed a Municipal Poet before.... He is the Mentor type for these parts, at that.... What a dandy man. This is real 'high baptist' oratorio. But sadly antique—don't you think?" In Rexroth's orbit Dorn observed a comfortable "ease" of locally-received opinions: a "one-directional circuit set up wherein you are the grantee of his spill-over ... not a possible relationship." Dorn represented himself as carefully keeping his distance in such circles, wary of the currents of local "taste." "The atmosphere here seems possible, albeit [there is] a latent surrealism in the ground and an idealized anarchism wandering from Coit Tower, the best smoke stack in town," he told his former teacher. The city seemed to have a self-satisfied, imperturbable "established" quality, as he would comment a few years later, that caused "the people [to] become obnoxiously egotistical, and nutty." Soliciting work from Olson for the journal project, he requested something that might shock complacent San Francisco into life, "to help ... shove this god damned mess off its silly mild accidentality." His best way to enjoy idle hours in the city, he found, was to avoid the nocturnal social life. "At least the day makes it. It always does, nice, fine, high mist. One ought to be able to play the trumpet or something appropriate. Piano. A plane ticket to see Miles." No matter where one was, the externals of the place could determine only so much. Dorn made an effort not to forget "just how god damned simple being in the right mood is."

After Dorn had solicited work for the *Moby* project from several poets, differences arose with the other editors, James Harmon and Michael McClure. At issue was an Olson poem, "As the Dead Prey Upon Us." When Dorn showed the poem to Michael McClure, McClure "deplored the length." When Dorn further urged the inclusion of another sizeable Olson poem, "The Lordly and Isolate Satyrs," McClure "mumbled, 'Does he think we're his nursemaid?'" Dorn's allegiances were being tested. It was "at best, a mean business." He told Olson the concept of the project had changed from a "huge collection" to an anthology, "more like a book," of a few hand-picked selections. "I hope I don't feel wrongly," he told Olson, "but I do feel like they want too much of something impinging on their own personal vanity." The publication, appearing early the following year, would feature writings by McClure, Rexroth, Duncan, Kerouac, Zukofsky, Ginsberg and Snyder; it would also include, in addition to Dorn's three poems cited above, material he had solicited from Olson, Levertov and Creeley.

The Creeley poem was "The Ballad of the Despairing Husband," hand-delivered on an April visit to the Dorns in San Francisco. The recently divorced Creeley spent his first three weeks staying with them on Grove Street before moving into a place of his own in North Beach. During this period Dorn introduced Creeley to his baggage-handling partner Ginsberg, who brought along to the meeting pal Jack Kerouac. There ensued a season of mutual visitation. Cabin-sitter Kerouac hosted Creeley and the Dorns at the Corte Madera hillside spread he would celebrate in *Dharma Bums*. Later the Dorns offered reciprocal hospitality to Kerouac, who dropped in regularly to talk and drink wine, then "just get out his bed-roll and go to sleep." After being shown "C. B. & Q." by *Black Mountain Review* editor Creeley, Kerouac proclaimed Dorn "a great writer," and paid him the ultimate writer's homage by interrogating him at length about the details of his wandering work-life. ("He wanted to know all about my experiences working on the Burlington in Wyoming, cutting trees in the Sierra Nevada and the Cascades—in fact he had an insatiable curiosity about everything.") Dorn was impressed not only by Kerouac's avid note-taking habit but by his predilection for "jumping up in the middle of any circumstance, talking or what-ever, at random," and doing handstands. "He believed in them very much," Dorn would later recall. "It was something about circula-tion, and also a matter of changing your view, turning things upside down." Kerouac eventually had everybody in the Dorn clan save two-year-old Paul working on their handstands.

Friendship with Robert Creeley was more complicated. Dorn had been befriended by Kenneth Rexroth; since hitting town Creeley had begun an affair with Rexroth's wife Marthe. Dorn carefully tried to maintain his neutrality, no easy matter once he was called upon by Creeley "to give him certain help, like transport their bags from some secret apartment to another.... I had a car, so I began to pro-vide transportation for them." Rexroth, meanwhile, appeared at the Dorns' to recite his anxieties over "where Creeley and his wife might be," leaving the younger writer "trying to find the key log to the pain and actual anxiety of this man, who was very hurt, insulted."

Creeley himself recalls the challenge of his testing presence in that period, which seemed to precipitate undercurrents of tension not only in Rexroth's home life but in the Dorns'. "I know my staying with them was hard on the household. Ed felt I was after Helene— and I am sure I was leaning on her for tea and sympathy. Ed's working the night shift at the Greyhound baggage job (from midnight to early morn) was hard on him and it made him expectably paranoid that Helene was being hounded during his absence. I recall taking Jack Kerouac up to meet them all after a night's drinking and my seeing Marthe, and finding just Helene there. So when Ed arrived, he found us all three together, his worst fears confirmed! Helene left their apartment in great irritation and returned with me. We found Ed and Jack intently talking, almost unaware of our return. Anyhow Jack and Ed recognized one another very particularly—and Jack's take on their family (children, etc.) was very sympathetic. Otherwise, having taken Helene from another man, like they say, perhaps Ed felt he was open to the same vulnerability—which leaves Helene sans vote, but it's sure a familiar male trip of the time (if not forever)."

Dorn's own measured and temperate May 7 account to Olson of recent social complications suggested both his interested observation of the scene and his limited patience with it: "Creeley stayed with us for ab[ou]t three w[ee]ks. He has an ap[artmen]t now in North B[each]. . . . He is delightfully harassed as usual and there is a whole new field. I hope it doesn't end until it should. No harassment no Creeley. I can hardly get along with him but sense that I can hardly not be a deep friend or whatever the score is that day. Or tomorrow. Another writer, Jack Kerouac, who is a great man, I am sure (I read some note-statements of his on prose that were as much as to say how you do it if you want with no bullshit) has become his friend, and they stay out at Mill Valley in Marin C[ounty] on the weekends in among the Eucalyptus trees and on the sides of hills. Listening to Indian (Asiatic) sounds. The whole place here appeals to C[reeley] very much because of an open interest in poetry and writing and there are lots of people at that, probably 100 who will open their mouths at any given point. It seems to be a very good place for him, and he says so too. As for myself, as you know, I can only take a certain amount, but am attentive, nonetheless."

Speaking of his life with Helene, Dorn expressed no such qualification of cautious distancing. He told Olson she was "very great these days, much at ease.... She has changed. You probably wouldn't know her. Her hair is quite long now and lovely." Between the two of them, "things [were] easy." Quietly they were preparing another passage, one that would involve withdrawing from the social complications of the urban scene altogether.

VII.

The Geography of
My Lunacy
(1956–1959)

I.

The Bright and Shining Hand (San Francisco to Seattle)

T HE DECISION TO PULL UP STAKES and head back to the Northwest came on the slim instigation of a postcard from Dorn's erstwhile lumberjacking comrade Bill Tindall bringing news of work prospects in the woods. "Bill's card came back to me when we were still in San Francisco saying, sure come up there will be a job for you. And we had gambled everything on that card. Had decided in an afternoon to abandon everything and go away. We counted the money. A hundred dollars or so. Not much to move three children. [Helene] called her brother long distance to see if we could stay with him for a while. My god! The suspense! And misgivings. ..."

The one immediate obstacle to leaving was the disposition of the Morris Minor, which had been through the road wars, over the deserts and the mountains. The Dorns had let the vehicle registration lapse; they discovered on the morning of their departure that the fine for late registration would be $90. "Here it was June and through some series of gestures we still hadn't any license for the car. The fine, and late fees I find out will be more than all the money we have. Nothing to do but leave it on the street. You can't sell a car either, without a license." The Dorns managed to get David Buck to take over responsibility for the car in its dilapidated and illegal state. They left it parked in San Francisco for him to retrieve, with a sardonic note from Ed listing mechanical defects and detailing needed repairs ("Don't let the low sonorous rumble coming from the universal or differential bug you. It's just the differential or universal. They say they go in a minute or years. Quien sabe?"). The car ownership papers were left with Michael McClure for transfer to Buck. Only after they'd left did the Dorns realize they'd neglected to include in the packet the expired registration card and the "cheap policy" limited-coverage insurance Buck would need in order to determine whether, once he'd got the car going and registered, he'd be insured to drive it. ("I'm afraid we handed you a liability rather than an asset," Helene would later admit to him.)

The whirlwind June 6 getaway was pulled off in a few hours. "That busy afternoon, called the bus station, packed and finally we were ready. What a group we were. At the station we took some pictures in one of those booths, for a quarter, the three kids, held Paul in range, Frederick and [Chan] below sitting on the seat. All three wide-eyed and staring. My hand and forearm were in the picture." So Dorn wrote in the draft of an autobiographical novel of life in the Northwest, the precursor of *The Rites of Passage*. The moment of anxious transit in the San Francisco bus depot would stand out in his mind, an emblem of the family's voyaging perils and exposures. He wrote about it again several times over the next few years, first in a set of unpublished vignettes called "4 Little Pictures of People at Work," then in successive revised drafts of the same material, culminating in the essay "Notes About Working and Waiting Around." In the 1962 published version of "Notes" (in the journal *Yugen*), his representation of the bus-station scene is titled "Departure" ("A Departure" in earlier drafts):

It was a day very much like this one, a bright sun and bold shadows on the buildings, and crisp air, when five people stood in the bus depot in San Francisco, all going somewhere together, going away. Three of them, children, stayed close to one another, holding hands sometimes. They looked about the station. . . .

In picturing the scene, Dorn adopts the perspective of the children, capturing through their wary but curious eyes a glimpse of the black Greyhound porters, "the people at work" whose calculated detachment and mysterious otherness are at the center of this section of the essay. The vulnerable and precarious outsiderhood of the huddled voyagers is linked through the "wide-eyed and staring" openness of the children's witnessing with the porters' impeccable, class-excluded "expertness." In final revisions Dorn converted the walking-dollar-sign who is the object of the porters' attentions from "a heavy set *man* in a rush" to "a heavy set *white* in a rush" (my italics) making it impossible to avoid his equation of race, class and money.

They looked about the station, watched the people eating sandwiches, playing with the gum machines, watched the porters carry suitcases and bags and sweep up cigarette butts from the floor. Watched the dark lazy-eyed Negroes lean casually against the walls or pillars, slight mysterious smiles on their faces, not eager to please but prompt, when a dollar hailed past, in the form of a heavy set white in a rush, or a lady whose luggage was too heavy for her slender legs and high heels. The studied casualness, and the promptly expert way, of discarding those who would not be willing to pay to have their luggage carried. The flick of a dark lash, over that mysterious eye, was all the registration of this expertness. And the way they dressed, those experts. Sharp. Work clothes are, by almost every one's speculation, rough, cotton, shirt, and pants, uniform, material and cut. But no. Not these workers. Sharp, and the hats. Soft soft sweaters. So clean, how do they stay so clean, for the kind of work they do, most of us would get dirty, dirt from the booming busted city carried in on the luggage, on the bottom of the shoes of these transients, in the palms of their meandering hands gloved and bare.

From the black porters the essay wanders with a purpose through a series of further subtle identifications with other displaced persons, with Mexicans, with Eskimos—the thought of "their distant removals, their shiftings, their dedicated stealth in foreign scenes" so resonant with the verities of the writer's own alienation. Dorn then comes back to his original structural plan for the scene, and his reason for elaborating it: to bring into focus the faces of the children themselves, no longer seeing but "seen" by the camera's uncaring historical eye in the unknowing hopefulness of the moment.

> And then one of the children, the oldest one, discovers an automatic photographic machine which takes four pictures for a quarter. The departure is an hour or so away yet, so the father relents and they take pictures. In one of the pictures the partial face of the father is visible, and also his hand as he attempts to hold the youngest boy in range of the camera, which governs itself and clicks along like an automatic thing. Their eyes are bright in all four pictures, and all the children are fair, have a high awareness look in their eyes, for they are all going away somewhere, not in search of trinkets, no, in search of the little nothings of searching, remember they are young.
> Searching, searching the world turns around....

Here the very understated, controlled distancing of Dorn's tone helps evoke one of the more powerful images of pathos in his work. Do the innocent, unsuspecting, excited children reflect some fugitive memory from the writer's own childhood of abrupt, unexplained dislocation and repetitive "searching, searching"?

For Helene and the kids the Greyhound ride up the coast seemed a pleasure cruise after their cross-continental road trips in the tiny Morris. "The bus ride was a snap, better all the way around than driving, believe it or not!" Ed however found himself lost not in his usual driving intensities but in vague reflections about what lay ahead, apprehensive speculations in particular about his ability to "provide" in this latest new kind of "exile." "It was a chattering trip in the bus, there was a toilet even. And when we arrived in Portland, we all got out and walked around the little square park lined with benches, near the depot. Then back on the bus for the last desperate swing up to Seattle and all the wondering of finally, would everything work out. What kind of exile is this? But most of all, could I provide the things it takes to live, for my family. Not easily, I hardly have the shackled spirit it takes to do any sort of work. But the desire, the desire."

The subject of his nocturnal bus-ride reverie was work: the clarity of his earnest desire for decent work inseparable from his wish for a decent life. Concern for the days ahead segued into memories of jobs he'd had in his youth, working in the cornfields, in the Villa Grove railway yards, on a tractor-factory assembly line.

> When I was very young I stood between the hot rows of hybrid corn in Illinois, pulling the tassels from the male stocks. Traveling down the same row eventually a half mile. And then, back again. The bright day and the bright young hand. The silence of occupation, when there is gay frivolous talk even, the resigned willingness. And later climb up into the dead locomotive to shake the coals down through the giant grates, the same bright hands around the six foot iron shaker. When Germany was quaking and the world in general was advancing through new segments of years. Working. My mother was more or less pleased. My friends were more or less doing the same thing. Most of the time we must have worked together. But why this dream? Of working alone. Why this desire to be. Why this desire to be together again. And later the hands not any longer so bright, the tractor factory, the bullhorn for lunch at 9:00 at night, standing the rest of the time before a 15-ton press, that so ponderously clipped the edges off the single pointed guide of the cycle bar; still held that by hand. But perhaps here, away from the city again in the open air ... it would be possible. And maybe later on a chance to live on a

farm, not to be a farmer, that stability, but that form of self-assurance. Possibly Hope, and the vision of the possible lead a man into grimnesses [where] he wouldn't otherwise set foot. But it was a new place for me, and away from the vast trickery of the city, where impetuousity and greed are the elements that keep the hand shining and the nails of that hand clean and twinkling as the stars above us. And now I have come into the land of green days worn out with wearyness of looking for a certainty to give my family; and more like the people there than I could have known.

2.

Hastening to a Dream

The Wymans came to the valley because of what they thought was a pressing need to leave the city although as time passed they saw this pressure had been largely of their own. Carl's old friend was then working as rigger at a lumber camp based at ... a village in the upper valley. Carl had been hired on this man's word. The logging lasted through that first summer and then there was a general cutting back of the new men in the fall, and Carl was out of work.

— *The Rites of Passage*

Hasten to your own kind, to your own dream, to your own
    land
Hurry while there is still someone to go with you there
        — Kenneth Patchen (quoted by Dorn as
        epigraph to a section of an unpublished
        autobiographical novel, 1956–1957)

ED AND HELENE WERE BACK in the city where they'd met three years before. That brief interval felt more like a lifetime. "It's a crazy sensation to be in Seattle again, I don't feel that I am, in a way," Helene wrote. In many respects they were different people now. "I am not a young man anymore," Dorn would declare a few months later at the outset of the projected novel about his migration to the Northwest. "Nor, really, am I old. Or even middle aged. But I don't look eagerly and with a swiftness at things, as does the interest[ed] and nervous youth. More, I glance off and am engaged by the impression as it already resides in the shelter of myself, equally as it resides upon the rampart of Earth. . . . Earth is my home and I love it, as deeply when I wake and see it lit for me, and my hapless doings, as I do the graduating darkness when I withdraw with the day, an abandoned man."

Older, but still hapless in his doings, still "vague and halting" in his ways, he felt exhausted by his search for the meaning of his earnest urgencies and brooding intensities. What he now wanted most for himself and his family was a respite from their wanderings, "a time when we stop a while and wait." The Northwest seemed as likely a place as any for reconnecting with one's purpose, storing up energies for a fresh start. And they were not entirely without contacts. Helene's brother's apartment on Lakeview Boulevard was conveniently vacant at the time of their arrival; it was "a godsend to have some place to come to," for once. Ed made plans to move them into their own place in Seattle, once he'd secured a logging job and temporary accommodations for himself at a company camp in the woods. By the end of the season, he calculated, they would have saved up a sufficient sum to get them to Europe for a while, perhaps Spain, where he'd heard the living was cheap.

Transportation was an immediate need. Dorn made arrangements to borrow an old black panel truck owned by his lumberjack/fisherman friend Bill Tindall—"Bill Elephant," in his writings. Collecting the vehicle from Tindall's wife, a waitress at a Seattle restaurant, he headed toward the "dim green realm" to the north. It was a drive and a part of the earth that would become intimately familiar to him. A gentle descent of the long sweeping grade from the uplands through Mt. Vernon, then the quick traverse of the five-mile stretch of the Skagit River basin into Burlington, then the turn east into the first rolling foothills of the Cascades: for the next three years, this verdant valley landscape would supply the restless migrant a refuge for his soul and a setting for his writings.

"Before you is the vast hand of a place spread out and altogether there," Dorn would write of the dramatic descent from the south "into this land where the days are green and dim.... If the day is clear, you will never have to look again, although that can be a new pleasure affirming the same great stretch that hangs in the mind, the plan of the river, the placement and direction of what poplars are there and the countless densities of orchards and minor ditches, the roads, paths, swamps and drainages. In all, it is an exact relief of breadth such as the mind wants very much for its own independent uses, to be gone for an instant from its welter of smallness. And having gained it, it will go back there again and again, as a place of rest."

That day of his first approach, however, the skies of the valley were not clear but clouded, atmospherically befitting the general uncertainty of his circumstances. "There was no sun in the usual sense at all.... The presence of the land under this canopy of grey air was very uncertain. It was not raining that day. The air was heavy with water nonetheless, and with a chill...." He would come to recognize such sodden, moody days as the more common weather of the valley—and of his spirits, while living in it.

On this first trip he continued on east through the grey, for stretches along the bends, then along the straight banks of the rushing Skagit, into the narrowing valley as far as Hamilton, a "remnant of [a] village" thirty miles up the river, where the Scott Paper Company logging operation had its base camp. There ensued some anxious moments when an initial search of the camp failed to turn up his friend among the "strange assortment of men," who ranged from "gangling school kids on vacation" to weathered-looking old-timers, "breathlessly thin, their hickory shirts giv[ing] way to the bones on the cliffs of their shoulders." Dorn had a brief premonition of disaster. "How painful to be there in the north waiting on hope...." Finally Tindall, who was working for the company as a rigger, appeared out of that green dimness. The towering figure of "Bill Elephant" was unmistakable: congenial, animated, this half-Irish half-Klikitat Marxist-"totemist" had "huge shoulders," "large arms and remarkably large hands," a constantly gesturing "great log" of an index finger that conducted his running conversations with expressive emphasis, and a nose "immense as a trunk" dominating "a face otherwise large." Tindall was well-read for a woodsman, and from Funk and Wagnall's Dictionary "had gotten the confirmation he needed that he was a direct descendant of Elephants." ("Now you," the "totemist" would inform Dorn with customary good humor, "you probably descended from a kangaroo—you're skinny, and kinda big-eyed, and don't say much.")

On Tindall's say-so Dorn was offered a job setting choker. The one hitch was that there were no open beds in the company bunk house. He'd have to find a place to live nearby, or face a long grueling daily trip. He resolved to move his family up into the valley, though he "hardly knew where to start searching."

The following week he went back north in the battered panel truck with Helene and the kids and "spent several days looking for a house to live in, in the mysterious little towns in the upper Skagit. And it wasn't so much a house we were looking for, at least I can say I, so much as a place to be in, to live in. Because I was already finding my peace, partly in the aloneness, partly in the wandering as such, and partly in the continuing acquaintance with small new things, like the streets of those small towns and the way they ran here and there, and the few people walking about or driving in their pick-up trucks."

After a long, fruitless day's search around Hamilton and Clear Lake, they were passing through Burlington on the way back to Seattle when one of the children noticed a House for Rent sign in a real estate office window. The place advertised was at 500 Anacortes Street, on the outskirts of the small town. "Five blocks from the main street, right up against the hill. In Burlington there is a prominent isolated hill, distinctly insular, existing as it does on a plain of farm-land, the rich soil of the broad[en]ing flood plain of the river. And this hill is at the edge of town. The house was at the edge of that hill." To Dorn, who'd spent much of his life in the doubtful spaces at boundaries and margins, it seemed a "remarkable location." The old frame house was modest but sound, with "actual floors" and a good roof; out back there was a barn covered with weathered reddish-brown cedar shakes; these buildings sat on an acre of land, surrounded by a cedar grove. A large front yard and a stand of half a dozen hemlocks separated the property from the nearest neighboring house. The place at the foot of the hill was "sheltered ... and had a happy air about it." The Dorns put down $25 for a month's rent ("fair enough") and drove back to Seattle "very relieved at having a house to live in." The next day they returned, bringing what few household things they had, sleeping bags, and a few pots and pans. Ed would take a few days to get them settled before starting work at the logging camp.

Driving north with their belongings his eyes were full of the new country, his heart abrim with hopes for a decent life to be found in it. The majestic bulk of Mt. Baker, with its snow-decked "fine blunt top," loomed off in the distance ahead to his right as he drove. "When you travel north of Everett, you encounter Mt. Baker from every angle and draw in that large north country," he would soon write, "and from out in the islands I later saw it at the end of sparkling grey bays and inlets, centered like a true picture. Mt. Baker came to mean something powerful to me, and I finally grew so close to it in the nature of my feeling for the strange lonelyness of that country that I would feel something on my back, on the back of my head, and turning would see it white and virginal in the sky.... It is a visual thing surely, but the entrance into the eye of the mountain's image is an awesome thing, and not to be forgotten. It exists with you as a strict and impersonal sternness of nature. I came to value the mountain for more practical reasons, because it came to be my *anchor*, when I tended to forget where I was, in the years to come."

3.

Homesteading
(Burlington)

The edge of town is cool. The wet air is heavy today but the sun comes out of the overlap of clouds as it goes down. Then it flashed through a group of hemlocks across the vacant lot. The trees surrounded an old house and the rays diffracted into spikes and hit the hills for a few minutes making the aluminum-sided grain elevator for a while a bright mirror. Then the sun was gone down into the Pacific, promising for tomorrow a clear day, which never came....

The neighbors had been hostile from the beginning. With the exception of a kindly old woman who was a character in the neighborhood, they had nothing to do with the Wymans. The house had been empty for five years before they moved in. It was little more than a shack. The surrounding houses were of the new tract type. The owner, who ran a lumber yard in the next town, was not very interested in it. He was holding the property for the land only; it was anticipated that when the east-west highway across the north to the Okanogan went through, it would go around the base of the hill in that town. That was where the house was.

—*The Rites of Passage*

THE FAMILY'S FIRST MORNING in the Skagit Valley began with dramatic proof they'd left city life behind. They were awakened by a loud bawling outside the house. Disconcerted pioneer Dorn "sat upright in my sack and looked at the window. The great brown curious head of a milk cow was looking right back at me, tongue hanging out. She was nonchalantly chewing her cud. At first I yelled Get Out Of Here! as tho[ugh] my privacy had really been disturbed. She gave one last chew and went back to her grazing. I went to the window and saw she was tethered right by the window."

The cow turned out to be the property of their closest neighbor, the "kindly old woman who was a character" and who seemed to regard the yard of the place at the foot of the hill as an extension of her pasturage. She and her husband, a drunken but amiable part-time house-mover, owned several patches of land in the neighborhood. They had a woodlot and milkshed in the stand of fir and hemlock across the large lot to the west of the Dorns' place; inveterate horizon-gazer Ed got into the habit of watching the sun go down over their woods in the evening. The thicket was dense with mid-summer undergrowth when the newcomers arrived, but later in autumn the lot revealed its curious contents: a "shambles" of disused house-moving equipment. "Great cables and shoring blocks. Huge rusty tandem trucks. Laying idle, the stuff looked like abandoned toys." The house-mover also employed himself as a sometime handyman and "junk man" around town, occasionally hiring Dorn to assist him with odd jobs. In emergencies this eccentric but friendly couple could be called on to help out with looking after the kids; they also proved an early source of invaluable survival information.

Though he was accustomed to defining himself as a wanderer not a settler, there were aspects of the place on Anacortes Street that provoked unexpected homesteading instincts in Dorn. He liked the stability and security projected by the great "heavy, sturdy" black iron stove that provided the front room with radiant warmth to combat a damp chill climate. A machinist who'd lived in the place some years before had built it out of sheet iron, intending it as a fireplace but never getting around to enclosing it with brick. The same predecessor had added on an equally imposing sheet-iron chimney, which ran up on the outside of the house by the front steps. On the other side of the steps there was a dying grape vine, a sign of futility standing out as mocking complement to that of iron self-reliance.

The front room fireplace and kitchen cookstove comprised the family's frontline defense against "the creeping chill which permeates Everything in the Northwest." Pieces of wood and dried dung Ed turned up around the place kept the hearth comfortably ablaze on summer nights, but with the first daylong rains there came the need to search further afield for fuel supplies. From the cow-herding woman he learned that he could purchase cheap wood scraps called "mill-ends" at the local saw-mills; or, more economically still, drive up to the mills near the logging camps in the mountains and fill up his borrowed panel truck with cedar scrap, the negatives of which (it "wasn't so good because it burns quickly") were easily outweighed by its positives ("it didn't cost anything"). Trial-and-error experimenting revealed to the new settlers that any but the driest cedar scraps retained lingering pockets of moisture, inducing periodic unnerving explosions that sent generous showers of sparks shooting out of the fireplace. Nuances of weighing the difference between a light dry piece of cedar scrap and one that was heavier and green therefore became a significant and highly delicate matter. "But the first few days nothing mattered but these things of living, for I had never had the necessity of doing everything for myself," Dorn would write with the greatest of seriousness. "Gathering wood, borrowing water, lighting candles for light, everything had to be done. Nor, might I add, had I ever had the opportunity."

To the kids, he observed, the half-rustic life of Anacortes Street "was like camping out only in a house. And they explored the hill in the daytime. Right back of the house they discovered a slightly raised shelf of ground, with several trees on it, and the entrance was obscured by the tangle of small alders, a path going through beneath them. And on the ledge of ground there were here and there slabs of rock making natural seats. Rising above the secret garden (that's what they named it) was a sheer wall of black rock 75 ft. high. It was a very secret enclosure."

He had planned their original, starkly simplified "primitive way of living" to be merely "temporary … until I started to work, then we would buy beds and tables, chairs and all the things you have in a house." The interim regime of spartan simplicity was hardest on Chansonette, who'd been ill and taking in very little nourishment since leaving Seattle. In Burlington her symptoms worsened; she "spent the day half alive looking out the window, mostly at the cow, and a worse thing was, we had no bed to put her in." By the end of their first week in the new place, Helene was forced to summon a local doctor. The doctor—a soft, insincere-looking middle-aged professional man in "sporty" powder-blue pants, parked his "vast Cadillac" in the Dorns' driveway and appeared with bag in hand at their kitchen door. Taken aback, Dorn saw the scene through this licensed intruder's eyes. "At once I noticed an embarrassment in myself … suddenly and for the first time I was aware our cupboard was bare. I was shocked for the first time by the fact we lived in an empty house. There seemed something illegal about it. There seemed a vagrancy about it, yet I remembered we had paid the rent.... My embarrassment grew as I further conceived his immaculateness. I myself was of course unshaven, water was precious to us. None of the so-called utilities had yet been 'turned on,' which may be neither here nor there, but is quite something else in the midst of civilization. And when you are not distinctly pauperous, it is a cause of mystery and conjecture in the witness. Because although people generally are unwilling to see into you, it is true they are quite willing to notice everything about you. When the doctor had absorbed his first shock at seeing our sleeping sacks laying about on the floor, and had noted our utensils and the further lack of absolutely anything else, he examined Chan. Who lay wanly I forgot to say on a rather rumpled couch near the fireplace, so we did strictly speaking have an article of furniture."

The doctor gave the sick girl a shot and prescribed vitamins. Before departing "he looked about himself again, and not being able to hold it, blurted out—'You can't live like this!... I'll send my wife around tomorrow.'"

The next morning another Cadillac pulled up. The doctor's wife, "a large woman, who moved with the ease of a mare," was making a good-deed visit. She would come again, bringing "things of practical use, like a large 15 gallon enameled pot, to wash things in. And ... lots of food. Chickens, and potato chips, butter, and large steaks from their frozen food locker ... things anyone would be happy to eat." The Dorns gratefully accepted these gifts, though Ed was not unaware of the meaning of the gesture. "Yet it was charity, lest I be misunderstood. But charity with an ease, carrying no embarrassment.... Who contrived for the benefit of the not quite pauperous but still poor man, the idea that to receive charity is dishonorable and mean?... The fact remains it is one of the mechanical strings by which an order is hooked together. For after all, arrange as you will, these things, like food and pots, remain simply things, and are at a loss to be confused with honor, or even that lesser quality, pride." The latter qualities indeed he was quite sensitive about keeping apart from all that was resulting strictly from need, in his present circumstance.

Still private charity without embarrassment would inevitably give way with time to the generalized, public and more humiliating kind. Once they were "sniffed out" as a temporary civic cause, there would be little pride left for the family to save. In *The Rites of Passage* Dorn represents his alter-ego protagonist, Carl, as "habitually suspicious of any efforts on the part of that sanguine body called society.... It had not occurred to him then that the doctor considered them 'interesting' people.... They had never before been propositioned by charity." The helpful efforts on their behalf soon extended to a local women's charitable organization—called "The Willing Workers" in Dorn's unpublished novel of migration to the Northwest and "Women for Good" in *The Rites of Passage*—which provided furniture, a stove, and boxes of "fancy" food: "roasts and butter, creamy pies, elaborately frosted cakes, some with coconut. In other words ... none of that plain food which is supposed to do the needy so much good." This, Dorn concluded, was "what is commonly understood by charity, and is an insult to the receiver." When all was said and done the goodwill campaign on their behalf made him distinctly uncomfortable, and he looked forward with more than routine anticipation to that semblance of independence which would come with his first paycheck.

4.

"1st Avenue":
The Formalized
Proletariat (Seattle)

O N A GREY, RAINY SATURDAY a few days after his hiring by Scott
Paper Dorn was taken in tow by his helpful woodlands guide
Bill Tindall "down to First Avenue and to Occidental" in Seattle, to
be equipped with the gear he would need for work in the woods:
wool clothing, tin hat, caulk boots, etc. "With Bill Elephant the great
bargainer getting them for me for next to nothing, in fact it was to
be very close to stealing." They stopped in at the Salvation Army,
Goodwill, St. Vincent De Paul, and descended to an obscure shoe-
shop Tindall knew of, deep in the under-levels of the Pike Street
Market; emerging from the subterranean regions, they cruised the
battery of taverns on 1st Avenue above the market, joining fellow
off-duty "timber beasts" putting in time "getting out the logs." Many
of the thirsty loggers proved to be Tindall's familiars—as, it seemed,
did many of the other waterfront denizens. As they sat on bar stools
drinking beer in the gloom of the Ketchikan saloon the totemist
acquainted Dorn with a drunken fisherman he knew from his other
life on the Alaskan sardine boats. This staggering seaman bummed
a quarter from them, while Dorn made mental notes on his story.
The bargain hunters moved on through the rain to a "sprawling sur-

plus store" that looked to Dorn like "a Hudson's Bay trading post" out of the days of the search for the Northwest Passage. There, in the actual event of negotiating for goods, "Bill's stamina for bargaining proved short-winded." The shoppers "haggled half-heartedly" a while, overpaid, then sheepishly hung around for half an hour roaming among "the canyons of used tarnished clothing, not willing to leave so soon after defeat."

After several hours of interesting searching Dorn had managed to accumulate a tin hat, a great pile of wool socks and underwear and various pieces of rubberized outer clothing, the "dull rain gear so necessary for the endless days of rain in the green land." Clutching his precious bundle he followed his friend to the haven of hard-luck and down-and-out woodsmen, Archie's Bar, for another round of beers, while "the loggers and drunks, the cripples and whores, the Esquimaux and Indians came and went, and the movement and noise was serene."

Dorn's account of the day in Seattle with "Bill Elephant" would become part of the 1956–1957 autobiographical novel of his Northwest migration—the only part of that work, in fact, ever to see the light; he would publish it as a self-contained piece, under the title "1st Avenue," in LeRoi Jones' 1963 anthology *The Moderns*. Among his most eloquent and exacting evocations of place, the piece would feature his elephantine guide as resident sage, the rainy Northwest city as a site of "commerce" of various kinds, and the "city rain" itself, falling on hills levelled and paved for business interests, as a sorrowful reminder of the displaced victims of that commerce—both the denuded natural landscape and the marginalized urban poor.

> The rain comes down softly. There are colors to be seen through it, blue houses, brown office buildings standing like dumb machines among the zealously laid out streets. It is said they washed the steepness of the hills of Seattle away with pressure hoses, they drove the summits right off into Elliott Bay, such a placer mine is civic interest.... When the hills were made normal the traffic started, no longer baffled. The rain

would never have achieved this. The rain would never have denuded the hills, not this soft eternal rain. The city rain is quite different from the country rain and the difference doesn't all lie in where it falls.... The major streets are named for early merchants.... This is an order born of commerce....

But there is a slender edge of the city around the great curve of the Bay, which is the halo of the city, the light grey rain making the shining arc, there the poor sometimes late in the night cry silver colored tears as they paw in the garbage cans: and then look up, the blue of the eye of the Scandinavian the brown of the eye of the Esquimaux, is diluted and washed another shade lighter.

An unpublished continuation of the "1st Avenue" sketch survives in the form of Dorn's hand notes on the remainder of that Saturday in Seattle. In this 2500-word extension the mood of the piece changes, sinking with the day itself downward toward a darkness that offers less prospect of rest than of troubled dreams. The movement of the principals, Dorn and his friend, seems no longer leisurely but strangely compelled, as if driven by the uncanny currents of this underworld toward the grotesque epiphany that occurs near the sketch's close.

There is a dreamlike air to the proceedings as the journey through the rain-slick streets settles into its later, lower stages. Dorn the narrator/observer leans for direction upon his unlikely Virgil, "the gesturing Elephant walking beside me, his great trunk wagging in the air, sidestepping we go, it is getting late and the mist has started to fall down through the dark buildings as we hurry on." Around them, mysterious denizens of the mist-distorted city seem to recede into wet twilight's growing shadows, "holding back, waiting in their myriad secrets" for the coming of the night.

This kind of city darkness is like a minus quantity; negatives define it. It is not, as we learn, the pregnant glowing dark of the prairie on "a bright singular Saturday evening with the people dressed in starched clothes coming in vehicles into a small town, girls stand-

ing on the Bank corner, straw yellow hair and red lips, raw unem-
barrassed legs swinging under cotton dresses, bright look, like a
child's drawing, the sun going down in back. No. No, the tone is
different here on lower 1st Avenue...."

In Pioneer Square, "the famous totem pole" rises "like a spar
tree" before a pavilion under which destitute old men and out-of-
work Filipino salmon canners sit like ghosts, "vacantly staring": "It
is a very different kind of Saturday evening here," Dorn signals, a
kind of Saturday evening that is an introduction to desolation. His
narration drifts with the hidden undertow of place, running off on
the flow of the Japanese current, following the movement of Pacific
salmon down the Northwest coast, "this thin green shoreline, going
from Oregon to Norton Sound," then returns to the moment of
notation: on Occidental Street in skid-row Seattle, outside Archie's
Bar, where derelicts and indigents now have gathered for a street
preacher's sermon. The sermon, Dorn ventures, offers less of peace
and hope than would a bottle of cheap wine, another form of decep-
tion but one that at least promises "a burning remembrance that
one is alive still." As the sermon ends, Bill Elephant comes up with
one last scheme for finding a good pair of low-cost caulk boots. The
pursuit yields chastened student of life Dorn "a lesson in what I later
recognised as 'human dignity'"—and the shock of an unanticipated
outcome to his yearnings for contact with the structure of reality.

> Bill & I were pulling away from the crowd of listeners, going
> to one final used shop he knew would be open and might have
> boots, when a man in a wheel-chair rode toward the curb. He
> was wearing only a t-shirt and khaki pants and I noticed it
> because of the coldness of the rain. His legs were off at the
> knees, they ended in great balls of flesh, so they had proba-
> bly been amputated at the joints. His pants were ragged and
> they stuck out. But the wheel-chair was strangely new, in shiny
> condition, no doubt a remote gift from the mass of architects
> living in the remote surrounding hills. When he reached the
> curb he hesitated, his strong hands began to ease the wheels

down one before the other. But somehow, on the edge of the slippery curb, the other wheel skidded and he went over forward on his stubs, tearing them both open. Blood poured immediately out of his legs, where all the great passages of veins had been turned back at the operation. Suddenly I didn't know what to do. Half-fascinated by the pouring forth of the red blood on the shiny wet pavement and also full of half-formed impulses to help him for he was struggling with one hand on the arm of the chair, which pivoted crazily back and forth as he struggled like a helpless landed fish. Bill was saying Jesus Christ! Jesus Christ! Then I was suddenly there, but with no strength, my arms were around his chest, lifting. He was so very heavy, with well developed arms, a powerful torso. And I, trying desperately at the same time not to get any of the blood on me. And I have since wondered over & over why? Why didn't I want the blood on my clothes? My face was so close to his. He was broken out in sweat. But he stared into my eyes, embarrassed for me, for my struggle to help him. And I wondered if it was possible I was doing something wrong. By the time I had gotten him back into the chair, I was embarrassed too. Then he thanked me for helping him, but I knew it was hardly the point. It was an object I had handled, no less to him than to me, and we were both, now, considering it. A simple "thanks" was all that was called for. And all the feelings I had secretly had, of heroic benevolence, at least to be genuinely able to help someone who needed it, were dismissed with a suddenness as I became aware, staring at the man, wheeling away in his chair, his legs bleeding, that here was a man isolated with that pain.

From this stark moment of unmediated encounter with the pain of the actual the sketch subsides to the quieter tones and chiaroscuro relief of an atmospheric scene in the "rich," mortality-drenched "old brown interior" of a final second-hand shop, where a "feeling for Earth, for shadow," replacing the weeping blue-greys of the mist and rain, envelops the weary shoppers. Browsing among piles of old army coats whose colors "are a ghastly deception in daylight, but here ... show a true hidden blood," and stacks of the spiked boots of long-gone Wobbly loggers, "sticking up at random as though those men had fallen here," they reach the end of their search. Haunted by the spirits of dead soldiers and lumberjacks, the thrift store appears to Dorn "a magically registered graveyard for lost tribes of former forest inhabitants & fittingly soldiers too: the formalized proletariat." Lost markers of a forgotten work force of the dead, these articles seem soaked through with a human historical meaning that goes beyond their exchange value. Dorn's quest to purchase objects of use ends in an ironic image of the ultimate emptiness of all such commerce.

5.

Rain, and More Logs
(Skagit Valley)

THE METAPHORICAL LABOR of "getting out the logs" in beer joints was one thing, the laborious daily grind of making one's way to and felling literal trees quite another. It took only his first Monday morning on the job to remind Dorn that logging was brutal, exhausting and dangerous work.

He had to be up in the damp, cold darkness at 4:30 A.M., out of the house at 5:30, and at 6:30 joining his five-man crew aboard the "crummy" or company conveyance, part of a ragged caravan of vehicles ranging from enormous tandem-wheel trucks to battered dwarf pickups, for the long slow climb through raw, exposed, mist-drifted "slash" country littered with fallen-down equipment sheds, "massive coiled up cables, rusted and waiting," and hulking, "huge dinosaurs of old machinery." On the "crummy" he discovered a rough segregation between the confident, talkative "home guards," hardy veterans of the woods, many of whom dwelt with their families in company row houses at the base camp, and the silent newcomers like himself, "city men ... dehorns, [or] drunks who have come up from Archie's ... worthless shifting material for the lumber companies." The home guard generally regarded the "transients" from a cool and watchful distance, leaving these inexperienced men to sort out for themselves the substantial difficulties of the job. The standard all-purpose advice to newcomers, issued with a grim smile, was "anything you touch can kill you." "Loggers are friendly enough," Dorn would observe. "But ... they are ultimately complacent, and very used to seeing men come and go. And all the years bring the same thing: rain, and more logs." After the long, rocking ride came the grueling half-hour hike, straight up a slope so steep that rocks rolled into one's shirt pockets, to the cutting zone, where the real work of the day began.

On that first morning the long walk on logs up the side of the mountain posed a strenuous test in itself. "The going was very tough on me," Dorn would write, "and I hadn't gone more than a hundred and fifty yards when my legs gave out and from there on up, I literally forced myself, although the pain was terrible. I hadn't had anything but low cut shoes on all the years since I had first worked as a logger. Logging boots weigh a ton if you aren't used to them. But the spikes saved me from falling into a twenty-foot hole of brush and rocks once. And at last, not thinking I would ever be able to do a day's work, we arrived at the spar tree." Collapsing wearily on a log to get his second wind, he attempted to take stock. "I had known I would be weak, and that it would take me several days or even weeks to get back into physical shape to be able to take that kind of work in my stride but I had forgotten how really exhausted a few steps up, in that altitude, could leave you when you aren't used to it." Peering down the great valley into "the noisy silence of the forest that rose when everything was quiet, when the sound of machinery lulled," he heard "a huge subtle roar com[ing] up into the air from the wind around the unending millions of branches of hemlock, fir and larch," and thought of his family down below in Burlington, "and how far off in the wilderness I had gotten since getting up this morning."

DOWN THERE BELOW, a new life was taking shape for the family. "This is really a beautiful valley," Helene declared enthusiastically to David Buck after a few weeks in their Burlington home. "We promised ourselves peace and quiet for a space before moving on...." By all appearances the promise had been kept. They had a "good place, really ... complete with fireplace, wood cook stove, raspberry bushes, a barn & our own 'mountain' & secret garden right back of the little barn. We're on the edge of town, so to speak, have the country but can walk 3 blocks to the grocery store. 'Baseball field' across the road & we got us a ball & bat & have family games, by the end of summer we should all be fat & healthy." In a situation that otherwise "seem[ed] heaven," the sole note of concern was contributed by the challenge of Ed's job, with its demanding physical labors and seemingly endless hours of daily transit. "E's work is pretty bad.... If you want manual labor for a change, *don't* pick logging!... But it pays well & soon he'll be in shape so he doesn't look like death every night." The woodsman/writer had started a novel about their latest migratory adventures, but though there was plenty of material to write about he was unable to do it justice, "mostly because of the physical exhaustion. We're praying he'll get used to the work & can do more than fall into bed when he gets home at night."

Even once Dorn had made himself fit for the physical rigors of logging, however, the monotonous, time-consuming ordeal of daily travel to and from the job remained a formidable problem—in the long run one he would not be able to overcome. From Bill Tindall and other forest cognoscenti he learned that the issue of arduous travel between camp and work site was "as old as the Wobbly insurrections." In the days of the Wobblies the camps had been located considerably closer to the work, at that: the first law of commercial production held that "the desirable wood is always receding from the site of the old original camp." From his homestead in the lower valley Dorn put in three hours every day just getting to and from the camp at Hamilton—"there and back two hours, with the other hour spent waiting about in one way or another, then when you got to camp it was an hour each way to the timber. Then there is the eight hours of work. Thirteen hours in all, but I never understood where the time went, it was fourteen hours the day lasted."

Among the other men who lived away from camp in the towns of the lower valley, Dorn found, the trials of transportation were regarded as a necessary evil, "taken as something common and not as a difficulty exactly ... [but something] about which they merely grumbled, more or less continuously." The combination of stamina and resignation displayed by these long-suffering fellow workers seemed to him a wonder. As the weeks went by he gradually despaired of similarly accustoming himself to the grind, acknowledging he would never be able to match the sheer endurance of part-time stump ranchers who milked cows in the dark before climbing into the hard muddy seats of the company conveyance, or of the stolid, stoic "war hoops," Fraser River Indians who commuted over 200 miles to the camp from shacks across the border in British Columbia, passing back and forth "from one world to another, every day."

6.

Chicken Feed

D ORN WORKED STEADILY in the woods through the summer until the dry season set in and with it fire dangers on hot days that forced earlier shifts and temporary layoffs, cutting into his pay check but providing a welcome opportunity to rest and write. "E[d] has either been not working or doing the night owl shift (leaves here at 2 A.M.!) and the time has somehow slipped by," Helene told David Buck in acknowledging his August support check. "But yesterday it rained at last so there should be steady work from here on (they can't log when it's so dry).... E. says the woods should remain 'logable' now till it snows." With Ed now earning a decent wage, Buck had requested a reduction in his monthly legal obligation from $200 to $100; the Dorns countered with a plan to reduce the amount in increments over the next year, and Buck had consented. The mutually-desired weaning from their dependent situation, however, would be postponed by unexpected events, which would force upon them an even greater reliance on Buck than before.

Dorn went back to work for Scott Paper at the end of September, but in October was "driven out of the woods by snow." He took a layoff for what was left of the season, but kept up payments on a company insurance policy that would all too soon prove precious. With his exhausting daily grind ended, there was time at last to begin work in earnest on the novelized account of the family's migration from San Francisco to the Skagit Valley and his subsequent experiences with "Bill Elephant" in Seattle and lumberjacking in the old-growth forests.

The family meanwhile was taking to country living with growing enthusiasm. "We are going to buy a cow as soon as Fred & Ed have the barn roof patched & the milk stall fixed," Helene announced. "The kids are excited about it—F[red]'s *sure* he'll be able to do *all* the milking! You would die to see us all sitting on a bench at the local livestock auctions—never dreamed I'd sit for hours looking at cows & enjoy it!" She hinted to David Buck that his prompt sale of the Morris Minor was being anxiously awaited: the deal was tied into their farm plans. "After we get the cow & necessary equipment, then, if you sell the car, we're going to hunt up a pony. (Have pasturage, for both.) We're doing the Northwest 'living' scene & the kids will at last see their 'farm' dream come true."

The outlines of the "'farm' dream" changed slightly in mid-September after Ed picked up a job near Mt. Vernon, five miles from Burlington, with John Smith, a flamboyant Bible-banging "spiritualist" he would caricature in *The Rites of Passage* as the hypocritical rural evangelist Albert Wonder—"a hellraiser in his youth," who upon marrying and settling down had "got religion and was very much a Hell and Brimstone quoter of the Bible." The work consisted of "gathering eggs, cleaning out from under the roosts, and filling the trays with feed." Within a few days of taking the job he'd been helped to decide he would be better off trying chickens on his own place than cows, which this late in the year would be a more economical investment (he was told) in the freeze locker than on the hoof. "To try to take the living thing by a different handle for a while we have bought a half of a beef @ $.20 per lb. We figure the meat will last six months at the inside. The freezing locker will cost $8 a year. Decided not to buy whole cow on advice of venerable farmer near by that it is better to buy in the spring and not feed it all winter. So chickens instead. We have a chicken house which I have been fixing up. I have been working for a chicken farmer, also a Spiritualist, for the last few weeks. We will have 10 or 15 chickens."

The connection with the "Spiritualist" farmer, Dorn allowed, was affecting his life and work in some curious ways. He was "writing a great deal" at night after work, he told David Buck. "Reading the Old Testament and all that fury and brimstone. Different slant on god and his children. Ectoplasm, Familiar Spirits, &c. We had a Seance one night after dinner and the spirits spoke to Fred. He thinks it's too crazy. We all hold hands you know in the manner of the Seance, in total darkness, the table raises and lowers by itself. Chanson, who is all too communicable with that world anyway, was afraid we wouldn't be able to handle it. Paul played on the floor with plastic Indians, in the dark. He doesn't care, or it's old stuff to him probably." ('I do remember the seance we tried," Fred Buck says. "I got a little spooked when the table started bumping, but I could tell Ed was doing it with his knees, so I broke the hand chain and turned the light on.")

Dorn would put in more than one stint working at the chicken farm in Mt. Vernon. Eighteen months later he found himself back there again, as he told Olson, toiling "like Isak, he who carried the stove up from a village in Lofoten" (on the Isle of the Maelstrom, in the Arctic Circle). Treading his own "endless circle" like that of the mythic hero, toting not a stove but "chicken feed on John Smith's farm," by then he had reason to view the routine humiliations of migrant farm labor as a kind of eternal recurrence of an early fate.

He told Olson in late November 1956 that with "time, and peace, here, to cool off, i.e. untangle, write a bit," he'd begun work on "some prose, not much to look, but coming along, I think." The writing, he said, was "quiet, simple, I mean plain, somewhat strange, but consummately easy. It's about a chicken farm I am intimate with not far from here. And the milieu of pentecostalism, local rollers. Christ's Teares over Jerusalem something to go by, not to touch." This first reference to early work on *The Rites of Passage* preceded Dorn's completion of his final draft of the novel by a full five years:

the chicken farm / "local rollers" material from this time was later on incorporated without substantial alteration. His stylistic model for the chickenhouse oratory of the womanizing preacher Al Wonder, as he indicated to his former teacher, was a work discovered in the course of the tutorial they'd done at Black Mountain on the Elizabethans, Thomas Nashe's *Christ's Teares* (1593). This obscure satirical tract, composed in a hyperbolic mock-apocalyptic tone, lent in Dorn's parody a "somewhat strange" subtext to the extravagant "fury and brimstone" preachings of the self-righteous chicken farmer in the novel. Nashe places his condemnation of a vicious, plague-ridden London in the mouth of an angry Christ: "Those that have been daily Fornicators and Fornicatresses ... Monstrous creatures are they, mervaile it is fire consumes not London, as long as they are in it...." For Dorn, the example of this vilifying extravagance provided "something to go by, not to touch" in casting the speech of chicken farmer Wonder to his migrant hero, on "the great advantages of getting with Jesus":

> The strange mix in Al of the practical, aspiring businessman and the evangelist, and how he could talk on for hours inside those loud contradictions. It amused Carl, and sometimes irritated him, that Al could assume such wisdom in the detailed consideration of what was wrong with Carl's way of life. One day, with some avid plagiarism of the Sermon On the Mount, Al told Carl that his loyalties were divided, he could not serve two masters at the same time, he had to choose, and in the end, when this show is up, it's going to be one way or the other and the man who loved *this* life is going to find out to his great dismay that the jig's up, that's all she wrote, all transitory, and what good is fornicating after all but the silliest smallest briefest little pleasure, a pleasure turned into an everlasting pain to be paid off forever, more than the unjustest debt any man around here could demand, a debt of pain unknown but to be believed, oh yes, you must believe it! And do you know, he looked Carl in the eye, Do you know the

one little thing you have to do to make it right? Humble your-
self to Jesus, to God! man, just humble yourself that's all,
that's *all*. Ask and it shall be given you! Just knock, and it
shall be opened unto you. That's all in the world you have to
do. But I've told you, Carl said, I like Christ very much, I can
say I love him. He is one of the best men I ever heard of, I've
told you that Al, I always thought so, from Sunday school
class on. I can hardly disagree with you, but I don't know
what you want. I've told you I think you live in a self-deceiv-
ing world, you run this farm like anyone else would run it,
and then you preach all this renunciation of life on earth that
you read about in the New Testament, you support usury
every day with those loans you have to have to keep going
and Jesus put that use of money down, why don't you walk
into the First National Bank and kick the president's ass out?

In *Rites,* Dorn's double-barreled satire turns Nashe's admonitory
rhetoric inside out, redirecting the zealot's reforming wrath back
against itself with an artful levelling relish. Carl/Dorn's exposure of
the evangelical farm-boss Wonder's "contradictions" is a moral
recognition around which the novel would in time be framed.

Ed's chronic skepticism and mistrust of proselytizing and evan-
gelism were plain to those close to him. "The good book came into
our house ... only as a source of story and parable and psalm," Fred
Buck remembers. "Worship was never part of it, but Jesus was def-
initely respected and Christmas was his birthday and we sang his
songs and gave him his due." Dorn's "own" Christ of these years
was not the self-appointed scourge of *Christ's Teares* but a sacrifi-
cial victim, a lowly underdog, a perennial loser in the eternal class
war—"a figure of great suffering, sympathy and tenderness," as he
would put it in *What I See in the Maximus Poems,* "infinitely manip-
ulable": less like the righteous overlord Al Wonder than the exploited
migrant laborer Isak, too tired for speech as he treads the "endless
circle" on the Isle of Maelstrom for chicken feed.

DORN'S WAGES ON THE CHICKEN FARM fell well short of what he'd been earning in the woods, and it was soon obvious that the transition to "country" self-sufficiency was going to cost money. By the end of September he was already reduced to soliciting an extra payment from David Buck in advance of their October family support check: this only a few months after they'd agreed to begin their "independence" campaign by the end of the year. Though he tried to veil the request in a birthday salutation to Buck, the birthday had already passed; Dorn also inquired delicately but persistently about possible funds from the sale of the Morris Minor, and enclosed a dollar bill for postage on a box of stored books he wished to have shipped on from Menlo Park. "Of filthy lucre" was the theme and refrain of his letter, which shifted in and out of self-conscious Biblical parody. "Of filthy lucre. Even with my working and all such as that ... we can hardly stand the initial investment it takes to live cheaper." Even $25 would help so that "if something happen[ed]" there would be something to eat "besides raw beef" when Helene's mother came to visit in October. "Of filthy lucre. This investing in the more economical and meaningful life probably has you in your eyehole with admiration. This is not all: we go about to farms and pick bushels of blue plums, ripe lush things in white bowls. In the end though, it is all worldly wisdom and should be acknowledged as such."

"Life is like the Song of Solomon," Dorn suggested to David Buck. In truth, however, their fruit-gathering bore little resemblance to the psalmist's paradisal vision of abundance: the reality had less to do with Biblical poetry than with economic necessity. "We were picking up fruit from the trees along the road as part of our diet," Dorn would allow twenty-five years later. "The last vestiges of nomadic habits collliding with modern waste." By then he had already spelled out the hard facts of the matter in some detail:

> This gathering process was a minor way of making ends meet.
> In that land there seemed such an abundance of edible things.
> If one went to a farmhouse and asked the woman if she would
> allow someone to pick the plums falling off her tree by the

road, she would usually look incredulously at the inquirer and then at last say, Why yes, if you want them. Oh lands of abundance. They are more cruel than those lands in which there is a scarcity. To see the suspicion come into the eye of an owner of trees who does not care about the fruit, but is trying to calculate whether or not the people who are asking for it will be trustworthy on the land, is an awesome thing. And in that land of abundance, begging was not the question, because these people or any other could have picked up the fruit without asking, but they felt obliged to make it legal. No matter what they felt about the waste of fruit, they respected the authority of the owner. But was it respect, after all. Perhaps it was simply a commonplace and casual fear.

These sentences come from *The Rites of Passage,* a book Dorn would cast as fiction, yet later speak of as though it were a true history, "masquerading as a novel ... simply a sociological study of the basement stratum of its time: the never ending story of hunger and pressing circumstance in the land of excess." The true-history aspect of *Rites* is confirmed by Fred Buck, who shared the trials it chronicles ("our life, our story, our friends, our suffering, our joy, our novel") and who still regrets Dorn's later decision, after separating from the family and remarrying, to "reconstitute it in his new life" in a reissued edition by changing the title (to *By the Sound*) and withdrawing the original "richly deserved" dedication "To Helene & the children, Fred, Chan & Paul."

7.

Animals ("Hemlocks")

They were pressed closely to gather fuel, food, or make compromises in a thousand ways for alternatives to what called for money....

There was a small barn in back of the house close under the hill. Someone gave them a pair of rabbits, and since there were hutches already, they raised them. At first Carl found it so difficult to finally kill one for food that the rabbits multiplied beyond feeding them. Some were turned loose. After a while, as things pressed the family more, Carl killed them a little more easily if no less anxiously. He could never stand the soft cracking sound the skull made when it was struck with a club. And the awful expectancy of the rabbit which grew into what he thought was a cognizance between himself and the animal....

Killing the chickens bothered him less and he thought now about why that was. He had been raised on a farm in Illinois. It was impossible for him to remember exactly how many times he had seen his mother wring the neck of a young rooster or old hen. It must have been several hundreds. He could still see her come out of the chicken house with the bird under her heavy arm, the thing would calm down slowly with short nervous sounds from the throat, a mixture of clucking and rasping gasps from its beak, almost a part of its breathing. Sometimes he would let him hold it and he could feel its swift heart beat. He could control the frenzy of its squawking. . . .

THE CHAPTER "THE EARLY DAYS" in *The Rites of Passage*—the book he would describe in a 1972 interview as "like a biography of myself"—spells out the complex associations of farm life for Dorn. "He was thinking about animals. It seemed a fixed cluster. . . ." In this confused train of thought and memory, "so vague and wandering now," he related animals to killing, cruelty, humiliation, the first stirrings of sex, poverty, work, and "the desperate loneliness" of his childhood. "That damned debased relationship raising animals," he found, still haunted him. "Feeding, eating animals . . . I look at animals and I think of my own life. A rabbit's eyes reflect my own life back to me." In this moment of truth he saw the creaturely domain intersecting human history in a brutal exchange of use and abuse; uneasy executioner gazing upon his helpless victim, he felt an obscure but palpable sense of identification, "a cognizance between himself and the animal."

"But he had grown up with animals. . . ." Keeping animals in Burlington, however, was not what it had once been in Illinois. Dorn was far less easy with slaughtering than with sheltering. His harboring of stray cats earned him the sarcasm of a roughneck construction worker he befriended, who upbraided him on the subject in a conversation recorded in *The Rites of Passage:* "Carl, you're sort of touchy about animals, aren't you? I mean, you have some sort of idea that animals are sacred, don't you? You think they should not be killed, I got that idea, but you eat the meat . . . what about that?" Indeed creatures acquired as a prospective food source tended to become members of the Dorn household, as is evident from family snapshots in which the children comfortably share photo opportunities not only with cats and a collie but with rabbits and goats.

In one photo a young black billy goat perches atop the cedar-shake roof of the Dorn's root cellar; in another, what appears to be the same goat, grown larger, accompanies Paul, Chan and a shirtless, cigarette-smoking Ed in a field of tall grass and wild flowers. In photos taken during the October 1956 visit of Helene's mother, the two younger children take turns cuddling a black cat. And Ed's mother is pictured on her February 1957 visit holding a full-grown Toggenburg goat as the animal is stroked by Fred. In another shot Ed and the children appear in the "secret garden" behind the house, Fred holding a very large white rabbit, Ed with one arm around Paul and the other resting on the flank of the large and noble recumbent collie. That "magnificent" collie, as Helene relates, was Laddie—acquired from a local pound, later run over on the large highway that skirted their house, and greatly mourned.

The family's proliferating rabbit population was memorialized in *The Hareling,* a children's book done as a cottage project, with Ed producing the text—about a newborn rabbit found in the fields—to accompany Helene's drawings. The best-remembered of the family animals, though, was the Toggenburg goat, Nanny, featured in Dorn's memorable 1959 poem "Hemlocks," an elegiac look back at the family's life in the Skagit Valley. "We bought her at a farm auction, thinking of sustenance but of course she became a pet," recalls Helene. "I even learned to milk her! The kids hated her milk but liked the cheese I made from it. We let her roam free in the yard and she used to come up when I was sitting out on the steps having a cup of coffee and chew on the buttons of whatever I was wearing. Goats are wonderful. Nanny gave us a lot of laughs and provided food as well. We got a billy goat to keep her company and provide us with kids which he did.... But taking them to be slaughtered was a nightmare. The billy goat tolerated me but did NOT like Ed. He peed on him whenever he approached, and billy goats have enormous pee power! We finally had to get rid of him. The house in Burlington had been a small farm at some point and we used it as such. The barn housed chickens, had a rabbit hutch outside, and we had a garden on the road side of it. We did, literally, 'live off the land.'"

That shared living would be kept vivid in the clear wet colors and bittersweet retrospective distances of "Hemlocks":

> Red house. Green tree in mist.
> How many fir long hours.
> How that split wood
> warmed us. How continuous.
> Red house. Green tree I miss.
> The first snow came in October.
> Always. For three years.
> And sat on our shoulders.
> That clean grey sky.
> That fine curtain of rain
> like nice lace held our faces
> up, in it, a kerchief for the nose
> of softest rain. Red house.
>
> Those green mists rolling
> down the hill. Held our heads
> when we went walking on the hills
> to the side, with pleasure.
> But sad.   That's sad.   That tall grass.
> Toggenburg goat stood in, looking, chewing.
> Time was its cud.
>
> Red barn mist of our green trees of Him
> who locks our nature in His deep nature
> how continuous do we die to come down
> as rain; that land's refrain
> no we never go there anymore.

8.

Interlude:
Is "Hemlocks" a Poem?

DENISE LEVERTOV, who as guest editor of *Origin* in 1954 had
accepted Dorn's first published poems, was serving in the same
capacity at *The Nation* in early 1961 when she took "Hemlocks."
The appearance of the poem in the magazine brought Dorn an
unusual letter of response from a New York attorney named Harold
Cammer, who wrote to say he'd "carefully read" the work and
remained unable to "see why it was published as a poem." The dis-
appointed reader detailed his frustrations in attempting to discern
a rhyme scheme, a rhythmic pattern, or a meter. "I feel I am miss-
ing something since the poetry editor of *The Nation,* which I respect,
obviously considered this a 'poem,' but I cannot find any basis for it.
I would be grateful if you would enlighten me about the theory of
poetry under which this becomes a poem...."

Dorn, it seems, was less offended by the lawyer's querulous tone
than flattered to learn that in his isolation he was reaching at least one
reader. His remarkably tolerant and thoughtful reply, running to
over a thousand words, comprises a serious defense of his way of
writing poetry. "Your question is fair," he wrote back, "but I am
unable to answer it with anything like yes or no as to whether 'Hem-

locks' is a poem. Personally, I do think it is, but then I am a poet, furthermore I think all my poems are poems."

He did not quarrel with Cammer's account of the liberties he'd taken in the piece, his departures from "normal construction," but suggested that in light of "a background of some fifty years of practice on the modern poem," such variations should be viewed with a certain "latitude of consideration." "Poems," he argued, "have a necessity in time and materials as does science or I imagine law"; his interrogator had overlooked this fact in judging poetry as though it were a uniquely timeless medium exempt from historical necessity. Such "measuring devices as once prevailed, and to a certain extent applied" had been rendered obsolete by the achievements of Ezra Pound and other moderns. "In the early part of the century the preoccupation continuously shifted from problems of feet and strictly scansionable lines to problems of what was then called image and is now not called anything with consistency. The freedom would seem to lie now in a search for Right content, form rather following that. Robert Creeley has said *Form is the extension of content.* I am simply putting that another way."

In fact the idea that the basic building block of poetry was not the metrical "foot," the syllable, the line, or the rhyme-scheme, but the *content,* was Dorn's particular—and curiously anti-modern—emphasis. He would reiterate his intent to re-valorize content in other statements of the period on his practice of the craft, for instance in a 1963 radio interview: "I know what meter is, but the way I write is usually in clots of phrase, and that usually comes out to be Idea, in a vague sense. I don't think Ideas come in units. When the individual line ceases to have energy for me, in those terms, I usually break the line there.... I don't think about measure and line, in a technical sense, that much. Clots of phrase, really. And not Olson's 'breath,' because ... [it's] a false problem ... I think it will become less important as the content of our speech becomes more important— as what we're saying becomes more important to all of us."

In this formulation, it appears that content is not, as in the legendary Creeley dictum, simply "extended" by form; content rather *is form,* or at least dictates all formal considerations. Prose, as implicitly defined in Dorn's response to Harold Cammer, is a centrifugal medium, has extension, travels and covers ground; poetry is a centripetal medium, has depth, is centered and returns constantly to its necessary places. The latter characteristics, moreover, are exactly those of "Hemlocks"—as Dorn patiently attempted to explain to the New York lawyer: "'Hemlocks,' to take that piece, is my attempt to govern a sense of place with certain recurrent properties of that place. It is not prose because the strictly emotional recall continually re-enters its own sphere, whereas prose is essentially an expansion of its materials, an attempt to embrace a given area, no matter how large or small...."

"Hemlocks," in Dorn's terms, is demonstrably "not prose." The poem's strictly emotional recall continually re-enters its own sphere, as repetitive as rain's steady, gentle, dying fall over sodden northern hills or a remembered life in a red house in a green mist. Dorn's expressive content here is the recurrence of the heart's desire for an endeared place, a desire whose fulfillment or denial is subject to the remote determinations of a mysterious absent Presence (or present Absence?) "who locks our nature in His nature." By foregrounding these key images in his insistently recurring return-lines—"Red house, green tree in mist"; "Red house. Green tree I miss"; "Red house. / Those green mists..."—Dorn makes "that land's refrain" serve both as central content and governing form. The *rentrement* becomes a refractive element, which, like a wave breaking back, repeatedly qualifies what has gone before.

Such use of a repeated element of key content, recurring through the poem with slight variations of wording appropriate to immediate context, and deployed in such a way that its significance develops from one recurrence to the next, emphasizing or reinforcing meaning by catching up, echoing and elaborating a crucial image or theme, comprises one of poetry's oldest formal devices, harking back in English to the medieval carol. Dorn greatly admired the poetry (as well as the novels) of Thomas Hardy, whose revival of late medieval return-line forms like the villanelle, the rondeau and the triolet as expressive vehicles for elegiac occasions provided an approximate formal precedent for "Hemlocks" (though Swinburne had been the more innovative versifier, Dorn proposed to Harold Cammer, "regardless Hardy was a finer poet"). Dorn's formal yet emotional recall in "Hemlocks" revolves around a paradoxically apart yet centered place where the empty spaces left by distance and absence are repeatedly filled up by the heart's echoing images.

In defending his own way in poetry to Cammer, Dorn stopped well short of suggesting that *that* way was *the* way, just as he carefully avoided attempting to "sell" "Hemlocks" as a poem to an avowed skeptic. He pointed out simply that he had improvised upon traditional iterative forms in a "modern" way, to express a feeling for place which could be expressed as well in no other fashion. "In that poem I tried to manage a line of variable rhythm length, of my own invention, to a constantly reiterated feeling about a place, a necessity of transmission. What is privately necessary is for any man to decide for himself, likewise what it is necessary to receive. Those are major terms with which to consider a poem today, it is my belief. If it doesn't set that way as a poem for you, then I can't see that any amount of explanation would make it."

9.

Legends of Resistance

DISTANCE FROM CITIES and from writer friends seemed to whet Dorn's intellectual hunger.

In an October 1956 letter from the Skagit Valley he told Robert Creeley he'd decided it was "better to be a Ghost in exile than to be eviscerated flesh meaning on concrete." For the site of his ghostly exile he could hardly have chosen a more remote spot: "a small obscure town resting ... on the left extremity of the land mass," as he described Burlington in one of a projected "*volume* of short proses called 'Bums & Drunks'" on which he began work late that year. In the tale, "Willis Moran," a barfly's persistent interrogation provokes from the autobiographical narrator a comically convoluted statement about his origins: "back of this question, and in a sense on all sides lay an immense geography of Hesitation, the forms of devil's towers and Dakotas...." He ponders a series of tentative replies— "grasping avoidances such as California ... and solid facts—Illinois ... "—before coming up with his answer.

> Where do you live? WHERE DO YOU LIVE?
> In a hole my dear sir where nobody is anything but shiftless, and the shifting of *where,* shiftless most...

In the fictional space of his tale Dorn was placing himself in the uncertain geography of his own history. Behind him yawned a vast emptiness of trekking, "three thousand mile stretches hauling wife and children hither and thither on top of the continental divide"; ahead loomed "Death ... a mere turn of the dial [to] great Colorados of endless waiting." Instead of merely covering more ground, he'd decided for the time being to dig in where he was, in his "shiftless hole."

He resumed his self-driven studies in isolation. Burlington became his graduate-school-in-exile, as he would suggest in a 1988 reminiscence.

> The big post graduate library for me was small town, not that different from the Villa Grove library in atmosphere but more advanced and more connected. Burlington, Washington. A narcotic little town of idiot savants and peckerwood survivors.

The local intellectual presence, as Dorn had discovered, was largely a rough-and-ready extension of the region's old Wobbly heritage.

> They were already shooting.... They would [have] deal[t] with the Aryan Nation and the whole Ft. Smith crowd by blowing up the bridge they was crossin' on. In the years I lived there they blew up the bridge at Sedro Woolley once a month because they got tired of waiting for the light to change. The rest of the time they just shot anything that moved, whether it changed or not. Nobody around there was interested in ambiguities. When I wasn't winding cable around hemlock I was reading the works of Wyndham Lewis and the volumes of *The Golden Bough,* through interlibrary loan, and the North-

western writers who were on the shelves. Archie Binns, rough realistic stuff with a romance angle superfluous and calculated. Wobblies, labor strife, verified by a lot of oral "input" riding out to the job, the legend of resistance—how a tightly rolled newspaper can become an effective club and gouge. In this age of high-[caliber] machine guns blown in on the zephyrs of smooth Peruvian kooka, all that's hard to imagine.

Dorn was discovering "the legend of resistance" in its modernistic literary aspect in the writings of Wyndham Lewis, whose prescient analysis of the tendency of machines to bring destruction would inform his view of the meaning of work—and of his own working experiences—during these years. (See for example the climactic chapter of *Rites,* "The Tunnel," which concerns a terrifying dam-construction accident.) Defining the plight of the alienated creative thinker in a mass-produced, robot-standardized anti-intellectual society, Lewis seemed to Dorn to be diagnosing the enslavement of human consciousness by the ruling-class technology of the future. Not surprisingly, it was the riskiest of Lewis's works which most excited him, even before he'd had a chance to check it out of the library: "Lewis's *The Art of Being Ruled.* I can remember the day it came in, wrapped in butcher paper and twine, official blue stamps all over it. I just screamed. I knew it was going to be the greatest book I'd read up to that time. It gave me the gift of sight."

In the months after leaving San Francisco Dorn had almost no contact with other writers apart from that maintained by correspondence. "We were lonely in Burlington despite all our oddball friends," Helene recalls. In these months Ed returned to his distances. He picked up again the Elizabethan study begun under Olson. "Have been reading in the more known minor Elizabethans lately. Nashe, Breton, Dekker, etc. Wild writing. But I stopped from sheer exhaustion with that language that was aborning, and of which every syllable gives forth its birth pangs." The preoccupation would before long stimulate him to assay verse in a long, expansive poetic line that would earn him a strong accolade from Olson, giving credit to his "Elizabethan ear."

Much of that winter Ed and Helene were at home together in their country exile. They began reading aloud to each other by the fire—a custom that would extend over the years. (They would eventually read their way through the works of W. H. Hudson and Thomas Hardy, among other writers.) That winter their "author" was Joseph Conrad. "We read together something [by] quite a man, this time Victorian I guess, have you heard of him, Conrad's the name?" Dorn half-joked to David Buck. "I had never read *Victory*. A too too much novel. Left us profoundly affected, I should say. Passages, many passages are branded forever, so to speak, on my mind, so called. I have never been so completely engaged in the last five years. It is certainly a 'great' novel, altogether, but I haven't heard anyone say so, at least not to me."

Working on his tales of migrant laborers, vagrants, drifters and outcasts that winter, Dorn followed Conrad, projecting a disquieting sense of betrayal and alienation in a world whose powers are uncomprehending, intolerant and exploitative. But his characters were his own, the characters of an immediate life. "You must understand that his stories and poems from that time were really autobiographical," says Helene. "We spent a lot of time in the bars drinking beer with the 'lowlies and outcasts,' making many friends among them like the hobo wino who loved the kids, ate sandwiches as fast as I could fix them, and one time when he knew he was going into the d. t.'s demanded Ed get him away from our house, 'I don't want the kids to see me.'"

The tales in the unfinished "*volume* of short proses called 'Bums and Drunks'" (as he described it to Olson) reflected Dorn's ongoing observation of life, conducted in the taverns and hiring halls of Burlington—"that town populated by loggers, migrant workers, tramps and construction people." Much of the speech in them came from the routinely downtrodden people of the place, to whom he felt obscurely compelled to give voice. He was still having difficulty finding his own way of speaking. "I can't open up my mouth quite, my old trouble," he would complain to Olson, to whom he'd shown several of the "Bums and Drunks" pieces—"Willis Moran," "Leonard's Wife," "The Polar Bear," "A Question of Hope." "And I can't bluff existence because I am NOT the raucous type, you know. 'Willis Moran' comes to a settling somewhat, as beyond 'Leonard,' but again, as a form, it closes itself up, at the end. I have trouble with what people say. I.e. should they at all *say,* or what. I have a bad ear, afterwards, but a damn good ear at the time." Contained narratives with dialogue, the tales presented him with problems of tone and structure; he felt constrained by the short story's implicit demand for formal perfection ("it closes itself up, at the end"), and daunted by the challenge of "posing" as a maker of fictions. Set aside during the life-trials of that winter, the *volume* was left unfinished; like most of Dorn's early work in prose it has remained unpublished to this day.

IO.

"The Rick
of Green Wood"

he/s avoided all cop-outs ... he/s woodshedded in illinois,
the northwest, the southwest, the south, and, i take it, the
value of woodshedding is that it lets you find out where you
are after you/ve gotten lost....
> —Joel Oppenheimer, reviewing *The Newly
> Fallen* in *Kulchur,* 1961

WHAT WOULD PROVE the fateful determining moment of the
Dorns' first year in Burlington occurred in the midst of their
otherwise happy early months. That August, Helene recalls, "we
were playing 'keep away' with the kids on the gravel road outside
the house. I slipped trying to catch the ball and went down on my tail-
bone. The pain was exotic, I actually cried, but ten minutes later
was back in the game and it wasn't till a couple of months later that
the effects started."

In late September she began seeing a Burlington physician—the
same one who'd treated Chan in their first days in town, and initi-
ated the "charity" drive—"for treatment of a pain, an intense pain,

at first irregular but increasingly constant, in her back," as Ed would later report to David Buck. The doctor, ignoring Helene's account of her injury, "insist[ed] that she had a lingering infection settled in her lower back." The Dorns would eventually consult another Burlington physician, and finally a local osteopath. "Our hope in this direction turned out to be just as fruitless," Ed would lament after the latter visit. "I am afraid I didn't pay close enough attention to my instinct, which told me that witch-doctors, in our society, have perhaps only changed their name." Helene recalls a series of "hopeless visits to doctors: 'remove your uterus,' 'go to Arizona' (that one sent me home with a huge bag of phenobarb which I took thousands of). And finally a chiropractor and his son—'I found it Jack!' Obviously they did. They also sent me home with phenobarb.... By that time I was crippled, couldn't stand, Fred stayed home from school to keep the fire going in the cook stove and fireplace."

Keeping the fires going was by this time a major chore in itself; with the extending and deepening rains of late autumn and early winter the repetitive wood-gathering routines turned into a central survival ritual, symbol of the family's subsistence economy. "We'd totally underestimated the amount of wood to stockpile," Helene says, looking back. At a low point in this long cold season of uncertainty and trial Dorn would report to Olson that for some weeks he had done nothing save "pretty much empty my interiors on getting wood to keep us warm by the fire." "Wow, there's a scathing rain here today," he would write in another letter of that winter. "Cold, wet, miserable, you know. Last week we got two cords of good wood, fir, and some cherry, and larch, fairling dry ... we keep the fires going."

A light, dry brightness or singing quality pervades the late 1956 Dorn wood-getting lyric "The Rick of Green Wood," which offers the modest warmth of the laconic poet's interior weathers as a charm against that creeping Northwest chill.

> In the woodyard were green and dry
> woods fanning out, behind

a valley below
a pleasure for the eye to go.

Woodpile by the buzzsaw. I heard
the woodsman down in the thicket. I don't
want a rick of green wood, I told him
I want cherry or alder or something strong
and thin, or thick if dry, but I don't
want the green wood, my wife would die

Her back is slender
and the wood I get must not
bend her too much through the day.

Aye, the wood is some green
and some dry, the cherry thin of bark
cut in July.

My name is Burlingame
said the woodcutter.
My name is Dorn, I said.
I buzz on Friday if the weather cools
said Burlingame, enough of names.

Out of the thicket my daughter was walking
singing—
backtracking the horse hoof
gone in earlier this morning, the woodcutter's horse
pulling the alder, the fir, the hemlock
above the valley
in the november
air, in the world, that was getting colder
as we stood there in the woodyard talking
pleasantly, of the green wood and the dry.

Five years later, on a visit to New York to promote his first collection of poems, *The Newly Fallen,* Dorn would tell a radio interviewer that "A Rick of Green Wood" represented for him the intensely local knowledges his lyric poetry of this time had sought.

> I don't have anything obscure in me to say. What's obscure in me is what I know. And that's what I try to get at. It may seem a waste of time to try to get at something you know, and only that, but I think that is a limitation I have, and if I can exploit anything, it will be that, as fully as possible.
>
> When we lived in Burlington, Washington, poems like "A Rick of Green Wood" came out of a direct influence of what I found myself in. Still then, I wasn't able to feel myself in relationship to a larger world than all those very small valleys and rivers that exist there. And still, I think the first sensible thing I did was to try to make it that way, at least, as a beginning. . . .

In fact he had left the poem out of that first collection, in part because an influence of Robert Frost, a poet whose disposition he did not care for, had been detected by some readers. ("I can't stand the thought of that!" he would one day tell me, irate at even the memory of the suggestion.) Among his peers, however, "The Rick" was credited with a particular singularity. "I like your poems," Robert Creeley would write that December, "I like particularly 'The Rick of Green Wood'. . . . I like the play of rhyming in it, and the good nature you have in it—the 'old song' finally, of it—which at moments I nearly despair of, for myself." And Creeley would return again to the poem, singling it out in his preface to Dorn's 1978 *Selected Poems:*

> Charles Olson used to speak of Edward Dorn's *Elizabethan* ear for the sound of syllables. That is, he was very respectful of this poet's ability to make every edge of the sound in words articulate. He didn't just go pounding along on the vowels,

o sole mio, etc., he obviously enjoyed all the specific quality of sound that one could also make sing, e.g. .... "I don't / want ... cherry or alder ... would die." It's not easy to make "or alder" feel so comfortable a thing to say, and you'll see, or rather hear, how he goes on playing this sound in the next line of this first poem, an early one indeed....

But the most thoroughgoing craft-tribute the poem would receive would come from the poet Robert Duncan, who "reviewed" it in an unpublished essay after seeing it in John Wieners' magazine *Measure:*

> "The Rick of Green Wood" is a poem devoted to the rich pleasure (lasting) of sound and simple sense.... Here, the woodyard is a woodyard; cherry or alder are cherry or alder: just this freshness and directness counts. Melodies of tone leading "fanning" to "valley" or "slender" to "get," of full rhyme sounded in beautiful changes, against changes of measure within the line. Its complexities are in the tonal pattern. It is a song of delight in the changes rung of single syllable words and their compounds ("wood", "yard", "green", "dry", "buzz", "saw", "thin" and "thick" ... "enough of names") with two-syllable words ("fanning", "valley", "pleasure", "cherry", "alder", "Friday", "daughter", "thicket", "cutter") that sends "SINGING" in turn three three-syllable words ("Burlingame", "november", and "pleasantly", this last the only qualitative adverb in the poem) ... keeping single meaning (thus: actual things, clear as a line drawing might render them). It is in the same a song of delight in expected and unexpected rhyme, expected and unexpected movements, as after "walking"
>
> "SINGING"
>
> comes "backtracking the horse hoof". These are simple excellencies that come from complex attentions.... Dorn's words

disclose a pleasure for the eye to go allied to the pleasure of the ear, a place, Bruegel clear, of green dry woods; beyond, a vista; just there, out of the thicket, his daughter walking: and a time, that was getting cooler, november. These are natural to the word.

I I .

The Blue Cowboy

As full winter descended Ed could no longer keep up with the increasingly demanding wood-getting regimen. "We started using coal which took less space and was easier to keep in a smoldering state," Helene remembers. Despite her worsening back pain, Christmas was celebrated around the open fireplace. A box of toys for the children from David Buck contributed to the subdued festivities, helping "to make this a wonderful Xmas despite odds." Paul, the youngest, got a cowboy outfit. "I wish you could see our house, most any hour of the day, and you'd know you really made it with P's present," Helene wrote to her ex-husband. "There is an eternal cowboy on some arm of some chair forever vigilant—and I am being run across by horses—all day long." While the rain fell outside, colorful cowboys rode a wild range in the kids' crayon drawings. The Dorn poem "Vaquero" dates from this time—"Ed's response to a crayon drawing of a cowboy done by Chan or Paul in Burlington," as Fred Buck recalls. Helene preserved the drawing. "I sent the drawing to Paul, I am pretty sure it is his." (Later on, one of Paul's western drawings would win the grand prize in the Rodeo de Santa Fe poster campaign—"I still have the newspaper clip," says Helene:

"'a seven-year-old first grader ... beating out all other student con-
testants including high school entrants.'")

The cowboy stands beneath
a brick-orange moon. The top
of his oblong head is blue, the sheath
of his hips
is too.

In the dark brown night
your delicate cowboy stands quite still.
His plain hands are crossed.
His wrists are embossed white.

In the background night is a house,
has a blue chimney top,
Yi Yi, the cowboy's eyes
are blue. The top of the sky
is too.

Dorn sent the poem to Olson, who dubbed it "the Cowboy in
Blue" and cited it, along with the tales "C. B. & Q." and "The Polar
Bear," as an objectification of Dorn's resistant temperament: "the
p[iss] o[ff] ... makes you an eternal object (that you know) ... but
it also defines objectively whatever it is that makes you p. o.'d ...
it's this ... which you ... exploit." The evidence of family history,
however, suggests Olson may have been mis-reading (or reading-in).
At any rate the poem made an immediate impression. Creeley, to
whom Dorn sent a copy, asked to publish it in the *Black Mountain
Review*'s eighth issue. When the *Review* expired and the issue died
aborning, the poem was taken by editor Donald Allen for the *Ever-
green Review,* where it appeared in the summer of 1958. It has com-
manded a loyal readership among poetic cowboys and others ever
since. (At a memorial tribute in San Francisco after Dorn's death,

his friend the English poet Tom Raworth recited "Vaquero" from memory, testifying that had it not been for that poem, he himself would not have taken up writing poetry.)

12.

A Mean Business

THE DORNS' OWN HOLIDAY GIFTS to faraway loved ones that year consisted of boxes of eggs produced by their chickens. The only box that did not arrive broken was the one sent to Helene's family in Duluth—causing Helene to suspect her folks had lied about that one to save her feelings. "We gambled and lost," she told David Buck, apologizing for the imperfect packaging.

The broken eggs bespoke the fragile state of things at the house beneath the hill in Burlington. Helene's condition did not improve with the New Year. "I am still a cripple," she admitted to Buck. The seriousness of the situation could no longer be disguised. "We've waited on 2 m.d.'s and an osteopath for 6 months now and it is just getting worse—to hell with THEM!" By the third week of January, as Ed reported to Buck, she was "unable to get up. Out of bed, stairs, in the morning (no novelty, I must say), etc. There is no doubt at all the pain is exquisite." A few days later she couldn't "even straighten her legs."

Dorn was forced to quit his job on John Smith's chicken farm so as to look after matters at home. Normally reticent about personal concerns in his correspondence with Olson, he now dropped vague hints of trouble. "A mean business," he summed up the current state of things on January 10. "The weather is not nice. And it isn't very often possible to exercise the ancient gesture of looking up at the sky to see what might be there. The days are broken by the nights and that is a comfort. The houses I care to go into here are a comfort from the shocking weathers." A week later he was more specific about the problems in his own house. "Helene isn't feeling so well.... The local doctors have unanimously fucked the dog for these past four months and she is in considerable pain—located in the back, lower." He was now "frightened enough" to search out further options—"almost, in my own harassment, ready to recommend a head-shrinker," as he told David Buck. The latter idea "infuriated [Helene] of course," and was quickly dismissed. At this point of crisis friends suggested the Virginia Mason Clinic in Seattle; he made an immediate appointment. "Hope it will work the magic button and tell me what's wrong and I'll be able to sit, stand or walk again," a worried Helene told Buck as they prepared for the worst.

After an initial examination at the "high powered clinic" she was hospitalized for tests—"two days of x-rays, chest, rectal, lumbar, barium and finally a kind [of test] in which a needle was stuck into the spine and colored fluid injected and then the needle tapped in various places." This "nitemare spinal check" yielded a preliminary diagnosis from the neurologist in charge of the case: "either a tumor, or, and he thinks this is *extremely more probable,* a ruptured disk," as Dorn, plainly alarmed, reported to David Buck.

Exploratory surgery was recommended. The operation took place on January 28. "It was what they thought it to be," a relieved Ed relayed back to Buck. The disk was removed, "a laminectomy as they say—'as large as a strawberry' ... the neurologist judged it was 'bad' enough to cause all the pain she had." "One of the nation's first laminectomies," Helene now says. "I'm sure it cost a fortune, but we did have some insurance otherwise they'd never have let us in the door!"

Ed's having retained the Blue Cross coverage provided by Scott Paper—a precaution that was "unlike myself"—indeed constituted the "one happy note" in their otherwise bleak situation. But Blue Cross was "good for only half the hospital bill," as he was soon faced with explaining to David Buck. The $50 he'd had to "plunk down ... to get her in" had broken the back of the frail family budget. He was reduced to begging another "advance" from Buck, and to hinting to the surgeon that they would not be above accepting charity. (Buck sent $50; the surgeon agreed to "knock some off the operation.") So as not to tempt fate or further charges, he took pains to "strictly avoid the front desk" on visits to the hospital—even though, as he confessed to Buck, "my children make a playground out of the lobby."

Helene spent twelve days in the hospital. Of a total hospital and surgical bill of $750, the Dorns came out owing only $150. "Not so bad, considering we could owe $750 a sum I don't have too much familiarity with." Meanwhile Ed remained out of work, and the family was all but out of money. He'd spent "an unbelievable amount ... on going back and forth to Seattle, baby sitters, canned soup (uhg!) and paper plates." On the day before Helene's release he screwed up his nerve and asked to "borrow" another $200 from Buck, proposing in exchange to "skip one [payment] later on in the spring or summer." There were some things "beyond the cost of living" he had to arrange for Helene's return, such as acquiring "an 'easy chair.'" He told Buck he was exhausted by their recent struggles, but that with the family coming back together and the worst presumably over, "things seem possible, no matter, the sun pricks our horizon at last." Once more Buck saved the day.

13.

"The Hide
of My Mother"

WHILE HELENE WAS AWAY in the hospital the weather in the valley got meaner. During a fierce spell of cold and snow from the north, Ed, unable to keep two fires going, spent the nights huddled with the three children "on a makedo bed on the kitchen floor by the heat of the cookstove." The daily burden of dragging the whole brood with him to Seattle aggravated the stress of the medical uncertainty, leaving him, as he admitted to Buck, "a bit bitchy." In a poem he recognized the small blessing of a neighbor's kindness—"the graciousness / of the woman of the junkman"—in taking the two younger children for a day:

> the junkman's
> woman had been so good to us
>
> a truss as it were, had kept the children
> when it was a hardship
>
> the condition had been foul, sleet,
> masses of air, a raw affair,

dumped out of the Yukon upon
us, roving bands of weather

sliding across British Columbia
a kind of dementia

of the days, frozen water pipes
and the wringer on the washing machine

busted, no coal.
Our house split in two like Pakistan.

Making arrangements for child care was now an urgent priority.
The women Ed knew in town all had "children of their own, fami-
lies, and so are pressed already." Hiring a live-in nanny, he discov-
ered, "would cost at least 8 dollars a day ... which is of course
unthinkable." Out of options, he turned to the one caregiver he
could count on and most trusted, writing to his mother "to see if
she would be willing, or could at all come, out here, and help." To
his immense relief, Louise agreed to come immediately. She arrived
in Burlington by train a few days ahead of the convalescent Helene,
and quickly took command of the household. Within a few days she
was exerting her characteristic opinionated but concernful presence,
"saying to my little boy, / like to go home to Illinois with grand-
mother?" and offering caustic comments on the abundant Dorn
household fauna ("why don't we throw them all out the door!")
and the sodden climate ("well now, there's more rain here / than we
have in Illinois in an entire year"). Ed reassured David Buck that
there was now much less to be concerned about: his mother "would
be here to insure the whole thing wasn't for naught, and she will do
the work."

Helene came home, "apparently, all mended," at the end of the
first week in February. She had been told she would not "be able to
do one simple bloody thing for one month." Outlining the prospec-
tive rehabilitation process for David Buck, Ed attempted a wrinkle

of humor in a bleak moment. "And for 6–8 months will have to take the utmost care to not lift anything over 5 grams, not twist, jump or play golf … all these problems will have to be worked out." Neither partying nor playing could be indulged for a while. "Recuperation from my surgery was a bitch," Helene recalls. "I sat helpless in a chair, did a lot of sewing by hand, clothing and quilts for the kids." The first major activity to occur in the house after the surgical patient's return was the highly practical flurry of pipe-fitting that went on when John Smith, the scripture-quoting chicken farmer, taking the part of the Good Samaritan, pitched in to help Ed install a hot-water heater—"prior to which," as Helene says, "our supply of hot water was in a big pot kept on the back of the wood cookstove."

Confronted by the reality of Helene's slow, lengthy recovery, Ed had to put on hold once again the vague graduate-school plans which had intermittently occupied him for the past three years. Earlier in the winter, before the severity of Helene's health troubles had become fully apparent, he had again extended inquiries to the University of Washington, and had obtained a copy of his Black Mountain transcript from Olson. "I am going to try to make a master's degree," he told his former teacher. "Will see where that leads, naively enough. I am having to work at altogether nagging occupations anyway for long enough to make me sick of it." To David Buck, whom he was counting on for funding, he admitted that he did not "look forward to reassociation with 'modern educated man,'" but felt he "had better get to it, before the fire goes out altogether."

In the present circumstances there could be no thought of academics. Once Helene had recovered sufficiently to cope with the household tasks, he would have to find work close to home. There were rumors among Burlington's casual labor force about well-paying construction jobs opening up at a new refinery near Anacortes, but word had it only union men would be hired. A grizzled concrete-finisher named Leonard with whom Ed had grown friendly went to bat for him. "A friend heard of our plight and went to the union, got Ed accepted," Helene reported to Buck in late February.

"[He] even thinks he can get them to dock $40 off the $100 [union] initiation fee." The thoughtfulness shown toward them in their time of need by the rough-hewn local working people made a powerful impression. "These people, workers around here, are so great. I don't know whether they still have strains of the pioneer 'we're all in it together' or what, but they sure replenish one's faith in humanity. We've even been given a TV to help along my convalescence." The kids and Ed's mother appreciated the new appliance, even if Helene and Ed, still distrustful of the one-eyed beast, wished privately that "the damn thing were a thousand miles from here."

The promising refinery work remained only a hopeful gleam in the sometime worker's eye. With Louise looking after the kids, Ed canvassed the town for odd jobs. After a windstorm at the end of that month he picked up a few days' employment with his neighbor "the junkman," helping repair downed television antennas. The modest pay represented his first earnings in six weeks; "you know the saying about every little bit," Helene ventured, trying to sound cheerful. After three weeks at home she was "slowly but surely making progress," could once again dress herself and with the benefits of Louise's cooking had added some needed flesh to "the uncomfortable 109 pounds I was when I got home." "The toughest month of the six months' convalescence is now behind me, or should I say us, spring is on its way...."

Dorn's spare, dry, offhandedly rhyming humor in the poem "The Hide of My Mother" is his moving memento of this time of courage, perseverance and trial:

> Tho winter's at term
> it still gets cold
>
> in the evening.
> My pets are warm
>
> because I have set a fire.

My mother is arranging some ferns
and young trees, a little too big

she found in the mountains.
A jig, of a sort must be going

on in her head. It is raining
outside ...

14.

The Blackest Hour

NEITHER THE HARD NORTHWEST WINTER nor the Dorns' struggles were yet quite "at term." "Strong March winds trying to keep spring off" raked through the hemlocks and cedars. Helene, trying to resume household chores after Ed's mother left, "overdid," and suffered a discouraging setback ("neurologist says no bending and lifting for maybe months"). With Ed still out of work, meanwhile, every penny had to be counted. "One-half this month's allowance," as Helene told Buck, had been spent on a ticket to ship Louise back home to Illinois. They'd already borrowed from Helene's mother, who anyway had been sending "money every month to help out." Dorn's work prospects at the refinery in Anacortes remained in doubt, with hirings repeatedly postponed. "Pray for us that this construction work isn't just a dream. If it is, the snow will soon be off the mountains and Ed will have to go back to the woods." They investigated the possibilities of getting county welfare, and found they could not qualify until they had a year's residence. Whether out of principle or fear, they remained reluctant "to lie in such a case," even if it meant starvation. "We've nothing left," Helene announced in late March, requesting the next month's support check in advance.

They were "simply rather desperate."

Her recuperation, it was plainer by the day, would not be speeded by praying. Though reassured by her doctor that her persisting pain was "something some patients do go through," she faced a "long road ahead." A trip by Fred to visit David Buck in Palo Alto had to be put off because in the event Ed did find work, she would require the reliable lad "to be here to do my lifting." In their straitened circumstances the Dorns strained to extract hope from little things. By mid-April there were finally real signs of improvement in the weather: "Spring is upon us inside & out and we all feel light because of it." They gathered wild flowers in the fields outside the house and placed them in bowls to brighten the surroundings. Ed, unemployed and at home, commemorated the long-awaited burgeoning in a small lyric titled simply "Bowl of Flowers":

> unwise self, will while
> it all, dwindle the hours
>
>   pick
> a bowl of floweres
>   leave
>
> a water bowl of floweres
>
> disk of yellow, upon the shelf
>
> before I go

With the spring flowers, however, came other, less pleasant events of the country season. The family goats, much beloved, had produced offspring which had become instant companions for the children, but now had to be sacrificed. "We have to take the kids to the slaughterhouse," Helene reported sadly to Buck. "Chan says she'll die before eating them (and I believe her, but our locker is empty)."

Dorn could be forgiven for comparing the fate of the sacrificial animal, born to be put to death, and that of "the unemployed man," who "has not been born to anything." His latest workless spell inscribed another chapter in an unheroic saga—what Helene called, in yet another emergency appeal for funds to Buck, "the seeming prolongation of 'the desperate Dorns.'" For the struggling writer it was a story whose psychic ramifications—shame, embarrassment, guilt, anger—were already too familiar. To Olson, on whose *Maximus* poems he'd volunteered to attempt an essay, he admitted he'd been stuck "a damn long time" (four months in getting started): "Things are rather knotted up for me right now." His efforts to write his way through his stubborn blockages, straining to untangle things, seemed only to tighten the internal knot.

> As for ourselves, I don't know whether we are approaching the blackest hour or have witlessly passed it, or what I would do if I knew. And as for our life here, it consists of that. It is most difficult to crawl up out of the hole when one can't even ... see the light that's supposed to come from the top.

He evinced disappointment over failing to make it to San Francisco that spring for Olson's appearance at the Poetry Center, explaining "there was no help for it": he couldn't afford a bus ticket, couldn't anyway get away from home.

> I think I am trying to find a job. It seems to be difficult. From what they say. I take their word, as if by habit, or helplessness. Sometimes I think I have a perverse built-in, inherited morality to be always so suspicious. Everyone can't always be grinning behind my back, or can they? Strangely enough, I would willingly do what they told me, if I could find the flaw in the gauze to crawl back into. I find the world can readily ignore me. I mean I find it all over again. The fantasies of how it would be if it didn't are rather plentiful, and this becomes an easy confession.

15.

No Success like Failure ("Like a Message on Sunday")

The plumber pours himself another cup of coffee.
> —"Notes About Working and Waiting Around," 1962

Out on the street of the world: its busy creeping. The helpless plight. Where the plumber who can't get on stares sadly at his dwindling supply of pipe....
> —Dorn novel draft, 1956–1957

If I had a wild chauffeur to drive me ... to wherever Dorn is (I think his poem about the plumber by the river with his daughter is one of the most mysterious yet clearest poems in the world)....
> —Jack Kerouac to Robert Creeley, February 16, 1962

LIKE HIS PROTAGONIST in *The Rites of Passage,* Dorn would pass many unremunerative workless days wandering the hiring halls, the taverns, and the contemplative banks of the Skagit. In the private code of his writings of this time "staring into the river" represented an idle, futile—but independent—way of life.

> Carl was staring into the river.... Across the river was a thicket of trees. Below, along the bank, a collection of small boats. They bobbed against the down river current. The sky had become pearl grey. Whether or not it would rain was a real but unimportant question.

The image receives its lyric inscription in the poem "Like a Message on Sunday."

> Sits
>   The forlorn plumber
> by the river
> with his daughter
>   staring at the water
> then, at her
> his daughter closely.
>
> Once World, he came
> to our house to fix the stove
>   and couldn't
> oh, we were arrogant and talked
> about him in the next room, doesn't
> a man know what he is doing?
>
> Can't it be done right,
>   World of iron thorns.
> Now they sit by the meagre river
> by the water ...   stare
> into that plumber
> so that I can see a daughter in the water
> she thin and silent,
> he, wearing a baseball cap
>   in a celebrating town this summer season

may they live on

on, may their failure be kindly, and come
in small unnoticeable pieces.

Fred Buck recalls the poem's occasion: "The plumber and his kid coming to fix the stove. He was drunk, smelled like a wino. She was skinny and very solemn. I think Ed happened across them sitting by the river doing some errand later that day, thence the poem. We all talked about them and how maybe we should be doing something for them, rather than the reverse, but the whole thing was so helpless and sad."

"These sounds mark the placements of an inner world," Dorn would write a few years later of the work of a fellow poet of small-town backwaters, Lorine Niedecker (in his introduction to her first chapbook, *My Friend Tree*). "Such notations of an inner world are a little touchy now.... It is distinctly unusual to speak of failure with anything but the rankest distaste. As if that were the point, as if any so called situation is possessed of success." His clear yet most mysterious lyric "Like a Message on Sunday" gazes back at us enigmatically across both the unheroic waters of the Skagit and the helpless plight of "that plumber" who came to fix the Dorns' big sheet iron stove one day at 500 North Anacortes. Discovering failure everywhere in a "World of iron thorns," both outside and in, acknowledging it, and saluting it as if that indeed were the point: this is Dorn's way in an eccentric lyric that perhaps more than any other bears his particular idiosyncratic gestural signature, linking the pun on his own name in "thorn" to the other key term with which it's made to rhyme, *forlorn,* from *for + laesus* (loss) = bereft, destitute, "the helpless plight." This poem of the Dorns' second summer in Burlington deftly carves the harshness of poverty out of the heart of "a celebrating town," an act of not-quite-random kindness that suggests there is no success like failure—one of the central paradoxical laws of Dorn's world of difference.

"It's one of my favorites, that poem," says Helene.

16.

Stolen Riches

New Years Eve Carl took Mary downtown for a glass of beer.... Mary turned once to find herself being stared at by the man on the next stool.... He said, You're Canadian. She replied, No, I'm not.... [He] asked more questions and was generally skeptical of the couple's local residence. To him they remained Canadian. This word, along the coast from Blaine to Seattle, is commonly used to mean odd ball.
—*The Rites of Passage*

THE MARKS OF THE DORNS' DIFFERENCE were easily noticeable if not always readily identifiable: "Canadian," as Fred Buck notes, meant "weird and poor" to the family's middle-class Burlington neighbors. In his writings of this time Dorn not only refused to conceal the evidence of their strangeness but took pains to flaunt it. In one of his most telling poems of the Skagit Valley stay, "The Argument Is," he adopted this against-the-grain strategy, perversely locating value in one set of distinguishing signs of material deprivation. In this poem the children's second-hand clothing is worn as "a secret burden" in the double sense, both as a social emblem of shame weighing them down and as a reverse badge of honor, declaring their innocence of "the ways of society" (and thus freeing them from responsibility for its complex injustices). The poem shows Dorn's "political" thinking at its nontheoretical concrete best, revealing an empirical truth about life in the sociological "basement stratum"—where, paradoxically, the only true grace, a careless, casually-fitting castoff or "stolen" freedom, is to be found.

Helene confirms the scene of the poem is Burlington, and that it is "definitely 'true to life.'" "Not sure who the little girl is," says Fred Buck, "possibly my sister."

> That worn clothes look
> as nice
> on the children down the road
> playing and running in the afternoon
> that these clothes are used,
> these castoffs
> we are castoff from—all the elegant
> running little retailers, here
> and in the next crossroads town.
>
> But the dress one little girl
> blithely wore, unaware
> an argument as to the ways of society
> was going on around her—
> a long yellow dress
> flowers
> pulled in at the waist, nearly
> sweeping the ground.
>
> Oh, they are now pagan
> these old castoffs,
> but as rationale one sees the grime
> sees the face broken in dark lines of consumption.

Of wearing secretly a burden,
costumes fitting as casually as though
they were stolen,
from the wealth
of the nation.

"We kids got shit in school," says Fred, "for dressing weird (Goodwill clothes etc.) and one of the taunts I got from neighborhood kids was literally 'Poor!!' Poor was weird then and weird usually meant poor, and as Ed wrote somewhere in the novel, weird and poor was also tagged 'Canadian.' So we were all of those and in isolation in so many ways in those Burlington years, not part of the town, hanging with the other weirds like Norma and Gordon in their pea shack, John the wino singing to us 'I'll buy you a rainbow' so sweetly and drunkenly, '202' and his toothless wife and their ragbag kids roaring up to our house in their banged up car and raising cain and roaring away again. True people and friends in the weirdness all melted away to whatever future we'll never know, but still in our heads and hearts and Ed's writing, bless him."

The fellow "weirds" Fred Buck refers to were to become key figures in the basement-stratum landscape depicted in Dorn's narratives of this period. Norma and Gordon appear in *The Rites of Passage* as James, a "desperately poor … flunky carpenter" with a drinking habit, and his equally hard-drinking wife Ramona, an Eskimo from Nome with a radiant smile. In the chapter called "The Difference," the struggles of this couple, shack-dwellers in a local migrant-laborers' "pea-camp," provide Dorn salient evidence of the multiple effects of class and race exclusion; particularly impressive is his drawing of the ironic contradictions of Ramona's character, candidly posing her "low" habits and qualities against her natural dignity and aspirations to a decent life. "202"—"no idea what his real name was, we called him '202' because he had a bumpersticker on his car saying Vote no (or yes?) on 202 [a union-busting 'right-to-work' bill]," says Fred—became another of the novel's main characters, Billy Hendersson, a temperamental, independent-minded hard-hat whose irrational explosiveness affords him a way to temporarily break out of the System, but also assures him trouble wherever he turns. Another case-study in ironic contradictions, this character figures in several pivotal scenes (in chapters "The Unemployment Office," "By the River," "The Deer," and "The Tunnel") as a latter-day manifestation of the frontier temperament now reduced to a self-destructive anachronism. (Billy/"202" also makes a cameo appearance as "Fletcher" in "Notes About Working and Waiting Around.")

Presenting "odd ball" images of scarcity amid excess, delineating scenes of actual poverty calculated to expose and undermine the easy assumptions of the Age of Affluence, it is little wonder Dorn found himself doomed to occupy a tenuous position in relation to the mainstream mass-market literary audience of the late 1950s and early 1960s. The very names of the ephemeral journals in which his writings were now beginning to appear—*Between Worlds, Migrant, The Outsider* (where both "Like a Message on Sunday" and "The Argument Is" would first see the light), *Wild Dog* (his own mimeograph magazine, done from Idaho)—bespeak this marginal stance. The characters of Dorn's writings of that era before the birth of the "counterculture" live out an edgy outcast/outlaw ethos; the lyric-realist graces of those writings seem "stolen," both in the sense that they must be stealthy (such is the outlaw attitude) and in the sense that they represent fugitive moments, precious time taken away from the central basement-stratum business of putting food on the table.

Fred Buck has a vivid recollection of casual food-gathering banditry undertaken with other children near "the pea factory where the peas Norma [Ramona] picked got trucked to. My friends and I would wait at an intersection up the street for the pea trucks to come by and slow down for the turn then grab a handful of vines off the truckbed. Good Eating! Sweet as candy. I guess they ended up in cans or birdseyed when they got to where they were intended." The sweetest of forbidden fruits, furtive pleasures "stolen, / from the wealth / of the nation," poems like "The Argument Is" were to my own generation (I started reading Dorn in 1959, as a college student) a secret sustenance, plucked fresh from a little-known writer's surprising and nourishing candor in an otherwise barren cultural moment.

I7.

Assholes & Elbows

D ORN'S UNION-MAN FRIEND Leonard was critical of his willing-
ness to accept almost any kind of casual labor. "Shitchew can't
fool around with that laborin there's nothin in that." Leonard's
observation reflected the general and intelligible view among Dorn's
working acquaintances that a smart young fellow like him ought to
be able to rise by his wits, sparing himself at least a little of the sweat
of common toil. In *The Rites of Passage*, "getting in with somebody"
is Leonard's phrase for the way the working game should be played.
"Carl answered that for all the time he had spent at the hall he had
not gotten any work yet so it was hardly a matter of having fooled
around with it anyway. Leonard said, Yes, I know, but shitchew have
to get in with somebody, you know that. I ought to getchew on with
me finishing concrete. There's where the pay is. Shitchew won't work
half the time at that laborin anyway, you know that. Shideye make
sixty dollars a day ora don't think I done anything." To prove his
point Leonard issues a drunken boast. "Shitchew oughta see the
money I got in my deep freeze.... Shideye never trusted banks." In
Dorn's "Bums and Drunks" sketch "Leonard's Wife," a dark-comic
tale of deception, betrayal and revenge among the rain forests, we

learn something of Leonard's buried history, and of the curious truth behind his boast.

But Dorn's own inclination was neither to hoarding nor to the particular forms of humiliation involved in perfecting the cunning arts of "getting in with somebody." (We recall Amiri Baraka's statement in a poem of posthumous tribute to Dorn, that "he'd rather / Make you his enemy / Than lie.") And indeed he had long equated all paid work with humiliation of one kind or another. In a passage of reverie about his farm childhood in *The Rites of Passage* he would trace the uncomfortable private meanings of the term "job" back to an early memory of the embarassment of accidentally seeing his stepfather outside a shed "with his pants down, doing his job"—i.e. having a bowel movement. A few pages later, he would comment that an unemployed man is able to think only of "money as the crux of his search," and "will never be misled by false propositions such as 'a good, steady job' or a slogan such as 'work your way up.'" Further care is taken to discriminate the humiliations of demeaning work done for money from the humiliations of false presence comprised in the forms of upward mobility known as "brown-nosing" or "getting in with somebody." The former kind of humiliation is the one Leonard accused him of "fooling around with."

In fact, however, Dorn's accounts of the many forms of taxing physical labor he performed during these years are hardly guilty of romanticizing the humiliations of such toil. In a brief stint at weeding strawberries for a farmer in the lower valley in early March 1958 he was acquainted by a fellow migrant with the vernacular phrase "assholes and elbows," which thenceforth became his chosen term for certain particularly demeaning forms of menial work which exposed the body to discomfort and embarrassment at once, compounding wage slavery with outright dehumanization. He shared the lexical discovery with Olson. "As a man said the other day, 'I wintered good'.... Crazy thing, when he is going down a strawberrie row weedin', his wife goes with her ass in the air, in his face, right next. He never seems to mind. There is a saying here, it may be in other places, but I haven't heard it—'I wanta see nothing but asses and elbows.' This is put in a boob's mouth, to indicate he expects an uncommon nice day's work. Wowee."

Although Dorn's union job at the refinery in Anacortes finally did come through, it proved "short lived as most construction is." Soon he was back in the halls again, waiting around. Another "laborin'" job that came his way would supply him a context for deploying the "boob"'s term in his "Notes About Working and Waiting Around." He was hauling and lifting large blocks of concrete at the construction site of a new Safeway store in Sedro Woolley.

> I am standing up, holding my back. It aches a little, having lifted blocks of concrete which were busted loose from the curbing-way all along the frontage and back of the new building. This concrete will be set in new, when the parking lot is made. Once in a while, if I can, I gaze out over the horizon, to rest my body. That's queer, come to think of it, they always say it rests thine eyes, to look afar. I just found it rested my entire body, the length of the stretch of the looking, over and beyond the dark green hemlock hills, a land of wet, where smoke rises all day long from chimneys, burning cedar scrap, or fir perhaps, burning away in an isolated far away country where progress is now coming, and new buildings, and where more things will be bought ready-made, in this new store, and where the man who now tries to keep a milk-cow will give up and work somewhere to buy milk solids. The pieces of concrete vary in weight from about 35 lbs. to 90 lbs. There is a vulgar saying workers have among themselves to describe a certain kind of work that is over difficult and in a sense ridiculous in manipulation of what they oddly enough still regard as *their* bodies. A kind of work that is mean in its confrontations. The saying—Assholes & Elbows.

18.

The Tunnel

D ORN WENT TO WORK with his friend "202" on a dam recon-
struction project at Baker Reservoir, located at the junction of
the Baker River with the Skagit near the town of Concrete, thirty-
four miles up the valley from Burlington. His duties involved setting
grout and tending a pump in a tunnel between the dam and a hydro-
electric powerhouse. It was a union job, a rare instance in which
"getting in with somebody" had actually led to employment. The
good pay and short (six-hour) shifts were positives. The conditions
of the work, however, proved alienating even beyond the scale of
insult that had come with "assholes & elbows" labor. The Baker
Reservoir experience was a laboratory of sorts for Dorn; the job was
perhaps the hardest test he'd faced in his years of migrant work.
There was not the backbreaking physical difficulty of breaking con-
crete, this time. The aspects of the work on which he would focus
in shaping his account of it into the climax of *The Rites of Passage*
were largely psychological: the long periods of enforced idleness, the
state of ignorance in which lower-echelon workers were kept as to the
overall nature of the project, and the anxious spells of risky activ-

ity underground, during which the monotony of the job gave way to a tense anticipation of substantial potential dangers.

> Men in the lowest position are usually uninformed as to the nature of the work they do, especially in construction ... they are kept standing about a great deal of the time. This requirement is the most difficult of all the situations a laborer has to put up with. On a highly mechanized project the carpenter is the only man who has a great deal of real, manual work. The laborer on the other hand is traditionally expected to look as though he is indeed working and when a foreman comes around he tries to look busy.... Men who run machines do not have this problem. They are an extension of the machine, and when the machine is idle, the man who runs it is expected to be idle too.... One speaks of "education" for adults and children. Instead of endlessly disposing of people as materials, it might do well to show them, for instance, the workings of a hydroelectric power system. This would not be too difficult since the system is near at hand and the largest class of ignorant workers have time to waste. Obviously, apart from the very interesting business of how water produces power, it would relieve those workers of the necessity to perform the rite of acknowledged cheating.... It would relieve the pressure, relieve and correct their sense of false presence, which relief is needed, false presence being one of the most prevalent of modern diseases. In effect, this planned policy to sequester men from work they are on the other hand forced to do, is one of the primary aims of the modern state: it is a planned murder beside which war is of little consequence. But in a world in which populations grow much faster than real work, such disclosures become pointless. As the world's cognizance, both technological and human, becomes greater, it ought to be able also to pause, and give that instruction which makes men feel less isolated from their surroundings. A state with a heart, if such a proposition seems reasonable, would

naturally be concerned with those men who are least able to understand anything.

In the denouement of Dorn's story, a nightmare sequence of subterranean terror, a tunnel in which the men are working collapses and the narrator's friend Billy Hendersson ("202") falls victim to what seems a violent retributive power of nature, "a subtle and terrible vibration of strength the men had never heard of or felt before [which] held grip on the powerhouse like a hand holds the lever of a powerful machine." Here, staging a scene of helplessness and horror that expresses in an intuitive, non-analytic way his perception of the truth of the worker's fate, Dorn resorts for once to fiction. The tunnel accident represents the sole significant episode in the novel which was strictly the product of the writer's imagination. "The Billy/202 accident was a fear we all lived with but it never actually happened," Helene relates.

19.

Piping Down
the Valley Wild
("A Country Song")

ALTHOUGH 1958 was another difficult year in the checkered annals of Dorn's employment history, it would prove a fertile one for his poetry. In early February he was felled by German measles, "sick as hell for 5 days throat rash spots / eyes for nothing but the ceiling." The affliction kept him out of work and at home until the middle of the month. Left alone, with the children off at school and Helene out doing errands, he stoked up the fire in the stove and allowed his mind the space to wander idly beyond the frosted windowpanes: "It must be wild / To get drunk on the country / In the cold burning air / When the orchard is empty / When winter stares with sloe eye / Thru bright windows...." The lyric mood of his sickbed notations was tuned to the lilting metric of Blake's *Songs of Innocence,* a "piping down the valley wild" whose light gravity seemed to fit the moment of his feeling.

A pure air of place filled the freshet of verse that followed over the next several days. Recovering, he rose unsteadily from bed, decided "Spring, is coming early," and went to work in the garden, turning over rich black topsoil prepared by the long months of deep soaking, clearing rows for planting in "the / Beckoning ground." Over this week of welcome false Spring, with daffodils coming up and cherry trees blossoming prematurely, he completed the six-part pastoral sequence "A Country Song," framing it with "a tag of Blake"— "And I pluck'd a hollow reed, / And I made a rural pen"—as epigraph. "A winter-time piece tethered / In his eye," these unhurried ruminations gathered and dispersed "Ideas of the land / Under a cold blue sky" evanescent as passing clouds.

The set represented "An obscure slight offering," a hopeful salute to Spring, capturing the plain and precious atmosphere of a life dwindled—or distilled—to an essential state of simplicity. "The country one is intended to be quiet, like it sometimes lovelily is here," he volunteered in sending along a copy to Olson on Valentine's Day. "But perhaps it is too much (quiet)?... [It] is just several hours old. It may still be wet.... Anyway, Blake is nice." With the typescript of the poem Helene put in a freshly fallen plum blossom—"from our (OUR) tree in the front yard," as farmer Ed proudly explained. Another copy went to Robert Creeley, who would single out the sequence for special praise in reviewing Dorn's first collection three years later: "Place is ... absolute ... in the variations of 'A Country Song'—as the last lines:

> Then in front of the fire
> We talk of Spring
> An obscure slight offering

The beauty of the thought, and line, throwing back upon the melody as it fades...."

20.

The Magick of Place ("Notes from the Fields")

P ERHAPS THE MOST POETIC of all Dorn's prose evocations of place, "Notes from the Fields: Skagit Valley" was written in response to a solicitation from the poet John Wieners (an Olson student from the final years of Black Mountain) for an issue of Wieners' journal *Measure* devoted to magic. In the thematic presentation of the magazine, Dorn's piece would appear under the rubric "The Magick of Place." The 1000-word sketch was his edited version of on-site notes on the activities of the numerous birds and occasional earthlings he saw in the farmers' fields where he was performing pickup labors that spring and early summer, tramping hay in silos and driving loads of it around to the feeding troughs and barns of dairy herds. "Here *are* some notes," he told Wieners in sending an early draft that June. "Wood notes perhaps. I call them field notes because that's literally what I think (about). As for magick, again I don't want at all to sound like the clodhopper I probably am but I can't, I still can't make it on that score." Once the proper province of religion and latterly pre-empted by psychoanalysis, magic, he suggested, had recently become a literary genre in the narratives of Truman Capote ("that goddamn decoining of content as practised by american realism") and the poetic "dream fantasy" of Robert Duncan. "I should think the forms of magick ... should be myriad.... You might even, profitably, go so far as to say what kind it is you want. But there isn't any MAGIC, i.e. one magick. It is made, on the spot. One *makes magic,* like love. This is man's gift to the Gods!"

Dorn's contemplative observations from the fields lived up to Wieners' set theme; he *makes* magic in the vivid clarity of his areal sentences.

> The meadow larks and the crows don't exist for each other. The lark is apparently always in flight. There is no question that the meadow lark is the loveliest of flying things. It has a slight manner when flying close to the ground, as one is walking across the field, of suddenly rising, sliding right into you with a turn that presents its blurred blue back, and the swift impression is that it is coming straight on back first, the outline of the tail, with the two streamers, the delicate feathering and quivering undercamber of the wings. But I suppose all it did was to turn, a bit, in its course. Then it flies with incredible speed two inches off the ground in a zig-zag line. But whatever manner it chooses, one's senses lag, in picking up the movement, a very sharp sensation, in this case. Or then, it seems, they will tumble together and roll over and over flashing the deep blue wings and the buff yellow breast, as it is with a slow color wheel. Everything flashing in the sun, low, over the green and yellow stubble of the field. What flying! The sheer exactitude of flying complexly and exhaustively, on the air, at that slight height, to the near ground. One sees how flying high in the sky loses its preciseness as flying and becomes, merely, "going someplace," as the crow does, who is better off on the ground, or the eagle, who is known for his nest, or as man, who created a considerable misery in the language when he spoke of himself as "flying," when all he ever did was transport himself in a straight line, a mostly mercantile endeavor from the beginning. Bad flight, in birds as well as

man, is curious. One hears of some birds being quarrelsome. And it is known that a crow has a suspiciously high number sense. Can discern as many as five men going into a building, and knows when only four come out.

*   *   *   *

Of all the marvelous gestures of an earthling one comes across in the fields, the gesture of waving to someone from afar is the most provocative. A sense of immediate and compelling loneliness. I have wept at it, but don't know exactly why. Because it is, when it is felt at all unusually, a lovely thing, almost thrilling. Certainly I wouldn't cry out in sadness. But this slight, distant act, the wave of the arm, could be a most dull recognition if it were unaloof or casual. Continuous contact is too shocking to ever disclose deep kinship. Anyway, it is an unusual happening, even if it happens several times a year. Superficially, the circumstances require that the person be a good distance away, and alone. It also happens that it is most often, a man, because men are alone in the fields here, working, not women.

Lucia Berlin, a particular friend (and later prototype of the heroine of the Dorn tale "Beauty") who would not actually meet Dorn until the following year, remembers the piece as her true introduction: "The 'Birds of the Skagit Valley' essay, Bob Creeley showed me that in New Mexico. That's when I fell in love with Ed. The writing, just so beautiful ... like W. H. Hudson."

Dorn had indeed begun the long project of reading Hudson's work, courtesy of the Burlington library's trusty interlibrary loan resources. He would eventually, over the next few years, read it all: from *The Purple Land, Green Mansions* and *Long Ago and Far Away* to *Birds in a Village, British Birds, Birds in London, Birds and Man, The Birds of La Plata*. With Helene and Lucia he would continue the project the following year in Santa Fe. "Hudson's bird books, even the wonderful *Birds of Richmond Park* (old age in England) all seemed new and delightful to Ed in 1959," Lucia recalls.

"Maybe he had read them before and was rediscovering ... seemed like each one was a new delight. I believe those early years were his finest years [as a writer]. His early prose, especially the wonderful 'Birds of the Skagit Valley,' DOES seem to have been influenced by Hudson.... I always felt that Ed saw himself not as a poet, but as a man of letters, as Thinker. Readings in history and geography always meant more to him than 'literature.' The literature he did love always had a strong sense of place." (One recalls in this context Carl O. Sauer's suggestion, noted by Dorn, that the finest geographers had sometimes been "literary" writers: Sauer cited Herodotus and Hudson. Dorn himself, had Sauer known his work, might have made an apt third entry in that list.)

21.

An Expansion of
Much Air and Tears

I know that peace is soon coming, and love of common
      object,
and of woman, and all the natural things I groom, in my
      mind, of
faint rememberable patterns, the great geography of my
      lunacy.
                  —"Geranium"

There are times when I pay too much attention to the absolute quickness and shortness of my energy, that I confuse everything on the basis of this. This is what makes me extremely limited, I think. On the other hand, I can't help, recently, i.e. new to me, deliberating my dis- and un-organized self, and how I get things to stay still and congeal.... I can't have things look common to me. No matter whatever I may say or believe about the common. For my own purposes I have to maintain, no matter how briefly, a "cocked eye." I slip back down to the pawn shop so easily, before I know what is happening. That's why ... the reply has to be quick or not at all.... I find

I cannot restrain tears, a madness, a fury, I can hardly stay at the machine, I can't on the other hand leave the room, and in the end I don't even get so much done, and at that in this precious spell I have. But thank the gods for the loose ingredients of my total disorganization. I have found something in it besides the goddamn psyche, which I found, kicked the shit out of and sent packing. I don't care per se to write like they do in books, even the best. Or want to make coherent sense, coherent sense being the bane of my existence ... there is a roar in the mountains into the valley and down my neck like bland soup. I am in the hands of every known element, but my honesty is that all that occurs to me anywhere is a man— located—I cannot stand the sight of "Material" in any form.
—Dorn to Olson, February 1, 1958

HIS OLD RESTLESSNESS RESURFACING, Dorn wrote to Wieners on June 21 that the future was up in the air, "i.e. whether to work or starve, leave or stay and in both cases, [in] what manner to do either alternative." "Nagging occupations" followed one upon another; some were all too familiar. There had been another brief stretch on John Smith's farm, hauling chicken feed like a "dull gull" treading an "endless circle." For a time in March the family had been reduced to "eating nettles. For true. The young shoots...." "We didn't winter so well," Dorn told Olson. "Ennui, I guess more than hibernation.... Spring brings work around here. If the 'unemployment shituation' don't become too bad I will make the loot to see us out on some other limb of the tree of life ... it would be nice to split for somewhere, some other miserable place, filled with some other miserable jazz."

Sending Olson "A Country Song" he admitted he had not "been writing posy for a long time." His efforts at narrative had foundered in the winter doldrums; he was now impatient with his work in both mediums, but was doggedly persisting. "The way it is with everything is long and dragging and much lassitude. And this seems the

meandering line, long. I haven't got it yet, but hope to. This is the
beginning.... What I don't want to do is scream, but when the lines
get slow, the life goes not so much dark, which I would like, but
rather ballooned-out inside, like bakery bread." That slow, self-elab-
orating "meandering line, long," which he felt was causing him to lose
his way in narrative prose—like the "Bums and Drunks" tales, "writ-
ten in process, i.e. one of sitting down to write and 'grapple' famously
with writing"—turned out to be much more serviceable in poetry.
By late summer he was declaring to his former teacher that he had
"dropped prose until another time ... in isolation one writes poems."

In June two remarkable long-line poems, drafted on successive
days, marked a new stylistic turning, and with it brought a new sense
of "the possibility of poetry"—as an empathic, redemptive "expan-
sion of much air and tears ... a grasping toward nothing, elaborated
by descriptives." "The first break into it," as Dorn would tell Olson,
"out of a candor of short metre," came with "The Air of June Sings,"
a country graveyard elegy precipitated by a tour with Chansonette
of the Burlington cemetery.

> Quietly and while at rest on the trim grass I have gazed,
> admonished myself for having never been here
> at the grave-side and read the names of my Time
>   Wanderers.

The poem develops slowly and deliberately as a reflection upon
the elegiac texts found in this "sacred place" in the form of tomb-
stone inscriptions. These texts are of two kinds: the modest, dated,
blurred-ink-on-tin common markers of the "unpreposterous dead,"
with their affecting sentimental messages—"I am moved to tears
and I hear / the depth in 'Darling, we love thee,' and as in 'Safe in
Heaven'"—and the more imposing, undated, coldly impersonal
stones of the "established local dead," like "Goodpole Matthews, /
Pioneer," whose signifying moves the poet in the opposite fashion:
"and that pioneer sticks in me like a wormed black cherry / in my
throat, No Date, nothing but that zeal, that trekking / and Business,

that presumption in a sacred place, where children / are buried, and where peace, as it is in the fields and the country / should reign."

"Reading" an endarkened spiritual history of the place in the material hierarchies of its grave markers, the ruminating poet positions himself as mediator between opposed symbolic locations, the endeared place of feeling revealed in the gravesites of his "Time Wanderers" (the long-forgotten children of the dispossessed poor, collectively brought back to life in his memorial) and the outrageous place of domination, revealed in those of the property-owning "established dead," with their greedy "trekking zeal." In Dorn's view of Western history, as suggested in a central passage from "Notes About Working and Waiting Around," it was only the jealous acquisitiveness of the original pioneers, their motivating "zeal" to acquire "furs, and farms, and land, and what ever fuel they could find for their amazing greed," that had made it possible for them to succeed in conquering great stretches of space. "What separates you from your desire" in the West had always been one kind of staked-out property barrier or another, set up by some prior pioneer. Just so, in the "The Air of June Sings," a glance across the road from the graveyard to a farmer's strawberry field gives a sudden glimpse of two poor children of the present age—that age confidently dubbed by the economist Galbraith the Age of Affluence—"stealing / their supper fruit, abreast in the rows, in the fields of the overlord."

Like all Dorn's finest work of this singularly productive period, the poem touches honestly upon the pathos of the common condition, finds reason to despair yet gambles in the end on some inkling however faint—as when the speaker realizes the graveyard is merely another kind of rural field, "where children are buried, and where peace, as it is in the fields and the country / should reign"—of a utopian hope.

> Lead me away
> to the small quiet stones of the unpreposterous dead and
> leave

me my tears for Darling we love thee, for Budded on earth
    and blossomed
in heaven, where the fieldbirds sing in the fence rows,
and there is possibility, where there are not the loneliest of
    all.

Oh, the stones not yet cut.

Appearing in the 1959 Grove Press anthology *The New American Poetry,* the poem would hold up as a kind of standard of Dorn's art for an early generation of readers. For many of these same readers the intellectual speed and verbal brilliance of mid-period Dorn, even (or shall I say especially) of *Gunslinger,* would not match that standard. I'll never forget my own excitement over the accelerated cosmic wit of that latter work coming up against the unanswerable objection of a fellow poet, John Thorpe (this was circa 1970)— "that's all okay, man, but what ever happened to 'The Air of June Sings'?"

Another early Dorn standard, drafted the day after "The Air of June," was "Geranium," that signature hymn to an unknown Indian woman glimpsed at a Skagit Valley bus stop—and to "the great geography of my lunacy." Discovering in the momentary apparition of his "pale sojourner" a "lapwing" beauty neither objectifiable nor commoditizable, not to be limited by a name or "purchased by the lust of schedule," the poet here locates also a sense of earth's natural value in the immanent presence of "a geranium and cherishable common that I worship and I sing"—a site where his lunatic difference can in this brief moment of recognition find its exilic asylum.

      And this is the last bus stop before Burlington
that pea-center, which is my home, but not the home of my
    mind.
That asylum I carry in my insane squint....

In a moment of striking self-disclosure, the craggy-browed visage of the author here stares uncannily out of his poem, exposing— as in some lines written twenty years later in England, "I knitted my brows too / an old response / and tried to look serious"—a deeply shy and private being's well-concealed secret refuge.

"Ploddingly, and out of tune," Dorn had found his own distinctive measure. "The 'news' is the *line*," Robert Creeley would write in reviewing *The Newly Fallen,* quoting the opening lines of "Geranium," which quite fittingly begin the book:

> I know that peace is soon coming, and love of common
>   object,
> and of woman and all the natural things I groom, in my
>   mind, of
> faint rememberable patterns, the great geography of my
>   lunacy.

"If 'lunacy,'" Creeley would comment, "it is gracefully apropos—and moves with the neat lightfoot way of quick sense and specific commitment. [Dorn] takes hold of things, common as the 'red Geranium' Indian woman of this first poem, and makes no mistake—nor invites you to any...."

A brief history of Creeley's readings of "Geranium" hints something of the uniqueness this new sound of Dorn's had in the minds of the most advanced fellow practitioners in his craft. "Your line is moving more slowly, clearly more to your purpose," Creeley had responded upon receiving an early draft in June 1958. "I am much interested in what can be done with this, and you show me a lot, in for example, the *size* of content here.... ['Geranium'] harks back for me to such ones as that vacant lot poem [i.e. 'The Common Lot']. Your positions, and feeling, really enlarge beautifully. I feel small in comparison, and relieved also, to read you."

Eighteen months later "Geranium"—along with "The Air of June Sings," which Dorn had by then also sent in typescript—were still on Creeley's mind. "I like that poem of yours ['Geranium'], and that long line, more and more [as] this registers...." Dorn, he proposed, was carrying forward the long line to new uses not anticipated by its great originator, Walt Whitman. Whitman had "treated [the long line] too much finally as an exhaust, trailing off" toward its ending; Dorn's way, closer in Creeley's opinion to the quantitative experiments of the Elizabethan musician-lyricist Thomas Campion, was to treat the line as a kind of springboard, "a lightness of pausing (lightly) through the line, not a cast of beats to the end thereof.... I think it is [in] that registration of light, collected diversities, emphases, that the line shows its uses." Dorn's long, slow line, Creeley concluded, had a classic ring, yet in its sturdiness, durability and variable "weighting," was authentically poetic "news."

Comparable attention was given the long-line poems by Olson, who went even further in detecting in them a reconciliation of archaic metric with the faint rememberable patterns of Dorn's invention. "Geranium," he proclaimed upon the publication of *The Newly Fallen* in 1961, was nothing less than a "Klessick." That poem was but one of several the poet's one-time tutor had determined to be written "in fantastically beautiful *hexameters!* A long 6 the like of which I do not know. And as a result (or anyway) you come out like a Donne—in Greek! Wild. Good lord what delicious language going on all the time ... with this crazy long parabola of length like a whip going on ... and like it isn't at all praise to say this, that is, I point it up because I believe ... you are unconscious of it, of the dominance of the 6 (and I say this because of your line breaks, which tend to obscure it also)...." "Mr. Ed Donne," he offered in a pseudo-solemn imprimatur, would henceforth hold poetic license "to take that Big 6 Anywhare."

Dorn wrote back honestly that the closest he could say he'd ever actually come to a hexameter was at second- or third-remove. "The Greek loses me, except insofar as I have been carried away by translated Homer and (don't hit me) Longfellow: 'This is the forest primeval; but where are the hearts that beneath it / Leaped like the

roe, when he hears in the woodland the voice of the huntsman?'"
He had conceived his long lines not by counting units of time but
by a pushing or stretching of his content to take up more space.

> It was literally a quest for more room ... and I can't say, tho
> I w[ou]ld like to of course, I had any [such] thing as a full
> (outsized) 6 in mind. But gradually over a period of the fol-
> lowing two years I did realize the extent of the beat, which
> led to a further use of it in "The Pronouncement" and other
> [poems], i.e. by that time it was deliberate.... It becomes obvi-
> ous I suppose that what interests me most of all in this pos-
> sible process is its Chant. And I don't even know how yet. I
> have the faith tho [that] I am right for my own terms. There
> is still a lot of slack and sloppiness that bothers me, i.e. the
> breaking [of the lines] is still dependent on my sense of the
> separation of ideas and their emphasis, which you must have
> noticed. Lacking a well defined and legitimate Ground, such
> as you have, and having one such as I have, one which is gras-
> pable *only* in its nebulousness, I can look only to the long
> adjectival line to stabilize my hold on the field. [Vachel] Lind-
> say, the only other Midwest poet I admire, didn't make it
> against that rock, and I think I see why, that he determined
> to use it as literal material, which will never work, and he of
> course got fucked up with a gew-jaw rhythm which is puerile.
> But [Lindsay's] "Tiger on Parade" is a great poem. I am still
> held by the possibility of writing poetry. Ginsberg isn't. That's
> hypnotic prose. He was born out of a centralized publicized
> ego, and his line reflects the normal machinations of a man
> caught in the public dentures, albeit he is remarkably straight
> for all that.... A shorter line exhibits bedrock always, with
> Williams I come to question that it is very interesting, with
> you I never doubt it, with Pound I rarely doubt it, with Zukof-
> sky I never understand it, with cummings I can salute it, with
> Creeley I pay attention—But, the line beyond five beats has
> not been practised properly since Whitman and for the same

reason nothing is really like Donne now, i.e. as a steadfast duty (but thank you).... Because from Donne to Whitman a poet could play around in his ground all he wanted it seems to me; how can you do that now and make any sense of profusion? There were heretofore always certain beginnings, even the romantics had them, the beginnings of what they took to be feelings, the beginnings Whitman hewed to were that he was nearly the only man writing at that time. *We* are beset by endings. If I am to have a line today and keep it going thru say 30 years optimistically, of course, how am I to do other than by an expansion of much air and tears? How am I to do it other than by a grasping toward nothing, elaborated by descriptives?

T HOSE EARLY MEANDERING-TO-A-PURPOSE long-line poems from the Skagit Valley, with their slowly developing, slightly archaic music, have survived as well as any of Dorn's writings the vicissitudes of postmodern critical history. The poet himself, always refreshingly self-critical, was less kind to them. In the mid-Eighties I once called upon him to read three early pieces to a class—"The Air of June Sings," "Geranium," and "Are They Dancing," a haunting ballad of the yearning distances and missed boats of his early adulthood. Dorn, who knew his own mind, said he no longer liked the poems; that in fact, he wanted to disclaim them; but that, if he must, he would attempt to read them. As if to prove his point, his attempts to summon a rhythm for "The Air of June" ended in exasperation halfway through. He struggled dutifully to re-create the fragile lapwing beauty of his bus-depot "Geranium," but, ending with a mighty sigh, declared its attenuated pacing simply just too much for him to stomach: the long lines, he said, now seemed "like Kay-ro syrup— very thick, takes forever to pour it out of the bottle." "Are They Dancing" he managed to invest with a little more commitment, but afterwards admitted he now thought the poem "totally sentimental." "Emotion in poetry is *cultivated,* in the botanical sense," he

said, "whereas emotion in life is *wild*. I know that now but I didn't
know it then. Those poems were sentimental. I was taking some-
thing wild and trying to cultivate it."

> There is a sad carnival up the valley
> The willows flow it seems on trellises of music
> Everyone is there today, everyone I love.
>
> There is a mad fiesta along the river
> Thrilling ladies sing in my ear, where
> Are your friends, lost? They were to come
>
> And banjoes were to accompany us all
> And our feet were to go continually
> The sound of laughter was to flow over the water
>
> What was to have been, is something else
> I am afraid. Only a letter from New Mexico
> And another from a mountain by Pocatello,
>
> I wonder, what instruments are playing
> And whose eyes are straying over the mountain
> Over the desert
> And are they dancing: or gazing at the earth.

22.

A Far Away Look
in Her Eye

In this season the long slow rains begin to fall, and the sun if it comes out, comes late in the evening going down into the Pacific, thus for a few brief minutes, as it passes between the horizon and the cover of dark clouds, it casts fabulous autumn shadows, and sometimes the rain shadows stop abruptly during that time, and then the sun shadows run swiftly out into every length of canyon and draw, down every town street and country road, shining through cobweb windows of barns on to the backs of sleepy cows slowly switching their tails, and it is a swift running, these shadows make, and they are soon gone, but sometimes the shadows lengthen and linger on in the heart, after the rain has begun again. Then one remembers the lostling smell of burning leaves, and the dryer shadows on other streets several years back, it is the pace that comes of sitting, and listening to the soul as it meanders back and forth through its former homes.

  —"Notes About Working and Waiting
  Around"

T HE LONGING FOR CONTACT with distant friends expressed in "Are They Dancing" would prove an uncanny augury. Driven by "an old hope," as a later Dorn poem would suggest, the family would continue for another half dozen years its ragtag circuit of the West's large empty spaces, "scour[ing] the ground / to start fires / in these rickety geographies / we knew better than to call home." ("Oh, Don't Ask Why.")

"Carl was out of work again ... they were thinking of leaving that part of the country as soon as they could see their way." The inevitability of further migration was the one certainty built into the otherwise infinitely contingent world of difference. The quiet, recessive close of *The Rites of Passage* marks the family's departure—which took place early in 1959, a few months before Dorn's thirtieth birthday—from the Skagit Valley.

> One morning, when the rain had turned to snow, five people stood on the platform with their luggage. Some of it had been checked, but they carried most of their possessions. The three children were laden with bags, and boxes held by the strings. The man carried three suitcases, one under his arm, two in his hands. The children leaned over the track looking to see if the train was coming. The mother pulled them back.... She had a far away look in her eye.... The children saw the train coming down the track and then slow to a stop. Then they all got on and the train pulled out.

Nomads once more, they would journey now to Idaho, stopping with friends for a few months, then move on to New Mexico for a stay of two-and-a-half years, then back to Idaho again for nearly four; Dorn would toil at a further series of obscure menial jobs, as a waiter, an assistant librarian, a lowly state college instructor.

If the catalogue of the family's travails and losses was not yet done, neither was the reckoning of their discoveries; nor would the "old hope" that instills Dorn's writings of these years with heart and spirit, the utopian signalling of a dream of freedom beyond resistance, annealing the old wounds of distance, soon fade.

Epilogue:

The Last Range
(1997–1999)

Wherever I went in California I was surrounded by a small crowd, like Christ going to Golgotha.
> —Dorn, after a reading trip to Los Angeles
> and Berkeley, November 4, 1997

Hector still possesses a free ego, the kind of circuit which stays in the human breast in the form of beauty (even such a thing as behavior was once beauty), but the ego, as well as beauty, and things abstract, are pagan. Whereas Christ was quickly utilized out of existence, Hector remained, precisely because he wasn't chosen. The chosen is the blackest fate of all, and that's why my heart still yearns over Christ.
> —"What I See in the Maximus Poems,"
> 1959–1960

It's either the Vatican or the Pagans. I'm with the Pagans.
> —after a trip to Rome, January 22, 1999

O N MAY 28, 1997, surgeons at Colorado University Hospital in Denver determined that Dorn was suffering from a nonresectable (inoperable) adenosarcoma of the pancreas, stage II/III (locally advanced).

Dorn had once written that he preferred the warrior figure Hector to the victim figure Christ: "Hector is not resurrectable. He lives in the manor of the mind and stands for unalienated beauty."

In his last thirty months, challenged with the most imposing of his many forced migrations, the hard trek into the mapless realm of the dead, the poet fought defiantly, a warrior like Hector, or like the great dissenters and heretics he admired, exercising all the stubborn resistance of his will in a protracted rebellious refusal of this ultimate imperial authority.

Out of the extended encounter came his poems of his remarkable last book, the "documentary" cancer journal *Chemo Sábe*. This chilling sequence, much of it composed in notebooks in the "cancer ward" even as the course of treatment takes place, scrutinizes the darkness and terror of the unfolding medical nightmare with an unflinching detachment honed through five decades of practice in the poet's craft. A complementary, more personal account of the harrowing struggle emerges in the letters I received from him in these final years. As well as showing the graciousness and generosity which never failed him, these letters reveal something of the courage—and grim humor—with which he approached the final confrontation. What follows is an attempt to reconstruct, largely from these sources, a kind of battle log or warrior's diary. At once painfully concrete in reference and, thanks to those passages where the expression glows with compressed metaphorical intensity, shimmering with more "abstract" implication, Dorn's last writing offers us a catalogue of the runes grasped before the door of death's hall by a poet whose visionary clarity—an image to outlast the all-too-human doubts and trials he inventories—recalls the proud, "unalienable beauty" of Hector dying in Homeric battle and the uncanny gallows wit of the Norse hero Ragnar approaching Odin's dwelling: "I shall not enter this hall with words of fear upon my lips. The days of my life are ended.

I laugh as I die."

"Entrapment is this society's / Sole activity, I whispered / and Only laughter / can blow it to rags...."—*Gunslinger*, Book III.

HOLY WAR

Actually I've finally had to admit I haven't been well since returning from England in mid-November ... lots of pain & can't eat i.e. the thought of food really repugnant yet with constant hunger ... if I survive I'll let you know.
—Denver, March 10, 1997

The sense has been grim around here and I feel even worse for the psychological burden brought to bear on Jenny. The uncertainty is the most awful.
—May 11, 1997

We leave for Taos tomorrow, Maya & Jenny driving. I'll read on Friday eve ... have booked a room in La Vida by the Spanish Peaks. On Monday I'll have another digital scan and on Tuesday begin taking either Gemcitabine or Marimastat ... 1 to 4 choices chosen by a throw of the dice by a computer in Baltimore (U. Colorado Med. Center the main place for all this), so it's all new and experimental and I think the point is it attacks the protein that is the Cause of Pancreatic C. Nothing to lose—
—June 11, 1997

Taos went OK. Reading useful to sort out where to go w/ current work and have got good concentration—had CT scan on Monday & started MARIMASTAT on Tuesday.... I feel lucky to have been randomized on the pill instead of the injection. Go in for scan on 8 Aug[ust] to check effect on tumor. So that's the deal so far.
—June 25, 1997

It seemed so amazing, he kept surviving. But it *was* a war. It was an incredible struggle, all through the chemo. There was one fellow sufferer we met at the cancer clinic who said, "We're living with it"—that was Ed's attitude, that it was something you were *living with,* not *dying of.* . . . It was only his determination to fight that got us those extra years.

—Jenny Dorn, February 13, 2000

There is a certain amount of mail unconsciously addressing me in the past tense. . . . I find that kind of morbid attention annoying.

—June 20, 1997

The we're-scared-so-shitless-we-assume-you're-dead people . . . gossip . . . but I'm not paying any attention to that anymore and I'm not dying—when I die I'll be dead but until then I'm living. Hope is beside the point and that's not what I believe in—I believe in my pill and my doctor and I'm going to Montana not on some "last trip" but because I can. I haven't been working with my present concentration and energy in 20 years. Went to the doc today—all is steady ahead.

—July 1, 1997

In [Yellowstone] Park our attempt to sitesee Olde Faithful was thwarted by being unable to find a place to park. That was cool with me, I can't take much sulphur.

—September 18, 1997

The scan of the 8th of October was not good—slight growth of tumor, but more seriously a slightly less than one centimetre spot appears on the liver. The growth is certainly slow for Pancreatic C. but it is in the wrong direction. Therefore I'll be put on the other form of the chemo gemcitabine—a half hour injection once a week.

—October 14, 1997

My blood was back up today so I got an infusion 11 AM …
it is an attack on the cells & I can feel it.
> —November 17, 1997

The attack is relentless.
> —Dorn, 30 October 1997, in conversation, on
> cancer pain

Having passed through my "free" week, I began the next set
of 3 gemcitabine infusions that past Monday. During that time
I seemed to have solved the chronic diarrhea problem for the
first time since this hideous misadventure began—this is mainly
the result of grinding up some of the [pig-pancreas] enzymes
in a mortar & pestle. And the oncologist prescribed a kind of
time release, 12 hour codeine tablet which has reduced the
pain problem a lot, altho not altogether.… You said at one
point that I seemed to be stoic in my suffering of this ordeal,
but in fact there are times of moaning and screaming and
involuntary weeping at my awful condition (obviously I try
to keep that as private as possible). But the effects, aside from
my own personal problems, are pretty strenuous for Jenny
and all that I very much regret. I have not given up hope and
I don't foresee giving up the struggle. I still have a lot of energy
if not so much strength—but I don't have to tell you of all
people that there are moments so bleak that everything is an
unanswerable question.
> —March 1, 1998

I went to university hospital this morning for a "procedure"—
putting a "stent" in my urethra. That's about a foot long (or
more) perforated plastic tube which goes from my right kid-
ney to my bladder. The channel was being pinched—the oncol-
ogist says by the tumor, the urologist says it's got nothing to
do with it.… I'm peeing blood (cherry red to tea brown) and
the pain from urination is a 10 on the scale—truly burning

and sharp deep ... where does it end or does it. If this is the preview of Hades, I'll take heaven, no matter how boring. I start back with the chemo, a different mixture, on Friday.
—May 26, 1998

I've booked us into the Colorado Hotel in Glenwood Springs—the hotel I "think" Doc Holliday stayed at when he went to take the waters and kick the bucket—I'll try to avoid the latter.
—June 9, 1998

Back from Glenwood Springs.... The Colorado Hotel has *very* wide corridors and some nice stairs with Venus-on-the-half-shell copies and stuff like that on the landings. The pool had a little too much sulphur for my taste.... Did my infusion/injections today—feeling wiped out. This new stuff (5 FU) is definitely strong medicine.
—June 15, 1998

At the cancer ward, 11:30 AM ... conference with the oncologist, Dr. Cohn.... Beautiful autumn weather—can almost be called Injun Summer, I reckon.... I can't tell you how great a relief getting your letter ... was. I worried about you and supposed you were going through a rough patch—as we were—last week was awful and I entertained serious doubts that I'd be able to make it through to Dec. 11th (last class—I'm teaching "Poetry as a Difficult Labor"!). But I somehow got past the pain with some calculated adjustments & guesses. I don't want to simply take *more* pills, oxycodone (20 mgs) being the heaviest beyond percocet I'm allowed at the moment. The really heavy stuff they restrict to the Hospital. But now I'm levelling off again and feel much better. I've stopped taking that fucking Zoloft for starters, and feel a *lot* better already. That has to be something invented by some New Age Torquemada, mindless nasty stuff. It is said, and I believe it, that the whole English dept. at CU is "on" it, and that theorists in general everywhere can't function without it. No wonder they detest the past in which it didn't exist. So then: I've made it through the 1st 30 days [of term]. . . . I hang out in my office with my French doors opened on the [letter ends in mid-sentence].

—September 30, 1998

The habit of considering personal expression or "lyric" as something that strives for compassion with all of the artifices which make up a poem, is in many ways a loathsome instrumentation that leads you into dishonesties and lies and pretenses that are damaging. It is damaging to the ability to absorb reality. In order to write a poem of any interest whatsoever, it should be beyond how one feels, which is largely a condition so freighted with lack of interest on anybody [else]'s part. You really have to educate yourself and the poem at the same time. That's where it's work, it's labor.

—from last lectures, on "Poetry as a Difficult Labor," November 1998

I was *so* thankful to get your letter ... it is just impossible to say. When the timing slips everything recedes with it. During that interval I was drifting deeper & deeper into the awful shades of *5FU*—a drug so terrible I'll have to save even trying to tell you what a living death it was. Finally the CT scan came &, who knows, ? in the main tumor of the Pancreas. I notice there is a novel or anyway something which heads the best-seller list titled the Seat of the Soul—which is what surgeons call the pancreas. About a year ago I wrote that as the title or subtitle for the journal I've kept on the [cancer] drugs— but then on reflection I saw the metaphor wouldn't be right for me.

—November 5, 1998

There are 3 or 4 "letters" to you, unsent, consisting of 2 or 3 paragraphs wandering into fragmentation … meanwhile, because I don't want my silence to be misinterpreted, this is a note to say I'm OK (+ or –) on a new chemo (taxol), but the side effects from 5FU which were *very* nasty are still lingering.… I'm feeling that slowly I'm emerging from the greatest nightmare of my life—But whatever that is, I'm *also* winding up the "semester" I owed for the year's sick leave—come Dec. 11th I won't owe anybody an hour's worth of anything. Free at last. Free, free at last. Well, I hope so.… On the 30th November I go in for "pre-op" … on the 1st stent replacement.… Every three fucking months—I've been pissing blood off & on for about 2 weeks. Still I crawl toward 11th Dec. Free at last? Well, not from the stent!
—November 19, 1998

We're going to Rome—"Roma non Futata in un giorno!!!"
—November 19, 1998

My bleeding fingers could certainly use the tropics. London/Rome is not going to do anything for that aspect—travelling 20° north a week & a half before the solstice is my contribution to madness.
—November 20, 1998

Finally walked along the river (very filthy)—in fact this is the dirtiest city in the world as well as the most beautiful. The two things so far I've got: you have to stand under the cycloptean hole of the Pantheon (which I did by shoving the Catholic Chairs out of the way—after that many tourists followed suit) and you have to be inside the colossal emptiness of St. Peter's to get it.
—Rome, December 18, 1998

The Pantheon is not just a great building—It's also a great gesture, since Hadrian's total reconstruction of it leaves Agrippa's name on the pediment above the colonnade. The theorists could take a page from that supreme lesson—reconstruction is infinitely nobler than deconstruction.

—London, December 22, 1998

I now have the means to see. I have stood under the cycloptic eye of the Pantheon, and that's what I needed to do. And I have stood in the great, vast, profoundly empty space of the Basilica and I also needed to do that. Oh, and I've also gone to the Protestant Cemetery too, which is where they leave the heretics when they've finished with them. Not a bad situation actually ... looks pretty good. Expensively maintained. Absolutely ... well maintained.

—comments at a reading, London, December 21, 1998

It's either the Vatican or the Pagans....

—Denver, January 22, 1999

Then there's still the weekly taxol infusions. The thing there is it turns you into a pine cone.

—January 28, 1999

The saline drip, / bridging the chasm to Taxus*, Latin for the yew / bridges the chasm of my senses. The conductor / to the ionic connexion, which produces / the violent interface at the holy war / of the short haired puritans with / the screamers and shouters / and yellers and scoffers and pushers....

*Pactitaxel, the brand name of the chemical derived from the yew tree bark [Dorn's note]

—"Chemo du Jour: The Impeachment on Decadron," from *Chemo Sábe*

... as the drip is connected to the pump I see W. J. Clinton
... / I see him in the Taxol pooling over my brow / move his
arky hand from the arm rest / to the Iraqi button ... / an
experimental / missile vibrates and flames and then launches
/ from the carrier, and Oh Good Lord, minutes later, / as the
nurse strips away the Medusan tubes of my oncology, / Amer-
ican dumb missile arrives with punity /in the southern sub-
urbs of Baghdad, ruined Cradle of Civilization, / just north of
the Garden of Eden ... / And Lo now the Taxol infusion clears
the atmosphere / where I see the Superbowl completely super-
seded / by the *superblow,* O yes, praise the Tree Lord, / now
it is time to go.

> —"Chemo du Jour: The Impeachment on
> Decadron"

This ["Chemo du Jour: The Impeachment on Decadron"] is the
best result yet of my attempt to render my chemo experience
in my documentary poem form.

> —February 2, 1999

On the 3rd of June I undergo my procedure re. the regular
replacement of stent, but this time I'm facing the music & let-
ting them install a medi-port, under the skin. My veins (and the
pain) have persuaded me. Still & all it is *one more thing* and
I've come to see more clearly that my existence is no longer
living, it's not dying. I'm not unique in that—maybe I've at
last joined the majority, the refugees.

> —May 25, 1999

Certain people try to make my cancer grow, / They seek to
feed it ... / I have / A list of them in my mind and when / I
exercise my blasting power / Against my tumor which was
environmentally / Induced and politically generated, I blast
them also, / Their portraits and vitas, their genomes. / These
are the megadonts, they want to chew on me. / I can draw

them in their molecular pointillism, / Their shadows Seurat
ghosts, / Under their molecular umbrellas ... / I will blast them
with the beam / of my centrifugal silence / In the flow of the
taxodiaceae.

> —"Enhancement," from *Chemo Sábe* (after
> July 12, 1999 scan)

Talk with oncologist resulted in his taking my suggestion that
the dosage of taxol be increased 10% until mid October....
This from not great scan results before we left for London 28
July.

> —August 25, 1999

Coming back here to my chemo roost is no choice. I've got
to go the Western rationalist/materialist route or not and I
decided to fight it and that's only possible here.... I went right
back to chemo on Wednesday after a month off & feeling a lot
better for missing it—plus I'm on a 10% increase in dosage on
the theory that it has (taxol, i.e.) a certain arresting effect so
we'll see—next scan in Oct....

> —August 27, 1999

"What is freedom but choice?" he had asked; but the literal
meaning of the word heresy *is* choice.

> —Christopher Hill, *Milton and the Revolution*

Returned Monday following Kidd's wedding in Dover New
Hampshire—at the ceremony in the "Catholic" church in
Dover Jenny & I read "Dover Beach"—I read the first stanza,
she read the philosophical/moral section beginning with Sopho-
cles and we read the final, ignorant armies by night stanza
together—it was pretty right on and well done, if I do say so.

> —August 27, 1999

Immediate future rather bleak—I have "dental surgery" come Friday—the teeth under my 20 + year old bridge which came out recently (due to chemo). I have teeth in front like a skeleton, or certain skeletons I imagine. I just had a stent change—deep anesthesia which messed w/ my mouth, nose, throat and lungs. The dental surgery will use intravenous—like lethal injection I suppose. Then following that I have to get Bone scan then regular scan after that. For the bone scan I have to be injected 4 hours ahead of time—woe is me. The only thing I'm looking forward to in that mess is I get to be off the Taxol for a while. Taxol is a rough chemo indeed—it just dehydrates the shit out of my already desiccated system.

—September 26, 1999

JUDGMENT DAY: TRIAL BY FIRE (THE SCANS)

Next scan, 3 October (Judgment Day, as I heard it called by a fellow sufferer).

—September 18, 1997

I had my scan this morning. 2 or three pints of barium was my elementary breakfast. Then, dropt off by Jenny, I entered the realm of the halt & the lame attended by African Americans in green shifts. At the CT-scan in the basement I was introduced to a new machine—still General Electric medical systems but the new mod, "much faster" and which takes twice the time. Iodine suffusion in I. V. Heat in the genitals & sphincter. Then the trip under the lazer, one millimetre at a time.

—October 3, 1997

Upon our return from Eastern Washington, I had a scan. I knew something was up immediately because the technician

started further up, just under my chin. . . . But obviously oncol-
ogist wants to check out my lymphs—no scan since late Octo-
ber. So when I start to take the Iodine feed it's not just my
anus & genitals this time but whole body *&* Brain—I thought
my head was going to flame out—the worst heat I've ever
felt—scary—beyond pain. As I was sitting up, resting on the
pad when I'd finished the scan the tech started to set up [for]
the next victim—a kind of hard-hat-looking casing where my
feet had been—a brain-scan setup—I shuddered to think of the
iodine for an actual brain scan—oh praise the Lord, may I
not repeat that incendiary heat.
　　　　—March 29, 1999

The power walkway to heaven / fed by the farming of heretics
/ roasted by fire, hell brought back / into the here and then
now, / the only place and the only time.
　　　　—"Albi, a Day Trip," from *Languedoc
　　　　Variorum: A Defense of Heresy and Heretics*

Throat ripping / Ball torching / Fire balling / Gut trenching,
war—/ the Iodine drift / In the trenches / The blasting of the
seat / of the soul, loading / Iodine fire, barbed / Wire snaking
through the veins.
　　　　—"Iodine Fire," from *Chemo Sábe*

The Seat of the Soul—which is what surgeons call the pan-
creas. . . .
　　　　—November 5, 1998

INFUSION DAY : THE LANCE

The bloodworker was in a bad mood / unreasonable as it
would be / to imagine she enjoys her work / if she enjoys hurt-
ing you as / an aspect of not enjoying her work . . . / I suppose

I made a smart remark / as usual, my tongue has been / my genius and my downfall. / The nurse began to collect the specimen / with ever increasing pressure on the split flesh / I nearly fainted, but not a tear / fell from my lid, and not a throb shook my throat / until I'd left the collecting station / and then I shook and wept, and jesus, / I'm sorry to say I hated that / bloodworker even despite the fact / that I knew she couldn't help / what she had a great irresistible / need to do, to hurt me deeply / because I was a bearer of cancer.
—"The Cocktail Party of March 1, 1999,"
from *Chemo Sábe*

On Infusion Day / every thing comes back ... / the voices of the unburied dead / and the satisfied symphony / of the truly dead, / along with the secret lurking / of the pure internal marks, / the passage of the pure week—/ life turned into a seminar. / The periodic bruise, / the exiting of the blood to work, / the cell count, the inventory / of the shelf life, meaning / the life of the shelf, the tear count / the involuntary drip account / the measure of the mystery of what / remains of the life and times / of the victim, condemned but not delivered, / just the keeper of the count, slowly / joining the counter.
—"Infusion Day," from *Chemo Sábe*

... getting a medi-port because I can't stand the pain of getting stuck no mo....
—May 23, 1999

... facing the music & letting them install a medi-port under the skin. My veins (and the pain) have persuaded me.
—May 25, 1999

RELIEF FROM GENERALIZED PAIN (THE WARRIOR'S SHIELD)

I've been on drugs for the last two years. But not street drugs, and so it's been a rather interesting, also unpleasant experience. And I've been writing about the experience. It's *not* about how the government pushes a really, when it comes down to it, pretty inferior quality product. There are, what, twenty-eight alkaloids of opium on the market.... The DEA dangles it out there just to see who in fact might be that unwise. So all these *oxy*s which occur in this piece—this is about some of those alkaloids.

> —London, December 1998, on the poem
> "Denver Dawn: With Ceiling Fan"

Oxycontin could put the dead to sleep—/ But Oxycontin can wake the living / just as well, Oxycontin can do anything, / Oxycontin can make you feel Nothing / and there are times *Nothing* is exactly / what you most desire to feel.

> —"Denver Dawn: With Ceiling Fan,"
> from *Chemo Sábe*

Tylox can put you out there for a while—/ relief from generalized pain. / Vicodin seeks the street, a pilfered bottle / here or there, which is a poor comment / on the cold forlorn rue, paved / by the engineering state.

> —"The Drugs Are Over-rated,"
> from *Chemo Sábe*

My ceiling fan whirls inside / The wind twirls in / The aeolian Colorado dust / The hand with the Ativan, / The keeper of the exit....

> —"Denver Dawn: With Ceiling Fan"

And then, / there's Ativan, Shelley Winters says / makes her
life wonderful, which is O.K. / but way low on Wonder. If it
is wonder / ye seek, knock on the door of a wizard / not the
hollow counter / of the pharmacist at Rite Aid.
> —"The Drugs Are Over-rated"

The Alien

"... an Adenovirus Mutant that replicates selectively in P-53
deficient Human tumor cells"—my kind of tumor....
> —June 25, 1997

... she's like your own private third world / she arrives and
breeds like guinea pigs, / evermore progeny and evermore food
/ and the priest cells / demand evermore progeny and then /
they all demand independence and this / is in Your
territory.
> —"The Decadron, Tagamit, Benadryl and
> Taxol Cocktail Party of 1 March 1999," from
> *Chemo Sábe*

I'll have to interview the alien / on that one. Sometimes I imag-
ine it yawns. / Life for an alien is not any better / than it is for
the subject.
> —"The Cocktail Party of March 1, 1999,"
> from *Chemo Sábe*

My tumor is watching all this. /My tumor is hearing all this.
My tumor / is interested in what interests me, and / she detests
who and what I detest. / My tumor is not interested in what
/ or who I love, / my tumor is not interested in love, / no neo-
plasm is—the blind cells thereof / are not interested in love
or affection, / she sends out little colonies, chipped genes /

mark their crossing by the river, they are / without variation, they keep time with terror.

> —"The Decadron, Tagamit, Benadryl and
> Taxol Cocktail Party of 1 March 1999"

Telling the truth will greatly amuse your alien / if you got one.

> —"The Cocktail Party of March 1, 1999"

They came in space ships / the size (i.e. dimension) / doesn't matter / smaller than matter / no matter—submatter—

> —"The Invasion of the 2nd Lumbar Region,"
> from *Chemo Sábe*

[The] reading was a valedictory for Dorn's 70th birthday.... Dressed in cool white on a very hot night, Dorn looked a little like Dennis Hopper gradually morphing into Buster Keaton, and his reading veered appropriately from angry railing against the evils of war to tragic accounts of treatment for cancer. "The poems are absolutely self-explanatory and rhetorically uncomplicated," Dorn began, and true to his word, nearly every word printed itself upon the mind.... The poems on cancer and its treatment were shockingly matter-of-fact and unsentimental.... "My tumor is watching all this," went one line, with a David Cronenberg-like concern to see the disease's point of view.... At the end I ... asked ... whether the cancer experiences were indeed his own. "Yes," he said. "The fright comes through, doesn't it?"

> —Phil Johnson, *The Independent,* London,
> 4 August, 1999, reviewing a Dorn reading
> at Bristol

When I read my own work [in public] now, it's like I'm *reading* my own work. It's like I didn't write it. And that's a great

relief. I don't want to take any responsibility for it. I mean I
don't even want to claim it, in a sense. It's just a great, great
relief. It's purely empirical. Reading it, it's the eye talking,
E-Y-E, rather than the tongue, or some other organ of per-
ception.

> —comments at a reading, Denver,
> September 14, 1998

What happened to I she asked / *his eyes don't seem right.* / I
is dead, the poet said ... / *We never knew anything much /
about him did we. I /was the name he answered to, / and that
was what he had / wanderin around inside him / askin so many
questions / his eyes had already answered....*

> —*Gunslinger,* Book II

In the Raven's Wood

The butterfly needle. The nurse patting the vein, / searching
for a wall to carry the load of Decadron. / Decadron sharp-
ens the senses / around the optic nerve and the neocortex, /
enabling one to see through walls and into / the present—
there goes the Pope, mobile as ever....

> —"Chemo du Jour: The Impeachment on
> Decadron"

And soon my vision tightened with decadron / the first of the
drips instilling you / with the fortitude to take the onslaught
/ of the now looming taxol....

> —"The Cocktail Party of March 1, 1999"

The optic nerve / visual disturbance [scintillating scotomata]
is a Taxol side effect—first you get the counteractive ophthal-
mic stimulation by the corticosteroid Decadron—that's the
first drip, then the Taxol. These ocular perceptions are an

"experimental" manipulation of your senses—or should I say (do I need to tell you) "my"?
—February 2, 1999

Charles Olson needs to be conceded / any incursions into human territory / he saw opening—his ocular / perceptions could not flourish / under the restricted (constricted) / "experimental" manipulation of modern science—the opposites / of carrying a lighter and lighter / light load—our eyes at / night. The direct call of communication / in the Raven's wood....
—"Notes on Olson, 14 October, 1999"

The vast light from the / green bay tree / now high yellow / increases the chances of perception / I'm reading Canto LXXXII / and that's what they were never / going to tolerate on these shores / any such increase, for long....
—"Notes on Olson, 14 October, 1999"

But that a man should live in that further terror, and live / the loneliness of death came upon me (at 3 P.M., for an instant) / δακρύων (weeping)....
—Ezra Pound, *Canto LXXXII*

INTERLUDE: STRANGELY FREE

Just returned from the Bob Marley Shrine & Mausoleum, only about 30 miles into the mountains south from the beach here but a *long* trip on these tortuous narrow & sunken, English style roads. We wisely hired a car and driver—no renting a car on this island or at least that would seem a stupid idea. In general the Jamaicans make it clear that it's cooler to let them be in charge in all all-important matters like getting from one place to another without a conductor. But other things are rented out—what a clean civilized country.... One love, no color really is playing everywhere, and the smiles are really real, as far as I can tell. We wish you were here. Kidd has his micro boom box set up on the balcony playin "Exodus" and "Natty Dread" CDs in the face of the surf. Great street parties—Xmas eve treated a bit like Mardi Gras, steel drum bands &c. contortionists, dancers.... At present we're laughing at having escaped the bitter cold of Denver.... More about the Shrine and Mausoleum when we get back—the pilgrimage was important for me—I'm still puzzling that one out....

> —Ocho Rios, Cutlass Bay, Jamaica, December
> 23–24, 1998

Christmas morning—The Flags on the Pier are waving in the cool yet humid tropical breeze—there's an arabic one—can't identify, Mahn, but one love, one spirit, no color, no mention, Bill [Clinton] should come down here for lessons before he presumes to go to Philly! Strangely free—1st 25th of my entire life there has been no tedious opening of trash package[s]— One spirit mahn, one love, no package, life *is* the present mahn!

> —December 25, 1998

To Separate Himself from His Body (Dorn, Keats and *Abba Abba*)

Is this thing made / with the end built-in / the component of death hidden only / in the youthful machine ... / ah news from the Great Manufacturer....

> —"Wait by the Door Awhile Death, There Are
> Others," from *The North Atlantic Turbine*
> (1967)

We dwell outside the city wall this winter / stone cold in the feeble sun ... off the Via Appia and come and go on the Metro / touching base at via Alba and casa Keats / rooms haunted still by his everlasting spirit / and the awful memory of the Roman / seizure and torching of his effects in public view ... / the secret pleasure / in the destruction of the great poet's very materials.

> —"Rome," from *Languedoc Variorum:*
> *A Defense of Heresy and Heretics*

The Spanish Steps are quite magnificent and Keats's room is elegant if still smelling of the very essence of death—the Oil of death—and the other act which so characterizes the Italian penchant for nastiness, the burning of all the contents.

> —London, December 22, 1998

I took some pretty good notes at the Spanish Steps and the Keats house. Keats's room is very haunting and deeply touching and I could weirdly relate to the struggle for & against Death.

> —Denver, January 4, 1999

Thanks for bringing the Anthony Burgess *ABBA ABBA* to my attention ... one of the strangest texts I've *ever* beheld.... But I understand the preoccupation—the Spanish Steps became a center for me.... I thought [Rome] was cold as anything—tho Jenny reminds me the days were sunny, I remember gloom & dank ghost ground.

> —January 22, 1999

Language itself was perhaps only a ghost of the things in the outer world to which it adhered....

St. Valentine's Day came, and with it Valentino Llanos to announce he would go to England soon. Then a week passed and two more days, and John knew his dying day had come, yet to achieve death might be a hard day's labour. Severn held him, as if he were carrying him to the gate, but he could not bear Severn's laboured breathing, for it struck like ice. To put off the world outside—the children's cries, snatches of song, a cheeping sparrow, the walls and the wall paper and the chairs that thought they would outlast him but would not, the sunlight streaking through the door—was not over-difficult. A bigger problem was to separate himself from his body—the hand worn to nothing, the lock of hair that fell into his eye, even the brain that scurried with thoughts and words and images. It took long hours to die....

The afternoon wore on into evening and his brain was fuddled and he groped for the essence he had called I. It fell through his fingers.

　　　—Anthony Burgess, *ABBA ABBA*

Clearing up came across your card of Jan 8th telling me of the Anthony Burgess *ABBA* and re-read, for which I thank you again. The book is so difficult & even annoying, but *so* beautifully touching on the struggle to die—there's a paragraph beginning "St. Valentine's Day came and with it Valentino Llanos to announce he would go to England soon...." It's truly haunting and brings tears to my eyes. I have a photo at the Steps Jenny took of me, one in front of the window to the room.... No lungs left, none. Otherwise the weather's pretty good and I'm finishing my book on the Droegs I'm on, *CHEMO SABE,* a play obviously on the Lone Ranger & Tonto's exchange....

　　　—January 28, 1999

I opted for isolation—/ a temporary suspension of my Mass Observation duties / and the chance to look over my recent notes / from Rome and to brood on the pallor / of the Spanish Steps and the moist brow / of Keats's struggle to die, still palpable, almost / visible through the window of his somber

room. / "... *a week passed and two more days, and John /
knew his dying day had come, yet to achieve death / might be
a day's hard labour. Severn held him / as if carrying him to
the gate ... To put off the world / outside — the children's cries,
snatches of song, / a cheeping sparrow ... the sun streaking
through the door ... / a bigger problem was to separate / him-
self from his body — ..."* /The butterfly needle. The nurse pat-
ting the vein....

> —"Chemo du Jour: The Impeachment on
> Decadron"

Thanks again for putting me on to [*ABBA ABBA*] because,
no doubt as a fragment of allied text, I certainly mull it, a lot.

> —October 23, 1999

After Ed got cancer, he changed as a person. He was made
incredibly sensitive. Part of it was physical—the pills, the
pain. But part of it was spiritual too, this growing sensitivity
he was feeling toward everything, especially toward the end
... he was already heading to the other side.... The very first
time he cried was after his surgery in '97. Later on, more and
more.... There was one time when Maya was here—in the
last year, when she was living in the neighborhood, and one
night she was staying over. He liked reading to her, he knew
she would be a good audience. He read that passage from
ABBA ABBA about Keats dying—read it aloud—and started
crying. He wanted to talk about death; he wanted to tell her
there was something beautiful about it. "Those who die sud-
denly or in sleep are so lucky," he said ... tears streaming
down his face.

> —Jenny Dorn, February 13, 2000

Life and Death are attributes of the Soul / not of things ... / Yet
the sad fact is I is / part of the thing and can never leave it. /
This alone constitutes / the reality of ghosts....
                    —*Gunslinger,* Book II

STILL ALIVE (LATE LETTERS)

I've been down but now I'm getting up—if you stumble after
70 yrs. They pick you up, prop you, stick you up, screaming,
stay up! in your face—all Medicare, Kaide, Aide whatever....
Just returned from the Bracemaker to my immediate relief. I
now move like a wind-up guy, only at the joints. I have a fur
hat on and red paste circles on my cheeks and a tin drum in my
wildly flaying arms—But from 2 weekends ago I'm still alive
after the radiation and the infection throughout my body. The
energy has returned. The fentanyl/transdermal is working.
The big oaf next door has *nearly* finished with our new Bath
(started in July) ... all is right with the world....
                    —"Little Book Letter for Tom and Angelica,"
                    October 21, 1999

Bright morning—it's been the most stretched out autumn.
Positively Hawaiian. Aside from bouts of Absolute terror re:
my weird fate, and mulling over the notes for some kind of
preliminary statement for your re-issue of Olson [*Charles
Olson: The Allegory of a Poet's Life*] ... I'm looking over the
Turners's book on the cannibals of the Southwestern invasion
[*Man Corn: Cannibalism and Violence in the Prehistoric Amer-
ican Southwest* by Christy G. Turner and Jacqueline A.
Turner]—a kind of re-thinking of *Gran Apachería*.
                    —October 22, 1999, from "Little Book Letter"

The stones rained down and they / were the bearers of the
new suns—/ were the news suns which coalesced / and when
they had finished their / repast by shitting in / the open cool-
ing firepits / they took out their long-stem stone pipes / and
burned the ceremonial / smoke of revolutionary / authority,
that is, conquering / and control by the consumption / of the
flesh of the enemy subject / so why did they consummate /
why did they relegate—? / because they could / because they
had assumed / the mantle of the host.

—"Notes on Olson, October 14, 1999"

I got some kind of basic Ideologized in the early part of the
summer—in June-July. First—from Dobro Dick, in which he
reported a conversation w/ a Jehovah's Witness up the road.
The Witness in his eternal Quest for souls was trying to sell
Dick the New Testament. Dick's insistence = *Nothing New!!!!!*
Reiterated over & over, nothing new, look around you, noth-
ing new—you won't see anything new—old guitars, old picks,
old banjos, old organs, pianos, old Dobros, old Hawaiians,
old old Plains Harps, old Jews harps, old pioneer cupboards
with tin flour bins, old measuring cups, old crocks, old ladles,
old labels, old ads, old old old, nothing new, nothing, no New
Testament! And then sitting in the kitchen in front of this open
fireplace in Devon cottage J. H. P[rynne] rocks back & says to
Jenny, No Images. No Images. No Images. = Two Ideolo-
gies.... I've got to say so long now with love to you both.

—October 23, 1999

The Invasion

I nearly what? / within days, / let the tumor / get past the 2nd
/ lumbar disk / to my spinal cord....

—"Linear Acceleration," from *Chemo Sábe*

I've been under deep infection for about a week—all revolving around a kidney stent—failure to have follow-up checks after stent change—on steroids & anti Biotics—I thought I was going to buy it a couple of times. I can still see this side of the wall though. Also, to reduce the swelling compression on my spinal column—2nd lumbar, I had 5 "treatments" of Radiation in Hans Bethe's linear accelerator—a devastation I couldn't have imagined.
—October 11, 1999

Finally I knew I wasn't Bulletproof / when I had my first true hit of a / Harold Urey way out / linear accelerator. . . .
—"Therapy Bombardiers," from *Chemo Sábe*

The linear accelerator radiation treatment took place in the basement of the University of Colorado hospital in Denver. It made him feel better at first, it relieved the inflammation and pain in the lumbar region. In early autumn he'd developed terrible back pain. . . . It got so bad we went into the emergency ward at CU hospital. They did a scan, and that showed the invasion of the tumor into the lumbar region. . . . From the time of that scan and the radiation treatment, we knew that we were really going to have to face the fact of his death at last.
—Jenny Dorn, January 28, 2000

. . . radiologists are / at least Wellsian / pragmatists— / their venues / are at least art deco / and make you feel / immediately better—/ for some reason / I'll never fathom, / when I was taking / the first 39-second hit, / expecting to smell / smoke, all I could / think of was Hans Bethe / and cream enamel / deep lacquered / in fifties June / jacket—the airvent / louvers, casting / now fifties noir / over the recent war. . . .
—"Linear Acceleration"

... the modernismo art set of Sao Paolo. The tone is gay &
trendy fascism, all black lacquer & cream....

> —Dorn, 1988, at the Havana Film Festival,
> reviewing the Norma Bengell film *Eternamente
> Pagu*, about the Brazilian poet of the Twenties
> and Thirties, Patricia Galvao

He was very impressed by the "creamy," striking art deco sets
in that film—the almost fascist architecture of Brazil, in that
period, too—which I guess he was "seeing" in that radiology
room.

> —Jenny Dorn, January 28, 2000

Staring up, / one's thoughts / alone on the cold hard bed / the
memoried map of ... / Los Alamos, with today's / new
ridges....

> —"Linear Acceleration"

And sitting here on my porch, one can see so far across / the
supporting hills to Los Alamos, a quietness almost too deep /
to hear, but one which gives its sound, visually, in the rising /
smoke of its various technical plantations of death / A slow
and unrevealing line about myself curls up from an Alamos /
chimney and my understanding darts like a borzoi away / such
a thing as humanity seems very relative, the final / abjuring
of any vision. Again to know: / What factor becomes like an
arrow to locate us?

> —"The Pronouncement," from *Hands Up!*
> (1964)

A lone crow / on the high wire / flies north / crossing the first
/ skylight north / and then arc'd low / crosses the 2nd / flight
now / skimming the bottom / edge of the frame / of time, the
reminder / Torn loose from / the human fabric, / adrift in the
human breeze

> —"The Invasion of the 2nd Lumbar Region"

... remember we passed the Trinity site, / where 15 years ago
we were led by the top gang / of all marching with their eye
protectors imagine / they covered their eyes thus those idiot
eyes / were not burned out by what they saw of their own /
creation. Only a man / will play god and refuse to look on his
own creation.

> —"The Biggest Killing," from *The Newly
> Fallen* (1961)

O ye sick and frail remnants / of the advanced life forms / who
built this thing

> —"Linear Acceleration"

THANATOPSIS

I wept my way through WHITE THOUGHT.... "Earthshine"
must be one of the loveliest poems ever written. "Surrender,"
the inventory of your parental existence through the objects
upon which their lives rubbed off then expands into a social
history of the time & place—but since I'm from that same
alluvial fan I might feel it more than some down river types.
Anyway Thanatopsis, the whole mode has been renewed.

> —February 8, 1998

Some last thing to be remembered by some sign / *(I was here)*
at all cost not to surrender / That last claim on life don't for-
get us they cry / From that other world of grey light and
shadow....

> —"Surrender," from Tom Clark, *White
> Thought* (1997)

Old moon yearning in the new moon's arms / Every loose
thread left dangling / At dusk Saturn rises out of the ocean /
Heavenly waters so tired of waiting ... / Venus ascends four

A.M. with the tide / White day opening not that far behind it
/ Swallows tossed wide around a calm sky.
   —"Earthshine," from *White Thought*

The Garden Wall

*Around Thanksgiving of 1999 we received by mail a small, rather
faint and wavery but quite lovely gouache Ed had done. It was
painted, he told us, in response to the latest in a series of postcards
we'd been sending him for some years. The cards were a collection
that had been assembled during her travels by my wife Angelica's
late mother, Louise Heinegg. In Ed's last weeks the large collection
had run out. The last cards we'd sent had represented churches, altar-
pieces and paintings of the Dutch and German Reformation.*

> Tom—your p. c.—the Jewel of Angelica's Mum's collection so
> knocked me out I gave up and did my own—the verso is titled
> "The New Wall," i.e. the wall between newly finished bath-
> room and my study.
>   —October 28, 1999

*Attached with the small parcel was his last note. He was now very ill;
it had taken him three weeks to get his painting into the mail.*

> Tom—this has been a long time leaving the premises—in case
> you won't recognize it and why would you—straight ahead
> shot water color of my new study wall—beyond which our
> new *de Lux* bathroom w/ imported Italian floor tile and bath
> tile top to bottom & months in the making.
>   —November 17, 1999

Modeled on The Garden Wall, *a John Singer Sargent water color Ed
had admired in an exhibition in London that summer — he'd sent
me a postcard reproduction — his 5" x 4" water color shows the*

view out through the door of his study to the pink marble tile wall of the "new" bathroom beyond. Whereas Sargent's garden wall opens into the defined receding perspective of the enclosed garden proper, however, Dorn's "New Wall" seems to look out into a watery salmon-colored empty space that goes on forever. The books lining the door-way-framing study shelves seem no longer part of the ghost world of language but the substantial props of the poet's waiting room of the beyond. Within a few weeks, the new wall would open out into all those distances Dorn loved.

THE GARDEN

Our garden is very lush and quiet after a cool spring with more rain than usual.
—June 25, 1997

The garden out back is lovely—I spend some time there reading &c.
—May 24, 1998

A few minutes before crossing South Platte to take my infusion—Daffs are out and the primroses.
—April 20, 1998

Lots of rain, garden is beautiful ... settled into not dying as substitute for living.
—May 23, 1999

It makes me sad / to see I go, he was / I mean I was so perplexed / I's obsessions were almost real / me and I had an understanding / I don't like to see I die.
—*Gunslinger*, Book II

We'll be into April—on the 2nd of course I'll be 70—I can remember, as a child, as soon as I could count, thinking, wondering, if I'd live to see the year 2000 ... now, it's all up in the air still or again.

> —March 29, 1999

What's your name? / *i I answered.* / *That's a simple name* / *Is it an initial? No, it is a single ... / Nevertheless, / it is dangerous to be named / and it makes you mortal.*

> —*Gunslinger,* Book I

When I die don't weep over my death. / I'll leave my body for you....

> —Patricia Galvao, *Album de Pagu* (1929,
> age nineteen)—trans. Dorn & Brotherston,
> *The Sun Unwound* (1999)

Rome was a big experience for me. I've shot my mouth about Rome a lot, but Rome's not like other places. If it's true that there's only one God, let's thank singularity for that. Otherwise our feet would be gone from those cobblestones.

> —London, December 21, 1998

Lord, your mercy is stretched so thin / to accommodate the need / of the trembling earth—/ How can I solicit even / a particle of it / for the relief of my singularity / the single White Rose / across the garden will / return next year / identical to your faith—/ the White Rose, whose / house is light against the / threatening darkness.

> —"The Garden of the White Rose,"
> from *Chemo Sábe*

The lights are going out all over the neighborhood.

> —Robert Creeley, December 11, 1999,
> upon hearing of Dorn's death

When Maya called with the sad news (Friday, December 10, 8 P.M.), the image that came into my nonideological mind was of an extreme brightness: a memory of cresting the Wind River Range with Ed on a long ago midwinter day in an ambient flash of the brightest luminosity I've ever experienced. I'd marveled, dazzled, seeing nothing, while Ed's craggy thousand-yard squint was fixed straight ahead out over the wheel into that overwhelming unspeakable light.

> We went up into the mountains, Maya and Kidd and I, to scatter Ed's ashes....
> —Jenny Dorn, December 17, 1999

> Thus this poor individual / like all the singulars of his race / came in forward and goes out sternward / and some distant starre flashes even him / an indiscriminate salute.
> —*Gunslinger,* Book II